MONSIGNOR WILLIAM BARRY MEMORIAL LIBRARY
BARRY UNIVERSITY
PR698.W6 R63 1989
Roberts, David, 1960-   010101 000
The ladies : female patronage

0 2210 0113521 1

D1526277

DATE DUE

DEC 2 4 2000	
GAYLORD	PRINTED IN U.S.A.

PR
698
.W6
R63
1989

208025

Msgr. Wm. Barry Memorial Library
Barry University
Miami, FL 33161

ROBERTS

LADIES

OXFORD ENGLISH MONOGRAPHS

General Editors
John Carey   Stephen Gill
Douglas Gray   Roger Lonsdale

EX·LIBRIS

BARRY
UNIVERSITY

PRESENTED·BY

PAT MINNAUGH
THEATRE ARTS

THE LADIES

Female Patronage of Restoration Drama
1660–1700

*

DAVID ROBERTS

CLARENDON PRESS · OXFORD

1989

Barry University Library
Miami, FL 33161

Oxford University Press, Walton Street, Oxford OX2 6DP

Oxford New York Toronto
Delhi Bombay Calcutta Madras Karachi
Petaling Jaya Singapore Hong Kong Tokyo
Nairobi Dar es Salaam Cape Town
Melbourne Auckland

and associated companies in
Berlin Ibadan

Oxford is a trade mark of Oxford University Press

Published in the United States
by Oxford University Press, New York

© David Roberts 1989

All rights reserved. No part of this publication may be reproduced,
stored in a retrieval system, or transmitted, in any form or by any means,
electronic, mechanical, photocopying, recording, or otherwise, without
the prior permission of Oxford University Press.

This book is sold subject to the condition that it shall not, by way
of trade or otherwise, be lent, re-sold, hired out or otherwise circulated
without the publisher's prior consent in any form of binding or cover
other than that in which it is published and without a similar condition
including this condition being imposed on the subsequent purchaser.

British Library Cataloguing in Publication Data
Roberts, David
The Ladies: female patronage of
Restoration drama 1660-1700.—(Oxford
English monographes).
1. England. Theatre. Influence of women,
1660-1700
I. Title
792'.0924
ISBN 0-19-811743-4

Library of Congress Cataloging in Publication Data
Roberts, David, 1960-
The ladies: female patronage of restoration drama. 1660-1700/
David Roberts.
p. cm.—(Oxford English monographs)
Bibliography: p. Includes index.
1. English drama—Restoration, 1660-1700—History and criticism.
2. Women in the theater—England—London—History—17th century.
3. London (England)—Social life and customs—17th century.
4. Theater audiences—England—London—History—17th century.
5. Theater—England—London—History—17th century. 6. Pepys,
Elizabeth, 1640-1669—Views on drama. 7. Feminism in literature.
8. Women in literature. I. Title. II. Series.
PR698.W6R63 1989 822'.4'09—dc19 88-22602
ISBN 0-19-811743-4

Typeset by Joshua Associates Limited, Oxford
Printed in Great Britain
at the University Printing House, Oxford
by David Stanford
Printer to the University

PR
698
.W6
R63
1989

208025

TO FIONA

Acknowledgements

THE pleasure of acknowledging the part of others in one's work sometimes exceeds the pleasure of the work itself; in this instance the discrepancy is owing entirely to the depth of my obligations.

Before the first incarnation of this book as a doctoral thesis two people were kind enough to talk for many valuable hours about territories to be considered and traps to be avoided: my former colleague, Dr Peter Davidson, and my former tutor, the late J. C. F. Littlewood, an incomparable teacher my real debt to whom there is not space to set down. Professor Emrys Jones supervised my work with an unfailing sense of detail and relevance, and, in recommending from the first that I should look upon the project as a book rather than a thesis, combined valuable stylistic advice with characteristically uncanny foresight. To my examiners, Michael Gearin-Tosh and Professor Bernard Harris, I owe thanks for much helpful comment.

During the completion of the book which arose from the thesis my colleagues at St Joseph's Hall were of invaluable assistance in tolerating occasional leave from duty. The staff at the Bodleian Library, The British Library, and the Public Records Office have been no less patient. I am deeply grateful to Kim Scott Walwyn of Oxford University Press for seeing the project through. The manuscript was copy-edited by John Callow.

My greatest debt is to my wife, Fiona Shaw Roberts, who, apart from helping to compile the index to this book, has given every support to its author since its inception. It is to her that the work is dedicated.

Fritwell, Oxfordshire   D. R.

Contents

INTRODUCTION

All the Gentlewomen heere, haue forgiuen me, if the Gentlemen
will not, then the Gentlemen do not agree with the Gentlewomen,
which was neuer seene before, in such an Assembly.[1]

Wee are persons of *quality*, I assure you, and women of *fashion*; and
come to see, and be seene ... we long to see Playes, and sit upon
them, as wee doe, and arraigne both them, and their *Poets*.[2]

THE female audience of English drama has been a subject for criticism for
a very long time. When Bottom the Weaver begged to add the lion to his
already full complement of roles, boasting that it would 'do any man's
heart good' to hear him, Quince had to remind him that there were others
in the audience to be accounted for: 'If you should doe it too terribly, you
would fright the Dutchesse and the Ladies, that they would shriek, and
that were enough to hang vs all.' The voice had, to use Bottom's own
memorable word, to be 'aggrauated'.[3]

Aggravation of a kind even further from Bottom's grasp than the
mysteries of the lexicon may be caused in some quarters by my emphasis
upon the age of the subject in hand. May no ladies shriek and call for a
hanging if I make the following statement of policy: because the particular
subject of this book—the female audience of Restoration plays—predates
by many years the current interest in feminist criticism, and because the
want of a proper study of it charges students of the period with neglect
rather than prejudice, my purpose is not to attempt the overthrow of any
patristic theory of scholarship, but to investigate the variety of interesting
facts which lies behind the disappointingly thin collection of recent
guesses at what women expected of the Restoration playhouses and how
they behaved when they went to them. I wish merely, like Peter Quince, to
lay before all those familiar with the subject of the Restoration Audience
(although it hardly seems fair to cast them in the role of Bottom) some
sense of the scope of their obligations.

[1] William Shakespeare, Epilogue, *The Second Part of King Henry the Fourth*, from *The First Folio of Shakespeare: The Norton Facsimile*, ed. Charlton Hinman (London and New York, 1968), 421.

[2] Ben Jonson, Induction, *The Staple of News*, in *Ben Jonson*, ed. C. H. Herford and Percy and Evelyn Simpson, 11 vols. (Oxford, 1925–52), vi, 279–80.

[3] Shakespeare, *A Midsummer Night's Dream*, from *The First Folio*, p. 165.

No one who has read the prologue or epilogue of a Restoration play can
be unaware of the lively consciousness of a female audience which
prevailed among playwrights of the time; equally, no one familiar with the
field can doubt how little of that consciousness (let alone its liveliness) has
imparted itself to scholarship. 'Criticism of Restoration Comedy begins
effectively with Jeremy Collier's Short View . . . (1698)', writes James
Sutherland.[4] The same might be said of criticism of its female audience,
but that *that*, with one or two honourable exceptions, *ends* with Collier
too. Occasional mention is made of the matter in nineteenth-century
studies of Restoration dramatists;[5] but it was not until after the last war
that anyone went further than that. The breakthrough was achieved in
1948 by John Harrington Smith, who argued, on the basis of prologues,
epilogues, and a small selection of other documents, that from the late
1680s onwards the 'respectable female patrons of the theatre' pressurized
the playhouses into presenting a more moral style of comedy: 'sentimental' or 'exemplary' comedy rather than 'laughing' or 'satirical'
comedy.[6] Smith's ideas have enjoyed wide circulation, and not only in the
field of English studies;[7] yet no one has, until now, attempted to fill in the
vast back-drop to the drama he envisaged by investigating who, precisely,
were those 'ladies' who are supposed to have changed the course of English
Comedy—which is also to say that no one has really challenged him. This
book is devoted, therefore, to considering the composition and character
of the female audience of Restoration plays, and to determining its
influence, if any, over the 'change in comedy' which incontestably took
place at the end of the century.

The first chapter deals with what Restoration authors would have
called the character of the woman theatre-goer. It examines the situation
of women in Restoration London—their economic position, their status
under the law, and their education—and proceeds to show both how the
dramatists' conception of their character as theatre-goers was determined
by it, and how it informed their actual responses and preferences.

Chapter 2 provides the first detailed examination of the best-
documented case we have of a Restoration woman who went regularly to
the theatre: Pepys's wife, Elizabeth. It looks closely at her reading and
theatre-going in the context of the 'character' established in the first

[4] James Sutherland, *English Literature of the Late Seventeenth Century* (Oxford, 1969), 460.
[5] See e.g. Otto Hallbauer, *The Life and Works of George Farquhar* (Holzminden, 1880), 1.
[6] John Harrington Smith, 'Shadwell, the Ladies, and the Change in Comedy', *Modern
Philology*, 46 (1948), 22–33.
[7] For example, John Harley, *Music in Purcell's London* (London 1968), 120–1.

chapter. Chapter 3 opens out the discussion into a consideration of the composition and manners of the total female audience, from aristocrats to whores. It describes the various patterns of attendance and attention among different groups of women, and considers the accuracy of the conventional terms of social description used in the prologues and epilogues.

Chapter 4 discusses the involvement with the stage of women at Court. It examines the patronage of the three Restoration Queens, and explores the occasional groups (or 'factions') which women set up at Court to pursue their interest in the stage. The differences between these groups are found to be so great as to make the idea of a single 'ladies' faction' (favoured by all recent scholars) somewhat implausible.

Chapter 5 tackles directly the question of the part played by women in the change in comedy. It acknowledges that the changes in attendance and patronage which led up to the late 1680s and 1690s encourage belief in a group of women capable of influencing the style of comedy, but finds all the evidence of such a group unreliable. It proceeds to show how certain 'sentimental' comedies really did cater for the interest of their female audience by taking advantage of the fashionable concern for women's rights, which is witnessed in a variety of publications. A 'ladies' faction' (the linchpin of all that is currently understood about the subject) is thereby shown to be a misconception which obscures the serious purpose behind a style of comedy which was designed to prize the interest of its female audience above all others.

I

THE AGE AND THE LADIES

I

FROM Mary Astell to Antonia Fraser, most commentators on the place of women in English Society have agreed in finding the Restoration period the nadir of the collective fortunes of the female sex. One ringing sentence written in 1909 distils a range of analysis:

Exposed to all the moral laxity of the time; deprived of the means of either intellectual or economic independence, they sank to a lower level in their own esteem and in the respect of the world than has probably ever been the case in England before or since.[1]

What reasons there were for this state of affairs, and how knowledge of them can help us to understand the female theatre-goer of Restoration England, it is the aim of this chapter to establish.

Much of the essential women's history of the period was written by people who lived in it. Sir Josiah Child twice argued in print that the economic success of the Dutch was partly attributable to the superior achievements of their women over the women of England.[2] Dutch girls, he observed, could generally write and knew arithmetic and accounts; at the very least they were brought up into the family business. The result, he claimed, was not only that they became more rational companions, but that they were able to assist their fathers and husbands in business and even to take over completely if the need arose.[3] Their skill and industry offered scope for jest as well as envy. 'Weighing soape, ma foy,' exclaims Monsieur in Wycherley's *The Gentleman Dancing Master* in recollection of a meeting with the family of an eminent Dutchman,

for he was a wholesale chandleer, and his lady was taking the tale of chandels wid her own witer hands, ma foy, and de young lady, his daughter, stringing harring. Stringing harring, jarnie![4]

[1] A. Beatrice Wallis Chapman and Mary Wallis Chapman, *The Status of Women under the English Law* (London, 1909).

[2] Josiah Child, *Brief Observations Concerning Trade and the Interest of Money* (London, 1665), and *A New Discourse of Trade* (London, 1694).

[3] *A New Discourse of Trade*, pp. 4–5.

[4] William Wycherley, *The Plays of William Wycherley*, ed. Peter Holland (Cambridge, 1981), 135.

Only in Holland could one expect to see such risibly unfashionable behaviour.

Had Monsieur known commercial London as well as Samuel Pepys did, he would not have been so sure of his cultural bearings. Pepys was used to doing business with Mrs Pley for canvas and Mrs Russell for tallow,[5] although there was a difference between those women and the Mrs Bland whom he met for the first time on New Year's Eve 1662:

above all, pleased to hear Mrs Bland talk like a merchant in her husband's business very well; and it seems she doth understand it and perform a great deal.

Her competence was surprising because she was encumbered with a husband; Mrs Pley and Mrs Russell were widows. So to understand her husband's affairs was beyond Pepys's own wife, her sympathetic ear notwithstanding. For a married woman to talk like that was startling. Pepys understood better than many that marriage in the London of his day was not likely to benefit a woman greatly. He knew well that what prompted his wife to persist in asking for a maid was a common affliction which could lead to a worse:

we had much talk and difference between us about my wife's having a woman; which I seemed much angry at that she should go so far in it without considera-tion and my being consulted with. So to sleep. 13. Up—and begun our discontent again and sorely angered with my wife; who endeed doth live very lonely. But I do perceive that it is want of work that doth make her and all other people think of ways of spending their time worse.[6]

The problem was not solved by the affluence which the couple enjoyed in later years. Six years on Pepys recorded the pleasure with which his wife showed him her 'stock of jewels', reckoned by her to amount to one hundred and fifty pounds' worth; he was glad of it, 'for it is fit the wretch should have something to content herself with'.[7] It was no impulsive act of kindness to buy her the four-volume romance, *L'Illustre Bassa*, the following morning. Pepys knew from personal discomfort what reformers were later to publish with philanthropic zeal: that marriage put an end to a woman's opportunities for useful work or thought, and that it might even encourage her in vice.[8] Little wonder that the proportion of men who

[5] Samuel Pepys, *The Diary of Samuel Pepys*, ed. Robert Latham and William Mathews, 11 vols. (London, 1970–83), 31 Dec. 1662, 10 Dec. 1663.

[6] *Diary*, 12–13 Nov. 1662.

[7] *Diary*, 23 Feb. 1668.

[8] For example, *The Case of Clandestine Marriages* (London, 1681); Mary Astell, *A Serious Proposal to the Ladies* (London, 1694).

nominated their wives to execute their wills declined considerably towards the end of the century, or that most of the 'female wits' of the day remained unmarried during their literary careers.[9]

One attractive explanation of the situation is offered by Alice Clark. Using the records of the London Companies, Clark has shown how the increasingly capitalistic organization of industry tended to move work away from the home of the master into separate premises. At the same time, legislation to restrict employment at the place of work to journeymen and registered apprentices prohibited the casual yet extensive employment of women which had been common earlier in the century and was still to be found in Holland. In the Restoration period, unless a woman was mistress of a business (she still could be, as Clark shows), she was likely to be consigned to a merely social or charitable function within the Company. As such, women had, in Mary Astell's words, 'nothing to do but glorify God and to benefit their neighbours'.[10] To this analysis even the more conservative David Ogg was bound to raise an assenting voice.[11]

If we confine ourselves to the evidence used by Clark it will remain, however, an analysis of limited range; it can hardly meet the case of the wives of professional men such as Pepys. We may extend it by referring to a well-known sociological work, Veblen's *The Theory of the Leisure Class*. One of Veblen's aims is to show how plutocracies conspire to rob women of useful economic functions, consigning them instead to idleness and ostentation. While the head of a household may aspire to that 'conspicuous abstentation from labour' which would show to the world his 'superior pecuniary achievement', his employment may force him to delegate his leisure to subservient members of the house: his wife and even his servants. They must then render him 'vicarious leisure', according to the demands of convention and, perhaps, fashion.[12]

The attractions of applying Veblen's ideas to the Pepyses are obvious. Elizabeth, furnished with maid and mask, and the object of her husband's scorn because she sometimes under-dresses for the theatre, seems to typify the bourgeois wife of Veblen's conception. She declares her husband's

[9] Alice Clark, *The Working Life of Women in the Seventeenth Century* (London, 1919), 45; *The Female Wits: Women Playwrights on the London Stage, 1660-1720*, ed. Fidelis Morgan (London, 1981), 5-61. Aphra Behn wrote as a widow; Katherine Phillips as a 'Platonick'; Catherine Trotter married after completing her last play; and Mary Manley enjoyed casual relationships and one bigamous marriage. Mary Pix apart, only the aristocrats, the Duchess of Newcastle and the Countess of Winchelsea, wrote during wedlock.

[10] *A Serious Proposal*, p. 145.

[11] David Ogg, *England in the Reign of Charles II*, 2nd edn. (Oxford, 1984), 126-7.

[12] Thorstein Veblen, *The Theory of the Leisure Class* (New York, 1925).

status by appearing at the theatre with her maid and a few friends and relatives, and in her interest in the trappings of fashion—masks and white curls—evinces the tendency of the middle-class wife to dress for show rather than for work.[13] The theory is less secure when applied to her husband. Pepys was obviously not content to let his wife render him vicarious leisure, but wanted the pleasure and distinction of it himself, particularly when it came to theatre-going. He was often, nevertheless, 'troubled' by his idleness, and resented professional underlings abstaining more conspicuously from labour than he did. He was, moreover, subject to a number of pressures which could prevent him from going to the theatre: the gossip of servants and the fear of being seen by colleagues, for instance.[14] Elizabeth had none of those worries; going to a play was an entirely acceptable thing for her to do. In that respect Veblen's theory of leisure does something to explain the presence of women in the Restoration playhouse; the idleness of the wife led her to seek distractions. The difficulty lies in Pepys himself not having been the assiduous labourer of Veblen's conception. Instead he occupies a grey area between leisure and labour, vowing to spend one week 'in seeing plays and pleasure, and so fall to business next week again'.[15] Elizabeth did not necessarily benefit from the consequent accumulation of leisure hours, and Pepys never felt so guilty about seeing a play as when he abandoned both work and wife to do so. Although she sometimes went to the theatre with her maid or family friends, Elizabeth did not have the wider circle of acquaintance which her husband's job allowed him, so she was entitled to think him selfish to go without her.[16] Alienated to some extent by the demands of his work, she doubtless felt robbed, too, of her one remaining right: to enjoy with him his hours of leisure.

That is one interesting upshot of the valuable work which has been done in recent years to show how many decent professional men went to the theatre in the afternoon; if Pepys's leisurely indulgence was typical, so, perhaps, was Elizabeth's lonely disenchantment.[17] It is no exaggeration to

[13] *Diary*, 8 May 1663, 25 Mar. 1667, 20 June 1668, 12 June 1663, 27 June 1664, 4 Feb. 1667.
[14] *Diary*, 19 Jan. 1661, 1 Jan. 1668, 19 Apr. 1667, 18 Feb. 1668.
[15] *Diary*, 22 May 1662. It seems to have been common practice for men in London to work for only three days each week: see John Houghton, *A Collection for the Improvement of Husbandry and Trade* (London, 1683), 383.
[16] *Diary*, 11 Sept. 1661, 18 Aug. 1664, 25 Sept. 1667.
[17] See Emmet L. Avery, 'The Restoration Audience', *Philological Quarterly*, 49 (1966), 54–61; Harold Love, 'The Myth of the Restoration Audience', *Komos*, 1 (1968), 45–56, and 'Who Were the Restoration Audience?'. *The Yearbook of English Studies*, 10 (1980).

say that a woman such as Elizabeth was consigned to boredom as much by the leisure as by the industry of her husband, or that while certain economic laws gave her every inducement to go to the theatre, her husband's wide field of professional acquaintance sometimes prevented her from going.

If Elizabeth does not fit easily into the leisure class identified by Veblen, neither does the typical 'lady' vilified by commentators of the day, in whom appears distilled all the historic unsatisfactoriness of Restoration womanhood.[18] For her, the daughter of the noble or genteel, economic uselessness was no bane but a boast, no divider of the sexes but a uniter. There were, to that extent, two leisure classes among the female population. If the one is typified by the lonely Elizabeth Pepys, the other receives its supreme expression in the supine accomplishments of Congreve's Millamant: the darling of a thousand; the artist of leisure, not its victim; capable of devoting a whole morning to curling her hair with letters in prose and counting it a strenuous day when she denies herself 'airs'.[19] To anyone seeking to identify the characteristic limitations of Restoration woman, Millamant offers a tempting case: unproductive except for her dowry; unable to enjoy the associations which marriage will bring; uneducated but for a smattering of song and Suckling; unwilling, even, to undertake the task of bearing children.[20] She is clearly, however, a different case from Elizabeth Pepys, who might equally be thought to represent those limitations adequately: a member, indeed, of a different leisure class.

Where Elizabeth acquired her leisure through exclusion from the world of men, Millamant could enjoy hers in something like a community of both sexes. Millamant could hardly be remote from the business or leisure of her male acquaintances because leisure was their business and she much of their leisure. She was not alone fortunate among her contemporaries; a 'lady' was almost by definition a woman who could command a range of male company when she required diversion. One manual of polite conversation divides men into three categories, whose members possess 'different degrees in the favour of the Ladies': 'the witty

[18] See Hannah Woolley, *The Gentlewoman's Companion* (London, 1675), 35–6; Elizabeth Elstob, preface to *An English-Saxon Homily on the Birthday of St. Gregory* (London, 1709); George Savile, Marquis of Halifax, 'The Lady's New Year Gift', *Complete Works*, ed. J. P. Kenyon (Harmondsworth, 1969), 269–313; Anne Killigrew, 'On a Young Lady whose Lord was Travelling', *Poems by Mrs Anne Killigrew* (London, 1686), 77–8.

[19] William Congreve, *The Way of the World*, ed. Brian Gibbons (London, 1971), II. 295–334.

[20] *The Way of the World*, IV. 188, III. 329–44, IV. 80–128, IV. 281–4.

man, the aery and conversable fop, and the sober and prudent man'. The favourite is the witty man, who can 'raise diversion' as he pleases and change the subject rapidly in order to forestall boredom; a diverting alternative is the conversable fop, who 'has always leisure enough to give a fair lady a treat, to wait on her to a Play, to a Ball, or to the Park; all of which will please the Ladies very much'.[21] In the world of this leisure class there was a breed of men whose lives were devoted to giving 'a fair lady a treat' (they are typified by Congreve's Witwoud), although the inferiority of their accomplishments compared with those of witty men was sufficiently evident to permit a grading of leisure hours according to company kept, even a refining of the term 'leisure' itself. In *The Way of the World* the first exchange between Mirabell and Millamant is a debate about the right of the use of time, about the manner in which the infinitely leisured should be allowed to be leisurely. He complains that she has denied him an opportunity of talking to her. She replies she was 'engaged', or not at leisure; he picks up the suggestion: 'You had the leisure to entertain a herd of fools—things who visit you from their excessive idleness, bestowing on your easiness that time which is the encumbrance of their lives.'[22] She must have been at leisure because she was talking to fools who had nothing else to do. Her leisure is the mirror of theirs.

Mirabell shared his frustration with a number of courtesy authors. On the question of diversion, Halifax remarked that 'those that are idle have no need of them, yet they above all others give themselves up to them', and he scorns women who are 'engaged in a circle of idleness . . . for the whole year, without the interruption of a serious hour' (these, furthermore, are the women who 'know all the players' names').[23] In like mood, Hannah Woolley advised her readers not to follow the example of those who existed 'for no other end than to dedicate the first fruits of the morning to the Looking-Glass, and the remainder thereof to the Exchange, or Play-house'.[24]

Nowhere does such contempt appear more frequently than in the character literature which was popular throughout the age.[25] A modest

[21] S. C., *The Art of Complaisance* (London, 1673), 133–4.

[22] *The Way of the World*, II. 383–9.

[23] Halifax, p. 311.

[24] Woolley, pp. 35–96.

[25] See e.g., *The Character of a Coffee-house* (London, 1665); *The Character of a Town-Gallant* (London, 1675); *Remarques on the Humours and Conversations of the Gallants of the Town* (London, 1673); Thomas Brown, *Amusements Serious and Comical* (London, 1700); Thomas Durfey, *Collin's Walk through London and Westminster* (London, 1690); Robert Gould, 'The Play-house', *Poems* (London, 1689), 55–85.

instance is a series of *Catechisms* published in 1703. The Beau spends the afternoon at the theatre, chatting in the side-box with a masker and then behind the scenes with the actresses, and in the evening he goes 'to the Ladies Chambers, where his professed activities include playing Cards and reading Plays'; presumably quite innocent activities compared with those he does not profess (the profession itself is of interest; what the Beau does to preserve the reputations of his lady friends is to claim to have passed the time in the most familiar, probable way imaginable).[26] The lady herself spends a good deal of time at the theatre and at cards, and on Sundays she indulges in 'Chit-Chat' about 'New Fashions and New Plays', and reads 'Lewd Plays and whining Romances'.[27]

What is portrayed in these accounts is a vacuum of boredom; the lady's leisure hours are indivisible, and she recognizes no qualitative difference between reading and 'Chit-Chat'. Yet Mirabell's charge against his future wife betrays the falsity of such accounts; he acknowledges that leisure within the mixed community of the fashionable as divisible in that it could be itemized and evaluated according to the kinds of people with whom one shared it. Distinctions of place and company were, indeed, integral to social organization. There were topographical sanctions: the chocolate house of the first scene of *The Way of the World* is a male sanctuary where Mirabell and Fainall can joke freely about its female counterpart, Lady Wishfort's house on a 'cabal-night'; while Millamant is convinced that such arrangements are essential to sanity at the private level. Her insistence that her closet remain 'inviolate' after marriage is designed to secure the prevailing distinctions of town life in her own domestic affairs.[28]

Even within individual activities the typical lady can exercise a considerable degree of choice. It is the variety, indeed the vitality of those choices which is most striking. Mirabell is anxious that Millamant will not be able to see a visit to the theatre in simple terms, but will want to use it as an excuse for alarmingly complicated stratagems:

I covenant that your acquaintance be general; that you admit . . . no decoy-duck to wheedle you to a fop, scrambling to the play in a mask, then bring you home in a pretended fright when you think you shall be found out, and rail at me for missing the play, and disappointing the frolic, which you had to pick me up and prove my constancy![29]

[26] *The Beau's Catechism* (London, 1703), 5-7.
[27] *The Ladies Catechism* (London, 1703), 4-7.
[28] *The Way of the World*, I. 45-55, IV. 184-97.
[29] *The Way of the World*, IV. 205-13.

Given possibilities like that, watching the play and giving it thought might be a grave matter; such possibilities, indeed, lend a seriousness, even a dignity, to the notion of a 'ladies' faction' in the theatre audience. The divisibility of a lady's leisure thus offers better material for analysis than the tiresome imputation of mere idleness promises. In fact, the view projected by Halifax, Woolley, and the author of the *Catechisms* seems more true to the situation of the disenchanted bourgeois, Elizabeth Pepys, than to the lady of fashion; for an Elizabeth, a visit to the theatre had a more constant significance than for a Millamant, and one more likely to savour of boredom.

Conspicuous leisure remained a predominant feature in the lives of many Restoration women; however diversely it could be employed it accounted for much of the low value placed upon women at that time. Other reasons must now be sought for the crisis of esteem. Once again, many of the important things have been said by seventeenth-century commentators. Throughout the Restoration period, but especially in the 1690s, many people lamented the poor provision of education for girls. 'Many Women equal us in the best talents of the Mind,' wrote Peter Motteux in 1694, 'and the weakness of some is the effect of the Education, which we have thought fit to allow them.' He went on to demonstrate that insufficient cultivation of the rational powers led to a ready capitulation to 'the alluring Joys of the Delightfull World'.[30] If the preciously tactful phrasing suggests that Motteux's readers had already capitulated, it shows too that the debate over such matters was not confined to the zealous. John Dunton added a gallantly regretful voice to proceedings: 'We unjustly deprive [women] of the greatest of all Goods; to wit, that of the Mind, whose fairest Ornament is Knowledge, the chief Good both of this world and the next';[31] an impressively latitudinarian view combining piety, gallantry, and righteous indignation. Mary Astell was more forthright in making a similar point:

according to the rate that young women are educated, according to the way their time is spent, they are destin'd to folly and impertinence.

Like Motteux, she draws a connection between poor education and moral laxity, and attends further to the dangers of instructing boys and not girls in the ways of the world:

if a woman were duly principled and taught how to know the ways of the world, especially the true sentiments that men have of her ... women would marry

---

[30] Peter Motteux, *The Gentleman's Journal* (London, 1694), 93–5.
[31] John Dunton, *The Athenian Mercury* (London, 1691–6), 4 Nov. 1693.

more discreetly, and demean themselves better in a married state, than some people say they do.[32]

There is every reason to suppose that these opinions were widely circulated; they appear in newspapers, printed books,[33] and even in plays. No play-goer could ignore their currency when so many scenes in Restoration comedy depicted husbands discussing their wives' education, or parents their daughters'.[34] What, then, did this lamentable business of a girl's education involve in seventeenth-century London?

Its structure naturally depended on the means and location of the family. A girl of noble birth might benefit from the presence of people who taught her brothers. A Mr Thornton, retained by the Russell family for that purpose, could usually spare an hour at the end of the day for the young ladies of the house.[35] Only in exceptional circumstances (that is, when the parents were exceptionally enlightened) was there any real plan of study. Lucy Hutchinson and Evelyn's daughter, Mary, were outstanding in their gifts as in their good fortune: at the age of seven, Lucy had 'eight tutors in several qualities, language, music, dancing, writing and needle-work; but my genius was quite averse from all but my book'.[36] In the latter—happily—she received equal encouragement. Mary, under her father's tutelage, became fluent in French and gathered some Italian, read a good deal of history, and played music with a beauty for which her father admired her scarcely less than for her piety.[37] Even in these unusual cases a lot of time was devoted to 'accomplishments'. Girls left to develop those in less auspicious surroundings very often did so indifferently and at the

---

[32] *A Serious Proposal*, p. 80.

[33] See *An Essay in Defence of the Female Sex* (London, 1696); Clement Barksdale, *A Letter touching a College of Maids or a Virgin Society* (London, 1675); Bathsua Makin, *An Essay to Revive the Antient Education of Gentlewomen* (London, 1673); Nahum Tate, Preface to *A Present to the Ladies* (London, 1694); Hannah Woolley, *The Queen-like Closet*, 5th edn. (London, 1684).

[34] For example, Edward Ravenscroft, *The London cuckolds* (1681), I. i.; and *The Citizen Turn'd Gentleman* (1672), II. ii.; Aphra Behn, *The Luckey Chance* (1686), II. ii.; and *The City Heiress* (1683), III. i.; Congreve, *The Way of the World*, V. 164-76; Thomas Shadwell, *Bury Fair* (1689), II. i.; and Wycherley, *The Country Wife* (1675), III. i. Many of these scenes have an immediate literary source: Molière's *L'École des femmes* and *L'École des maris*. See Molière, *Œuvres completes*, ed. Georges Mongredien, 4 vols. (Paris, 1695), ii. 32-7 and i. 355-62.

[35] Gladys Scott Thompson, *Life in a Noble Household* (London, 1937), 73-8; and *The Russells in Bloomsbury* (London, 1940), 77.

[36] Lucy Hutchinson, *Memoirs of Colonel Hutchinson*, 3rd edn., 2 vols. (London, 1810), i. 25-6.

[37] John Evelyn, *The Diary of John Evelyn*, ed. Esmond S. de Beer, 6 vols. (Oxford, 1955), iv. 421.

expense of everything else. Hannah Woolley was engaged by a young noblewoman as a resident tutor, the lady having wanted to make up the education she had not enjoyed as a girl. Whether Woolley's pupil considered herself properly educated at the end of her tutor's employment can only be guessed at. She was taught the arts of 'huswifery'—making Salves, Oyntments, Waters, Cordials, healing any wounds not desperately dangerous'—and of the making of ornaments: 'all kinds of Beugleworks upon Wyers, or otherwise . . . Rocks made with Shell or in Sweets, frames for Looking-glasses, Pictures or the like, Feathers of Crewel for the Corners of Beds, making sweet powders for the Hair, or to lay among linnen'.[38] That writing and arithmetic were given so little attention did not, Woolley suggests, reflect the lady's competence in those subjects.

Girls would fare little better at school. The Verney daughters, Molly and Betty, were sent to boarding-school at the cost of twenty-five pounds per year; an extravagant investment when they appear to have learned nothing but how to dance and lacquer boxes.[39] Thomas Durfey's satirical play, *Love for Money, or the Boarding School* (1690), is set in a sort of Restoration Dothegirls: two 'tawdry, hoyden, overgrown Romps' called Molly and Jenny have been kept there for longer than anyone can remember, forever attempting to trill (their mouths crammed with bread and butter) under the guidance of a lecherous violinist, Semibrif. How faithfully Durfey drew his school may be judged from the event mounted by its rumoured model in the year of the play's composition: in the summer of 1689 Josias Priest's academy at Chelsea put on the first production of Purcell's *Dido and Aeneas*, using largely home-grown talent.[40]

At least Durfey's play reflected accurately public suspicion regarding the boarding-schools. As early as 1661, when John Batchiler wrote his biography of Susanna Perwich, he published it partly 'to refute the opinion of such as greatly blame the *education* of publick schools, as if they were places of all other most dangerous to corrupt the manners of youth'. The school in question, said to inspire wonder among foreign visitors, was Mrs Perwich's academy in Hackney. Eight hundred girls were trained

---

[38] *The Gentlewoman's Companion*, p. 17.

[39] *Memoirs of the Verney Family during the Seventeenth Century*, ed. Frances Parthenope Verney, 4 vols. (London, 1892), i. 433–4.

[40] Durfey's dedication of the play traces the rumour to the 'malice of a prejudic'd party'. Details of the première of the opera are nowhere more tersely or elegantly given than in Richard Luckett, sleeve notes to *Dido and Aeneas*. With Emma Kirkby. Conducted by Andrew Parrot. The Taverner Choir and Players (London, 1981).

there in its seventeen years' life. There was a school consort led by the admirable Susanna (Mrs Perwich's daughter and later a teacher in the school), and sixteen tutors in dancing and music. Other subjects included the reading of scripture, cooking, and housewifery, while Susanna is said to have taught herself accounting. Even in this prodigy of a modern educational establishment, little was taught which could raise girls above, in Motteux's words (and he was not one of the more radical commentators), 'the low and narrow sphere of domestic management'.[41] Indeed, there was probably little difference between what Elizabeth Pepys's serving maid, Deborah Willet, learned at the Bow School and what Margaret, Sir William Penn's daughter, was taught at the school in Clerkenwell; Willet was quite as proficient in some ladylike accomplishments as her mistress.[42] Pepys's legion indiscretions with her may tempt us to the view, with other evidence to hand, that he regarded her as the perfect schoolgirl; in the space of a week in April 1667 he condemned the Putney schoolgirls because they were not as pretty as those from Hackney, and paid a special visit simply to look at the strange creatures appearing one day from their classes.[43]

The popularity of courtesy literature for young women may not reflect directly popular mistrust of the girls' schools, but it does provide a clue to the prevalence of a number of interesting attitudes towards female education. Hannah Woolley's *The Queen-like Closet*, a guide for servant-girls and maids, went into five editions within ten years of its first appearance, while Allestree's *The Ladies Calling* was printed five times in the first four years of its life.[44] If these and other such books supplied the educational needs of girls whose parents could not or would not send them to school or have them taught at home, they show how minimally those needs could be felt. Allestree sets out his approach squarely in his preface: 'Let it be admitted, that in respect of their intellects, [women] are below men; yet sure in the sublimest part of humanity, they are their equals'. Women were not to expect equality in this world, but in the next. Motteux's concern with allowing equal opportunity to equal talent would have seemed to Allestree one further aberration of an age bent on

[41] John Batchiler, *The Virgin's Pattern* (London, 1661), 1–2. Motteux, *The Gentleman's Journal*, May 1692, p. 10.

[42] *Diary*, 21 Oct. 1667; 23 Mar. 1668; 23 Dec. 1667; 22 Jan. 1668; 6 Mar. 1668. Clerkenwell School: 11 Dec. 1661; 11 May 1663.

[43] *Diary*, 21 and 27 Apr. 1667.

[44] Richard Allestree, *The Ladies Calling* (Oxford, 1673). The 5th edn. was published in Oxford in 1677.

confusing traditional distinctions between men and women.[45] In relegat-
ing female reason to the lower rank he was seconded by Halifax, who
admitted that his view was 'a little uncourtly', thereby implying that it
belonged to the fashionably gallant to claim that women might be as
rational as men.[46]

The principal concern of these authors was to develop their readers'
sense of the traditional virtues of women. Foremost among these as far as
Allestree was concerned was modesty, whose chief accomplishment,
beauty, was destroyed by boldness. Modesty imparted itself to all faculties,
for example to speech: 'A womans tongue should indeed be like the
imaginary Music of the Spheres, sweet and charming, but not to be heard
at a distance.' Its chief manifestation, however, was in the glowing cheeks
of the righteously offended, and in no instance was the 'degenerous age'
more at fault for ignoring the true character of women than in this: 'The
blush (tho formerly reputed the colour of vertu) is accounted worse
manners than those things which ought to occasion it.'[47] Jeremy Collier
went so far as to show how well attuned were the physical properties of
modesty to the moral probity which it served to defend:

Tis likewise propertion'd to the occasions of Life, and strongest in Youth when
Passion is so too ... The enemy no sooner approaches, but the Blood rises in
Opposition, and looks Defyance to an Indecency. It supplys the Room of
Reasoning and Collection: Intuitive Knowledge can scarcely make a quicker
Impression; And what then can be a surer guide to the Unexperienced?[48]

If the natural modesty of woman was so effective an instrument of moral
discrimination, why educate a girl to think? She had only to become, as it
were, expert in her own physiology to gain what knowledge of life she
needed. In a similar vein, Allestree contended that it was wrong even for
the pious to read 'whole Tomes of Disputations', when all that women

---

[45] Motteux, *The Gentleman's Journal*, pp. 93–5. Allestree, p. 12, remarks: 'Such a
degenerous age do we live in, that everything seems inverted, even Sexes; whilst men fall to
the Effeminacy and Niceness of Women, and Women take up the Confidence, the
Boldness of men, and this too under the Notion of Good Breeding.' See also Anthony
Wood, *The Life and Times of Anthony Wood*, ed. A. Clark, 5 vols. (Oxford, 1891–1900), i. 509.

[46] Halifax, p. 277.

[47] Allestree, p. 12. Congreve's Mirabell replies in a similar vein to Petulant's taking
blushing 'for a sign of guilt, or ill-breeding': 'Where modesty's ill manners, 'tis but fit / That
Ignorance and Malice pass for wit.' (i. 463–81). Mirabell seems an unlikely ally for Allestree,
and perhaps had more in common with the reformers of the stage than they themselves
realized.

[48] Jeremy Collier, *A Short View of the Immorality and Prophaneness of the English Stage*, 3rd
edn. (London, 1698), 11.

needed was to spend some hours each day examining the basic truths of their religion. The aim of this was primarily defensive; those truths were designed as an 'amulet against delusion'.[49]

So self-referential an approach to the education of girls seemed to some a capitulation to ignorance—the result, merely, of fear of the immorality of the age. Hannah Woolley reflected that: 'Most in this depraved later age think a woman learned and wife enough if she can distinguish her husband's bed from another's.'[50] There was doubt about the power of such an approach to achieve even its own limited ends. While Motteux and Astell warned of the dangers of ignorance, the unanimous verdict of the dramatists who wrote 'education scenes' was that experience was the best amulet against delusion; it is the Margery Pinchwife or Miss Prue who is most at risk. An alternative approach designed to accommodate the unavoidable fact of conspicuous leisure was proposed by Woolley. Her more liberal attitudes are reflected in her list of recommended reading. In the front rank are masochistically edifying theological works (even these might have been too much for Richard Allestree).[51] More daring is the inclusion of all the fashionable romances;[52] Woolley knew that some would find them hard to accept. Would they not, after such 'practical books of divinity . . . overthrow that fabrick I endeavour'd to erect?' Her case for their inclusion, however, is founded on evidence which might have satisfied their most obdurate opponent: 'There are few ladies mention'd therein, but are character'd what they ought to be: the magnanimity, virtue, gallantry, patience, constancy and courage of the men, might intitle them worthy husbands to the most deserving of the female sex'.[53] Thus stated, the value of romances could differ little from that of works of divinity; they were not escapist, because they showed that disappointment with a man in the real world could only be occasioned by

---

[49] *The Ladies Calling*, p. 35.

[50] *The Gentlewoman's Companion*, p. 288.

[51] Works recommended were James Usher, *A Body of Divinity* (London, 1645); George Swinnock, *The Christian Man's Calling* (London, 1662); and James Janeway, *Invisibles, Realities, Demonstrated* (London, 1673).

[52] Woolley included Gauthier de Costes de La Calprenede, *Cassandra*, trans. Sir Charles Cotterell, 10 vols. (London, 1652); and *Cleopatra*, trans. Richard Loveday, 12 vols. (London, 1652-5); Madeleine de Scudery, *Clelia* trans. John Davies and George Havers, 5 vols. (London, 1656-61); and *Artamenes, or Grand Cyrus*, trans. F. G., 5 vols. (London, 1653-5); Roger Boyle, Earl of Orrery, *Parthenissa that Most Fam'd Romance*, 6 vols. (London, 1654-69). She also recommended Philip Sidney, *The Countess of Pembroke's Arcadia*, new editions of which were published in London in 1655, 1662, and 1674.

[53] *The Gentlewoman's Companion*, p. 9.

insufficient desert on the part of the woman—the most perfect conspiracy of example, as Eliot might have put it. Hannah Woolley is not alone implicated in it. Sir Ralph Verney advised his god-daughter that the most stabilizing, womanly books were those written in French, 'for that language affords many admirable books fit for you, as romances, plays, poetry, stories of illustrious not learned women . . . and in brief all manner of good huswifery'.[54]

Against this must be set the familiar case of Mary Pix's Beaumont, who may speak for all those authors who, like that of the *Catechisms*, saw in romances a way of filling time which added to a lady's disqualification from normal life:

Too studious for her sex, she fell upon the seducers of the women, plays and romances. From thence she formed herself a hero, a cavalier, that could love and talk like them; whilst her father, without consulting her, provided her a husband, rich, but wanting all such accomplishments.[55]

Such disagreement over the worth of romances extended to everyday conversation; this, combined with the fact that one of their most conspicuous apologists, Hannah Woolley, disliked in principle the very things for which their opponents condemned them, must have made it a problematic and even subversive business for some women to read them at all. Pepys was aware of one simple kind of moral pressure when he sat down one Sunday to read 'some little French Romances'; he asked God's forgiveness for wasting his time so idly.[56] While Elizabeth may have been glad to have her hours taken up with some activity, the liveliness of the debate about its propriety suggests that other women may have approached romances less straightforwardly. Where they were allowed, a woman was to feel chastened by example; where forbidden, retreat was more likely into the private world which they were thought to foster. If the allowing encouraged feelings of moral inferiority, the forbidding facilitated a more complete withdrawal from a responsible consideration of the material world.

If Woolley's prescription of romances seems, after all, less than liberal, so too does her suggestion as to how they might best be enjoyed. Courtesy

<hr/>

[54] *Verney Memoirs*, iii. 74.

[55] Mary Pix, *The Spanish Wives* (1696), I. i. Cp. George Farquhar, *The Constant Couple* (1699): 'After supper I went to my chambers and read *Cassandra*, then went to bed, and dreamt of him all night, rose in the morning, and made verses, so fell desperately in love.' (III, i.).

[56] *Diary*, 10 Feb. 1661.

books of the earlier years of the century stress the importance of teaching girls to read aloud from the Bible; in the pious household it was a way of suiting the instruction of the daughter to the convenience of the father.[57] It is typical of Woolley's peculiar brand of toleration that she recommended an extension of the practice to less serious literature. One noble patroness would have her read aloud: 'Poems of all sorts and plays, teaching me as I read, where to place my accents, how to raise and fall my voice, where to lay the emphasis of the expressions. Romances of the best sort she took great delight in.'[58] In recommending the study not only of French and Italian, however, but also of Latin, Woolley was challenging a deeper prejudice than that against romances.[59] The hostility attracted by learned women in the seventeenth century is a well-documented subject, but it does seem worthwhile to point out how exactly the learned lady of Restoration Comedy catches the voice of those who, like Mary Astell and Elizabeth Elstob, saw the life of leisured women as one of vanity and idleness. Aphra Behn's Lady Knowell scorns the perpetual round of visits, park, and playhouse; in her own youth her 'looser hours' were spent in reading: 'if serious, 'twas Tacitus, Seneca, Plutarch's Morals, or some such useful author; if in an humour gay, I was for poetry, Virgil, Homer or Tasso'. She cannot, she protests, read those works in their original languages 'without I know not what emotions'. The generality of women 'have no other knowledge than that of dressing', a swipe by the dramatist at critics like Hannah Woolley who scorned the devotion of the morning to the looking-glass and the afternoon to the exchange or the playhouse.[60] It is scarcely surprising to find Lady Knowell's creator stating bluntly elsewhere that the only advantage which a male author had over a female one was in classical learning, and that there was no call for that in the

---

[57] Mrs Elizabeth Josceline, *The Mother's Legacie to her Unborne Child* (London, 1622); Mrs Dorothy Leigh, *The Mother's Blessing* (London, 1630); Richard Braithwaite, *The English Gentlewoman* (London, 1631); and *Time's Treasury* (London, 1641).

[58] *The Gentlewoman's Companion*, p. 13.

[59] The following plays of the period reflect contemporary prejudice against women of learning: John Dryden, *An Evening's Love* (1668) and *Marriage à-la-Mode* (1672); Richard Flecknoe, *Damoiselles à-la-Mode* (1667); Aphra Behn, *Sir Patient Fancy* (1678); Shadwell, *Bury Fair* (1689) and *The Sullen Lovers* (1668); Thomas Wright, *The Female Vertuosoes* (1693); Congreve, *The Double Dealer* (1694); W. M., *The Female Wits* (1697). See also Myra Reynolds, *The Learned Lady in England, 1650–1750* (New York, 1920). There is a striking contrast in the *Verney Memoirs*, iii. 74, between Sir Ralph's advocacy of French for his goddaughter and his horror of Latin.

[60] Aphra Behn, *Sir Patient Fancy* (1678) I. i. Woolley, *The Gentlewoman's Companion*, pp. 35–6.

playhouse in any case.[61] All this may show that those dramatists who parodied the learned lady in their plays felt that anyone writing a courtesy book for girls or recommending some adjustment in society's perception of women would find in the regular female theatre-goer a complete vindication of his opinions.

The truth of this may be determined if we look at what the courtesy authors said about the role of leisure and recreation in a girl's upbringing. The most proper recreations to Woolley's mind were dancing, painting, and music; without music, she declared, 'a lady or gentlewoman can hardly be said to be absolutely accomplish'd'.[62] Her opinion was a popular one. The liveliness of musical education in schools has already been noted, and a comparable breadth of interest was sustained informally. John Playford wrote of the large number of women in London who employed guitar teachers for their own and their daughters' instruction, while the Comte de Grammont's *Memoirs* indicate a similar enthusiasm for the instrument at Court.[63] Elizabeth Pepys begged for singing lessons, so her husband handed her to the hapless John Goodgroome for tuition.[64] Goodgroome's primitive method of teaching by rote did not endear him to Pepys, but according to Roger North it was a practice which could hardly be avoided given the voracious appetite of ladies for new tunes:

Ladys hear a new song, and are impatient to learn it. A master is sent for, and sings it as to a parrot, till at last with infinite difficulty the tune is gott, but with such infantine imperfect, nay broken abominable graces, in imitation of the good, that one would splitt to hear it. Yet *this is fine*, and the ladys goe to teaching one and other, especially if a little naturall lusciousness be couch't in the words.[65]

There were, nevertheless, sufficient numbers of the musically literate to permit the publication, in broadsheets and magazines, of popular songs, notation and all; while the concerts of music given first at his home in Whitefriars by John Banister and then at York Buildings by his imitators became a regular resort for the quality and the *beau monde*, if not so much as to challenge the supremacy of the playhouse.[66]

   [61] Behn, 'Letter to the Reader', *The Dutch Lover* (1673).
   [62] *The Gentlewoman's Companion*, pp. 83–4.
   [63] John Playford, Introduction to *Musick's Delight on the Cithern* (London, 1666); Anthony Hamilton, *Memoirs of the Life of the Count de Grammont*, trans. Abel Boyer (London, 1714), p. 177.
   [64] *Diary*, 25 June 1661; 1 Oct. 1661; 12 Mar. 1667; 9 Aug. 1667, *passim*.
   [65] John Wilson, *Roger North on Music* (London, 1959), 21.
   [66] Harley, *Music in Purcell's London*; Wilson, pp. 352–3.

In the theatres themselves the richness of London's musical life was strongly in evidence, particularly after the church had closed its doors to musical extravagance in 1689.[67] This should have presented the courtesy authors with a dilemma: how could one cite music as the supreme accomplishment and then deny your tutees the opportunity of enjoying it regularly at its most magnificent? It was only in the playhouse that one could listen to the most ambitious work of England's foremost composer; was it just to be severe to those women who picked up the names of all the players by going repeatedly to *King Arthur* or *The Fairy Queen*? In fact, the question never raised itself with sufficient force to reach print. People who wrote courtesy manuals did, nevertheless, ponder the suitability of the theatre in general as a recreation for gentlewomen, and their ponderings suggest strongly that dramatic opera presented no conflict of moral interest; not, perhaps surprisingly, because it was thought out of the question for a polite woman to attend the theatre in whatever circumstances, but because theatre-going was accepted as a suitable pastime.

None of the courtesy literature advises against going to the theatre. Woolley, Halifax, and Elstob certainly objected to ladies who did little else, but the bad habits of some did not diminish the value of the stage if used properly. Proper use in Woolley's book meant a studious attention to all the moral warning-signs which plays had to offer; in them a girl would find: 'excellent precepts for instruction, and sundry great examples for caution, and such notable passages, which being well applied ... will confer no small profit on the judicious hearer'. There is no comment on the productions of the contemporary stage (it is enough to note the triviality of some of its patrons) so it is difficult to know precisely where Woolley stands. She concludes that by allowing that the responsible parent will always use discretion in granting permission for his child to go to the theatre, and decrees that while the 'moderate recourse' of gentlewomen to plays may be tolerated, the 'daily and constant frequenting them' is certainly to be condemned.[68] Her taste for the exemplary quality of drama is not shared by others who addressed themselves to the rights and wrongs of female play-going, while her liberality in permitting attendance is. Halifax admitted that his daughter needed diversion from the oppression of sustained work or study. He was contemptuous of

---

[67] Mary Ede, *Arts and Society in England under William and Mary* (London, 1979), ch. 3; Franklin B. Zimmerman, *Henry Purcell* (London and Basingstoke, 1967), 185-210. Purcell suffered at the Court at this time because of his loyalty to James II and alleged Catholic sympathies.

[68] *The Gentlewoman's Companion*, pp. 35-6 and 84-5.

women who 'knew all the players' names' but he also envisaged a place for moderate enjoyment of the theatre in the lives of women who had other things to do, even without the requirement that it should be linked to instruction; it was the diversion which was important.[69] Similarly, John Dunton, when asked by one of his readers 'Whether it be lawfull to see plays?', replied first by lamenting the lewdness of the modern stage, and then by admitting that he knew of no recreation more profitable or enjoyable, even allowing for the aberrance of some playwrights.[70] Like Halifax, Dunton could readily conceive of an enjoyment which was quite proper though it had nothing necessarily to do with moral instruction; and if the allowance in these cases sometimes has the air of resignation to unalterable social habit, that shows simply that the regular theatre-going of many ordinary women provided no cause for alarm. It was demonstrably an innocent activity.

This review of the ideas and practice of female education and recreation has so far given ample support to the proposition of Beatrice and Mary Chapman which began the present chapter. Neither those who favoured accomplishments nor those who sought domestic competence and piety were interested in educating their daughters in any sense we recognize. Even so, the female community of London appears to have been literate to a substantial degree. One did not, as Aphra Behn pointed out, have to be learned in order to make a success at letters, and even serving-girls were capable of reading the romances and plays which their mistresses cast aside.[71] There were publications specifically for 'the ladies': historical works, newspapers, books of letters and tracts, apart from plays and prose fiction.[72] Women might even be praised for particular literary accomplishments, such as 'Quickness of Wit' and 'native Easiness'.[73] When Elizabeth Elstob found fault with her fellow women it was their casual literary abilities which she lighted upon:

They admire a play, a romance, a novel, perhaps entertain themselves a little with history, they read a poem gracefully, and make verses prettily, they rally and

---

[69] Halifax, p. 311.

[70] *The Athenian Mercury*, Tuesday, 14 Nov. 1693. Every Tuesday edn. of the paper was nominated 'The Ladies' Edition'.

[71] Shadwell, Epilogue, *The Squire of Alsatia* (1688).

[72] Tate, *A Present to the Ladies*; John Dunton, *The Ladies Dictionary* (London, 1694); Motteux, *The Gentleman's Journal*, June 1692; 'My miscellany is not only the Gentleman's but the Ladys Journal', *passim*. Some plays were dubbed 'Ladies' plays; see e.g. Nathaniel Lee, Prologue, *Mithridates* 1678) and Thomas Porter, Prologue, *The French Conjurer* (1677).

[73] Motteux, *The Gentleman's Journal*, April 1693.

repartee with abundance of wit and readiness; and with these embellishments imagine themselves perfectly accomplish'd.[74]

We might be forgiven for finding this an impressive list of attributes after reading Hannah Woolley and Richard Allestree. It is a comment on female education which underlines a previous comment on female leisure; the situation of the fashionable lady, thus figured, was very far from one of bored stupor.

Indeed, opportunities for developing literacy at least to the same degree as men multiplied the more a woman moved in fashionable circles. Woolley herself complained that the source of the intellectual difference between the sexes lay in the tendency of men to read one kind of literature and women another.[75] Such differences were more pronounced among the unfashionable: Pepys chid himself for reading the sort of book which was virtually designed to help his wife pass her time; and while the two of them could share the pleasure of Chaucer, Robert Wild, a number of plays, and some more specialized literature, Pepys's employment and education naturally gave him access to many books in which his wife could take no interest.[76] For the fashionable, whatever the quality of the literature, reading was more uniform. It is Sir Wilful Witwoud's breeding and not his sex which makes him stand stupidly by as Millamant quotes Suckling at him; the well-bred man can enter the room and complete a couplet with assured familiarity.[77] It was in the popular 'character' of the lady and the beau to go together to the theatre and to read plays in the evening; the same cultural opportunities were conspicuously shared.

Whatever the benefits to women of such an arrangement, however, other accomplishments and leisure activities tended to augment the sexual divide very much to the disadvantage of all women, 'ladies' or not. Elizabeth Elstob counted among the 'embellishments' of contemporary women the art of repartee, which many were able to practise with 'abundance of wit and readiness'. To read Jonathan Swift on the same subject is to realize that in granting women such readiness Elstob was bearing witness to a process of social change. 'Raillery,' wrote Swift, 'is the finest part of conversation; but, as it is our usual custom to counterfeit and adulterate whatever is dear to us, so we have done with this, and turned it

[74] Elstob, Preface, pp. iv–v.
[75] The Gentlewoman's Companion, pp. 1–2.
[76] Diary, 21 Nov. 1666; 23 Aug. 1663; 6 Dec. 1668; 29 Nov. 1661; 13 Mar. 1661; 23 Jan. 1661. Elizabeth's reading is discussed in detail below, in ch. 2.
[77] The Way of the World, IV. 80–128.

all into what is generally called Repartee, or being smart.' Raillery is not mere smartness, but to say: 'something that at first appeared a reproach or reflection; but, by some turn of wit unexpected and surprising, ended always in a compliment, and to the advantage of the person it was addressed to.'[78]

With the primacy of the baser art of repartee went an unprecedented egotism on the part of those who practised it; it was 'the character of being wits' which led some to seek admiration for their rudeness. One feature of this tendency was: 'the custom arisen, for some years past, of excluding women from any share in our society, further than in parties at play, or dancing, or in the pursuit of an amour'. This does not contradict the analysis of the fashionable world given so far. To Mirabell's disgust, there was a breed of men who lived simply to take part in those activities which Swift mentions; to Mirabell himself such things hardly constituted a negligible part of the day. The exclusion which Swift has in mind was that represented by the chocolate-house, where women could be spoken of in a spirit of free disparagement, if not of immodesty or indecency; qualities which were most to be feared when women were excluded from the conversation of men. One result of this was the phenomenon of the man who can only talk to a woman over whom he can claim social and sexual superiority:

it is observable in those sprightly gentlemen about town, who are so very dexterous at entertaining a vizard-mask in the park or the playhouse, that, in company of ladies of virtue and honour, they are silent and disconcerted, and out of their element.[79]

It was partly in the interests of good manners that the conditions which produced such monsters were brought about. The author of *The Art of Complaisance* went further than Swift in describing the benefits of conversing with ladies (it offers 'that air of the world, and that politeness, which no counsel nor lecture can give us') but he also drew emphatic limits to them: 'certain it is, we ought to regard the entertainment of the ladies, onely as a pleasant amusement, or a school of politeness, a man who makes it his whole business, renders himself contemptible'.[80] That code is

[78] Jonathan Swift, 'Hints towards an Essay on Conversation', *The Prose Works of Jonathan Swift*, ed. Herbert Davis, 14 vols. (Oxford, 1957-68), iv. 91-6. There is a useful discussion of Restoration codes of conversation in Allan Richard Botica's D.Phil. thesis, 'Audience, Playhouse and Play in Restoration Theatre, 1660-1710' (University of Oxford, 1985).

[79] Swift, p. 95.

[80] S. C., pp. 118-21.

witnessed by the contempt of a Mirabell for a Witwoud, and it seconds Swift's analysis: it was simply good manners to disdain the conversation of women except on particular occasions of leisure or self-interest. Only those who did not grasp the rules behaved otherwise; it was they, the 'conversable fops', who 'oblige the ladies no constraint or vigilance over their words or actions, having a full liberty to say what they please, without being thought vain, or foolish, by a man who knows not what it is in himself or others'.[81] It was, in short, good manners not to spend all of one's time in the company of women because one could not, as a man of sense, put up with for long with their stupidity; men such as Witwoud had to be dispatched instead to cope with the surplus.

Such an attitude bred strict rules concerning the subject matter of conversations with women. Learning is forbidden, and the topic must be changed frequently to avoid the fatigue of concentration. For ladies as well as men, grimaces and disagreeable gestures are not to be considered, and raillery is only to be employed 'as a delicious sauce, and not as a food'. Above all, the well-bred man must 'shun all manner of equivocation, since it is certain they very seldom please, I speak of words which have no certain signification, yet wound the imagination.' This sentiment was shared with a French contemporary, who thought any equivocation or ambiguity of expression used in the company of women 'an intrenchment upon civility'.[82] It was a sentiment, however, which had already begun to seem out-dated in 1673. One author claimed that it was pointless to observe such proprieties when talking to women because their own style of conversation had changed; in precisely the way, indeed, indicated by Elstob and enlarged upon by Swift. Swift wrote nostalgically of the means by which conversation had been cultivated at the Court of Charles and Henrietta Maria: assemblies were formed where 'persons of the best understanding, and of both sexes' met to discourse 'upon whatever agreeable subjects were occasionally started'. In later years the habit declined as the 'sublime Platonic notions' of its practitioners were ridiculed, but these notions, say Swift, at least held in check the 'sordid, vicious and low'.[83] Their demise came to the notice of the author of *Remarques on the Humours and Conversations of the Gallants of the Town*, who observed:

---

[81] S. C., p. 134.

[82] S. C., p. 42. See also *The Rules of Civility; or Certain Ways of Deportment observed in France, amongst all Persons of Quality, Translated out of French* (London, 1673), 71.

[83] Swift, p. 94. For a learned, comprehensive and early ridiculing of Caroline Platonism, see Walter Charleton, *The Ephesian Matron* (London, 1659), 48–9 and 66–7.

We are not now adays for lectures of Platonicks; since many of our women are grown as hardy as the men, and love a taste of the thing you wot of, to relish their conversations: they deride the formality of hearing long discourses of their beauty, of the achievements of their sex.[84]

Women's place in the art of conversation was in a state of flux; older rules of gallant decorum were challenged by a new refusal to recognize traditional distinctions between male and female conversation. Immodest raillery might be practised by women, but against a background of strict rules which had hardly accommodated themselves to its use by men. This made it difficult for some women to express offence at bad language without risking the charge of hypocrisy; to what standard could such women appeal, that of female modesty having been discredited?[85]

In the changing codes of conversational practice may be found a pattern to explain the status of Restoration women as sketched out at the beginning of this chapter. The author of *Remarques* goes on to report that no gallant of the town could be accomplished unless he was able to 'discourse on the intrigues of famous wenches'; an activity harmless enough but for its alliance with one thoroughly invidious:

The next great subject of their discourses, is the dishonours of women; those whom they have not overcome with their addresses, they will be sure to conquer with their tongues; and hardly leave an honest woman in the town: they are so charitable to think, there never was any such, but those who liv'd solitarily, and were never attacqu'd by a powerful courtship.[86]

It is a familiar phenomenon: the reduction of all women to objects of the sexual attentions of the fashionable male. In the mere fact of its promoting such an attitude Restoration society was scarcely distinctive. What was unusual was the intensity and sophistication of the means; such has been the subject of the first part of this chapter. The second is concerned initially with the peculiar role of the theatre in encouraging and diversifying that attitude.

II

The peculiarity of the role is partly in the peculiarity of the evidence. No one who writes about the Restoration Audience can shun the responsi-

---

[84] *Remarques*, p. 123. An example of the long discourse of which the author writes is John Shirley's *The Illustrious History of Women* (London, 1686).

[85] See e.g., William Wycherley, 'Epistle Dedicatory to my Lady B——', *The Plain Dealer* in *Plays*, 347–53.

[86] *Remarques*, p. 89.

bility of discussing its chief chronicle, the vast body of theatrical prologues and epilogues, though such an attempt extend no further than the breathless survey of scholarship which is offered here as a preliminary to some further observations. It is acknowledged that prologues and epilogues were popular entertainments in themselves; and that their popularity taxed sorely the ingenuity of the people who had to write them.[87] It is known, too, that they mentioned only a small proportion of the audience, and that those mentioned revelled in their conspicuousness though others laughed at them.[88] Dryden understood that no one expected a prologue to offer a great deal of factual information about the theatre or the intentions of the playwright; it was there to whet the appetite of the audience with a little raillery:

> You think yourselves ill us'd
> When in smart prologues you are not abus'd.
> A civil prologue is approv'd by no man;
> You hate it as you do a civil woman:
> Your fancy's pall'd, and liberally you pay
> To have it quicken'd, e're you see a play.
> Just as old sinners worn from their delight
> Give money to be whipp'd to appetite.[89]

The suave analogy with the sexual commerce of the town embodies the chief means by which the audience's fancy could be quickened.

This encourages one to regard the form less as a chronicle of the audience than as a means of conversing with it: an instrument for rallying and jesting which flattered the conspicuous with its attention to them and entertained everyone else. Some degree of exclusiveness was a precondition of its success, in that the majority of spectators were engaged merely as spectators. The shape of the playhouse must have helped; it was the people in the pit who received most attention, and it was they who sat,

[87] Stacy, *The Country Gentleman's Vade Mecum* (London, 1699) speaks of the role of good prologues and epilogues in securing a longer run (p. 45). See also Thomas Duffett, 'A Prologue', *New Poems, Songs, Prologues and Epilogues* (London, 1676) 65-7. For the 'tax on wit' exacted by the popularity of the form, see Sir Robert Howard, prologues to *The Suprizall* (1662) and *The Vestal Virgin* (1664), and Samuel Pordage, prologue, *The Siege of Babylon* (1677).

[88] See Avery, 'The Restoration Audience', and Botica, ch. 3.

[89] John Dryden, 'Second Prologue', *Secret Love* (1667). Only one recent commentator has held out, with predictably uninteresting results, for the literal accuracy of prologues and epilogues: Pierre Danchin, 'Le Public des Théâtres Londoniens à l'Époque de la Restauration d'après les Prologues et les Épilogues', *Dramaturgie et Société: XVIᵉ et XVIIᵉ Siècles*, ed. Jean Jacquot (Paris, 1968), 847-88.

surrounded by stage, boxes, and auditorium, half-way between playing and simply watching.[90] Given the conversational mode and its implicit exclusiveness, it is not surprising that prologues and epilogues were in certain respects subject to the same rules and failings as everyday conversation. The tendency towards male exclusiveness identified by Swift and others is there in abundance. One who complained about the imbalance of attention was John Crowne:

> The epilogue, yes, it becomes you well,
> You gentlemen! and why, I pray, to them?
> What, do the ladies merit no esteem?
> Good sirs! I know not whether 'tis your due,
> But poets still direct themselves to you.[91]

To neglect to address the ladies directly was in a sense to exclude them from a conversation with the gentlemen. In the town at large such conversations were often the occasion for disparaging comment about women, and the same pattern may be observed in the theatre. In Dryden's second prologue to *Secret Love* it is the men who are bored by their regular visits to the playhouse, the men who need to be enlivened by the raillery of a good prologue. In the same instance, raillery takes the form of two similes of uncivil women and flagellation; clearly women are excluded not only because they are not addressed directly, but also because they are made objects of rude fancy, mere referents of sexual experience, in the banter of playwright and male audience.

One effect of this exclusion was to banish the distinction of class usually observed in descriptions of the female audience, just as the distinction of honesty in women was banished from the conversation of gallants determined to conquer all in chat or in fact. Female spectators were generally allowed by the poets to be ladies, city-wives, or whores; whenever they were addressed directly, as if the same circle of conversation, those distinctions were respected.[92] It was when the poet was

---

[90] The best discussion of the relationship between the structure of the playhouse is to be found in Botica, ch. 1.

[91] John Crowne, Epilogue, *Juliana* (1671). The 'ladies' are mentioned in 40 per cent of the prologues and epilogues I have consulted, the 'gallants' in over twice that number.

[92] For ladies: Lee, Prologue, *Mithridates* (1677); Crowne, Epilogue, *The Ambitious Statesman* (1679); John Leanerd, Prologue, *The Counterfeits* (1679), *passim*. For city-wives: Crowne, Prologue, *Charles the Eighth* (1671); Thomas Dilke, Prologue, *The Lover's Luck* (1696); Behn, Epilogue, *The Debauchee* (1676). For whores: Crowne, Epilogue, *The English Friar* (1690), and Epilogue, *Darius King of Persia* (1688); Charles Saunders, Epilogue, *Tamerlane the Great* (1681). Francis Manning, Epilogue, *The Generous Choice* (1700), surveys all three types.

exclusively preoccupied with the men in the pit that they were forgotten, and a more generally imputed characteristic brought to the fore. It is well known that all the styles given to women—lady, mother, miss, and mistress—suffered peculiar stress at this time, and it was common for dramatists to joke that one could no longer distinguish a lady of quality from a whore, and that women were therefore all ladies or all whores.[93]

When begrudged direct attention, women in general (their lubricity taken for granted) could be seconded to serve as metaphors for the theatrical experience of the playwright, the actors, and the male audience. A poet might represent a new woman playwright as a bride unusually sullen and therefore incapable of giving pleasure; he might compare plays with mistresses, forever hankered after and soon cast off, or with wives, sent out into the pit among all those sparks to be debauched.[94] If he had an actress to speak his prologue or epilogue, the opportunities for titillation improved considerably. Favours could be offered to the first gallant to speak up for the play; a young girl could threaten to retire to the convent if the men were unkind, or she could lament her inability to please all those mature, worldly-wise male spectators.[95] The female prologue, so enthralling to the male audience, did little to arouse the female. The breeches prologue which Dryden wrote for Mrs Boutell confessed its want of tact:

> The ladies we shall not so easily please.
> They'll say what impudent bold things are these,
> That dare provoke, yet cannot do us right.[96]

The humour (such as it was) of these experiments in arousal depended on the assumption of universal female lubricity; that, irrespective of the

[93] Pepys (*Diary*, 30 May, 1668) applied the term 'lady' without flinching—perhaps even with a consciousness of propriety—to the chief among London whores, Mother Bennet, as did Wycherley. For 'mother' see also Dryden, *Sir Martin Mar-All* (1667) iv. i.; for 'Madam', *The Poor Whores Petition* (London, 1668); for 'miss' and 'mistress', Richard Flecknoe, *Euterpe Reviv'd* (London, 1675).

[94] Pix, Prologue, *The Spanish Wives*; Thomas Durfey, Epilogue, *The Fool Turn'd Critick* (1678); Henry Nevil Payne, Epilogue, *The Rambling Justice* (1678).

[95] Thomas Otway, Epilogue, *Don Carlos* (1676); John Dennis, Epilogue, *A Plot and No Plot* (1687); Durfey, Epilogue, *The Commonwealth of Women* (1685). Autrey Nell Wiley, 'Female Prologues and Epilogues in English Plays', *Publications of the Modern Language Association of America*, 48 (1933), I. 1060–79, counts 246 instances of the form from 1660 to 1714, 188 of them epilogues; an actress was more often employed to let her charms plead for the play rather than introduce it.

[96] Dryden, 'Prologue and Epilogue to *Secret Love* Spoken by the Women', *The Poems and Fables of John Dryden*, ed. James Kinsley (Oxford, 1970), 137–8.

social categories, was part of the character not simply of women in
general, but of women as patrons of the stage. Given that, women's
experience of the theatre could be described with rather disturbing sexual
intensity. Here is one version of what happened when women disliked the
play on offer:

> But here's the plague, they being of female kind,
> Have all the passions of a female mind:
> Their humours are as various as the wind,
> With fawning smiles they seem to draw you on,
> Till, when you think their favours you have won,
> The jilting jades turn tail, and straight are gone.[97]

They are, in other words, just as unreliable in the playhouse as their
teasing, lubricious instincts lead them to be in the park or elsewhere.
Charles Saunders even went so far as to portray his female audience as
ravenous sexual tyrants in their appetite for new plays; only the lusty
young newcomer stands a chance, he claims:

> You sly she-jockies of the box and pit,
> Are pleas'd to find a hot unbroken wit,
> By management he may in time be made,
> But there's no hopes of an old batter'd jade:
> Faint and unnerv'd he runs into a sweat;
> And always fails you at the second heat.[98]

The casual wit is entertaining enough, and not incompatible with the
raillery which, as directed to particular sections of the audience, was a kind
of compliment; but in its address to the female audience it merely
confirms the status accorded them in the public insinuations of playwright to gallant. It may not exclude them formally, but it bears all the
marks of exclusion. Jeremy Collier appeals to something other than
prudishness when he complains of the Restoration epilogue, 'Lewdness
without shame or example . . . This is the desert he regales the ladies with
at the end of the entertainment.'[99] The poet short of an easy simile for his
epilogue could turn to womankind with as great an assurance of success as
he could to Molière for a comic scene or two; a minimum of ingenuity
could wed the sex to any of the chief characteristics of the Restoration
stage: first nights, short runs, painted stages, and so on.
    If women in general could be so evoked in their capacity as patrons of

[97] Thomas Dilke, Prologue, *The City Lady* (1697).
[98] Charles Saunders, Epilogue, *Tamerlane the Great* (1681).
[99] Collier, *A Short View*, p. 13.

the stage, those who belonged to the class known as 'the ladies' suffered further wrongs of a similar (if more refined) sort. It was not only when social distinctions lapsed that generalized vituperation was permissible. The ladies were thought of as a critically homogeneous body of spectators; where it has often been allowed that the people of real critical influence in the playhouse (at least until the 1690s) were individual male wits such as Rochester, Buckingham, and Mulgrave, 'ladies' were believed to exert influence only corporately. According to John Dennis, it was those three eminent men who secured the success of *The Plain Dealer* when the rest of the audience was doubtful, while casual criticism from the lips of a brilliant man like Sir Charles Sedley could be more worth one's attention than the play itself. Such criticism ranged freely over a number of established, though not constricting, principles: plot, humour, wit, and so on. It was in the versatility and enterprise of their deployment of those terms that the leading critics excelled and led. Discussion could embrace a number of considerations, so dissent or approval was possible on a corresponding number of grounds.[100] The ladies were not so fortunate. Whatever discussion may have taken place in the leisurely round of visits and play-readings—there was clearly ample opportunity for it—the declared character of the ladies imposed its own regime: they were a single faction; and departures from the established rules of preference and aversion invited the charge of hypocrisy. Dryden could view such a departure with something more like astonishment than disgust when the controversy of Walsh's poem *The Confederates* divided the allegiance of the town: 'and there are really two factions of ladies, for the two playhouses';[101] but Sedley, disappointed by the failure of his *Bellamira* among the ladies, who had found it obscene, could not resist reflecting, 'I confess after the plays I have seen lately crowded by that fair sex the exception did not a little surprise me.'[102] Far greater would have been his surprise had it been objected that it might not have been the same lot of ladies, or that the other plays he referred to might have had other qualities

---

[100] The best formal example remains Dryden's *Essay of Dramatick Poesie*. See also J. W. H. Atkins, *English Literary Criticism: 17th & 18th Centuries* (London, 1951), ch. 1–4.

[101] Dryden, 'To Mrs Stewart', 23 Feb. 1699/1700, *The Letters of John Dryden* ed. Charles E. Ward (Durham, NC, 1942), 133. Walsh's poem is in *Poems on Affairs of State*, 2 vols. (London, 1703), ii, 248–50. It is a mock-heroic account of the support given by ladies to Peter Motteux's *The Island Princess* (1698), a dramatic opera after Fletcher's play; performed at the Theatre Royal, the piece drew crowds away from the previously more popular Lincoln's-Inn-Fields Theatre. Those who remained decried the plush vacuity of the new piece. See also *A Comparison Between the Two Stages* (London, 1702), 21–2.

[102] Sedley, Preface, *Bellamira* (1687).

to recommend them.' 'That fair sex' is indistinguishable in Sedley's account from the individuals who did or did not go.

A similar case is the scandal caused by Aphra Behn's *The Luckey Chance* in 1686. Plotting the play's failure, a number of 'sparks and poets' chose the most effective way of spoiling its reputation before it reached the playhouse: the magic words were circulated and a stock of pre-ordained critical objections released for the dramatist to contend with. 'When,' wrote the author, 'they can no other way prevail with the town, they charge [the play] with the old never failing scandal—that 'tis not fit for the ladies.' The force of this scandal-mongering was such that it could not be assuaged even by well-publicized reference to a group of discerning and actual ladies 'of very great quality and unquestioned fame' who found the play 'very far from scandalous'.[103] Evidently the popular idea of the lady as theatre-goer could not adjust itself to the heterogeneous composition of the real community of lady theatre-goers. There is some comfort for the student in Aphra Behn's misfortune: nothing could indicate more clearly that there was such a thing as a community of female patrons who took a responsible interest in the stage, and who exercised independent judgement in pronouncing on what was submitted to them. They may have been powerless to resist the imputation of conventional kinds of response, but such indications of critical interest must be valued if there is to be found in the lady theatre-goer anything more than what the courtesy authors usually found: idleness and frivolity.

In some respects, however, the stage went further than simply to adopt the base suggestions about women which the age was well-equipped to supply. It may seem implausible that anyone writing a theatrical prologue or epilogue should have been concerned to consider the political rights of the female audience, but the evidence is there. Dryden's definition of the political rights of the audience as a whole is a useful starting-point:

> To clap and hiss are the privileges of a free-born subject in a playhouse: they buy them with their Money, and their hands and mouths are their own property: it belongs to the Master of the Revels, to see that no treason or immorality be in the play; but when 'tis acted, let every man like or dislike freely: not but that respect should be used too in the presence of the King, for by his permission the actors are allowed.[104]

---

[103] Behn, Preface, *The Luckey Chance*. Crowne, Preface, *The English Friar* (1690) records a similar experience. Behn also won the approval of Charles Davenant, Charles Killigrew, and Sir Roger L'Estrange for her play. The ladies concerned cannot be identified; in the circumstances it would have been very impolite of Behn to disclose their names.

[104] Dryden, *The Vindication of the Duke of Guise* (London, 1683), 19.

It is in property that the right (even the capacity) to approve or disapprove resides. The qualifications of 'free-born' and 'property' claim a right not mentioned directly by Dryden but one which appears in the forefront of further evidence, the right to vote. That is a right from which women were, of course, excluded.[105] Dryden's concession, 'let every man like or dislike freely', is no accidental ungallantry: it merely matches the political balance of the playhouse with that of the country at large.

Where democratic rights were lacking, it was easy to envisage constitutional privileges. John Crowne refers in his prologue to *Juliana* to the 'Senate of ladies, lower house of men', a political distinction which was emphasized by the arrangement of boxes and pit in the theatre: the ladies were really aloof from the busy 'voting' of the men, and were no doubt enfeebled by their aloofness. The difficulty was apparent to Dryden. In his epilogue to *All for Love* (1677) he mourned the supremacy of fops and fools and hoped that the ladies might form a 'Grand jury' to sit in judgement on his play. Henry Nevil Payne, in his prologue to *The Fatal Jealousie* (1672), suggested a more conciliatory political solution when he called the ladies 'lawfull Monarches', which complimented them on their tactful exercise of power while reminding them of its origins and limitations. Such precision in a passage of raillery whose humour depended upon instant recognition argues for a measure of subtle political understanding among the audience, male and female, which enabled them to move wryly from the political scene at large to the particular routines and topography of the playhouse. Even greater precision is achieved by Thomas Betterton in his prologue to *The Prophetess* (1690). Here the ladies are appealed to *in loco regis*, and the appeal is made piquant not only by their destitution of ordinary democratic rights, but also by the conspicuous lack of interest shown by the recently enthroned William and Mary in the theatre. Betterton hoped that another dramatic renaissance might be fostered by female patronage:

> That our dead stage, revived by your bright eyes,
> Under a female Regency may rise.

'Regency' offers tactful encouragement while avoiding a direct slight to the monarchy. The ladies, unable to participate in the democracy of the pit, step carefully into the shoes of the absent rulers.[106]

---

[105] For a discussion of this, see Roger Thompson, *Women in Stuart England and America* (London and Boston, 1974), 162–9.

[106] Lee, Prologue to *Lucius Junius Brutus* (1680) envisages a sort of *coup* to overthrow the 'leading voters of the pit': 'Women for ends of government more fit, / Women shall rule

Barry University Library
Miami, FL 33161

It is interesting to compare these allusions with discussion of women's political rights as it existed at least in the memories of the theatre's patrons. Pamphlets celebrating the petitioning of Parliament by women show that the issue of female suffrage had been alive in the recent past, while the opposition which such publications received was invariably crude and reductive: the usual case, predictably, was that a parliament of women would merely offer rule by the over-sexed.[107] It is perhaps surprising (and certainly reassuring) that the political raillery of the Restoration dramatist with his female audience on no occasion reflects such a view. The rights of the ladies were a comparatively sober issue.[108]

It was not only in overtly political terms, however, that the political status of the ladies was addressed. The language of courtship which poets often used to beg favour implied an understanding of it:

> The poet now the ladies help does crave,
> That with a smile or frown can damn or save,

wrote Thomas Durfey in his epilogue to *Trick for Trick* (1678), anticipating Motteux in his epilogue to *Love's a Jest* (1696): 'You save or damn us as you smile or frown.' For William Davenant, the 'richest blessing of his fortune' lay in the 'gentle eyes' of the 'soft ladies', while Elkanah Settle hoped that the female audience of his *Empress of Morocco* would be as kind as they were fair.[109] The power attributed is royal (even divine) as it is sexual. The lady is a presence at once regal in her detachment (she has to be flattered

the boxes and the pit.' This discussion on the rights of the ladies redraws, from the point of view of the female audience, the boundaries of an argument first expounded by Leo Hughes in *The Drama's Patrons: A Study of the Eighteenth Century Audience* (Austin and London, 1971), ch. 1. I am indebted to Hughes's research into the preference of early eighteenth century dramatists for metaphors of government when describing the audience; a preference which, he argues, dates from the 1689 Bill of Rights. The constitutional conception of the playhouse, in so far as it explains the rights of the ladies, clearly dates from before 1689.

[107] Ellen McArthur, 'Women Petitioners and the Long Parliament', *English Historical Review* 24 (1909), 698–709; K. V. Thomas, 'Women and the Civil War Sects', *Crisis in Europe, 1560–1660*, ed. T. Aston (London, 1965); *The Parliament of Women* (London, 1640); Henry Neville, *News from the New Exchange, or the Commonwealth of Ladies* (London, 1650); George Horton, *Now or Never: Or a New Parliament of Women* (London, 1656).

[108] The notion of women ruling by lust is, however, conspicuous in libertine literature of the Restoration, especially in descriptions of the Court. See Roger Thompson, *Unfit for Modest Ears: A Study of Pornography in the Seventeenth Century* (London and Basingstoke, 1979), 121–30.

[109] Davenant, Prologue, *The Platonick Lovers* (1665); Settle, Epilogue, *The Empress of Morocco* (1673).

and petitioned humbly for the granting of the day's suit) and potentially
alluring in her command of the favourable nod or glance. The constitutional privileges accorded women in the theatre had that further security
of tenure; they proceeded naturally from the rules of gallant courtship,
and any notion of granting women democratic power in the playhouse
was bound to seem fantastic compared with that of allowing them the
beatific influence which they enjoyed as unpredictable givers of favour.
There were, inevitably, dangers. It was the ambiguity of 'favour'
(ambiguous in the expectation but straightforward in the disappointment)
which facilitated detraction when favour was withheld. In the words of
Thomas Dilke quoted above,

> With fawning smiles they seem to draw you on,
> Till, when you think their favours you have won,
> The jilting jades turn tail, and straight are gone.

Even where women enjoyed royal or senatorial status without the
burden of such insinuations, their power was admitted to be limited in a
way that of the gentlemen was not. If to the collection of encomia to
gentle eyes be added the claim of William Phillips's epilogue to *The
Revengeful Queen* (1698) that 'One tender look' from the ladies gave more
pleasure than 'when the pit applauds, or galleries roar', it becomes clear
that the usual appeals to female critical power do not permit the right of
vocal approval or disapproval: it is all in the play of the face, and a single
tender look can out-do applause or roaring, the young man's prerogative.[110] It is not fanciful to suggest that when the rule was breached—most
famously in the case of *The London Cuckolds*, when some women 'cried
down' successive performances—the consequent fuss was caused not only
by the familiar scent of hypocritical prudery but also by the fact that the
women concerned spoke up at all.[111] The convention was that they should
remain beatifically detached: constitutionally superior but without a voice
in the actual running of affairs. 'Not to be heard at a distance' was Richard
Allestree's verdict upon the voice of a woman; not that he would appear to
have much in common with people who wrote prologues for the theatre.
When Olivia, in *The Plain Dealer*, was mocked for grimacing at *The*

---

[110] See also Lee, Epilogue, *Sophonisba* (1675); Durfey, Prologue, *The Siege of Memphis*
(1676); Boyle, Prologue, *Mr Anthony* (1694).
[111] Ravenscroft, Prologue, *Dame Dobson* (1683). The offence caused to some women by
the appearance of *The London Cuckolds* lingered for years. See Behn's prose tale, 'The Court
of the King of Bantam', *The Works of Aphra Behn*, ed. Montague Summers, 6 vols. (London
and Stratford, 1915), v. 30.

Country Wife, she was found guilty of a crime against conversational deportment, yet she had also done her best to remain within the constitution of the playhouse as understood by a number of dramatists.[112] Grimaces could be the last resort for the truly conscientious.

This silent language of critical approval was sought by the playwright in the interests not only of the particulars of his play but of securing order within the auditorium; a precise reflection of the role of the King there, as Dryden envisaged it. The softness of the ladies' eyes in granting favour to the playwright becomes a more brilliant force when required to deal with his enemies:

> Disperse the storms with your fair smiles and eyes,
> That from the rage of burning critics rise;
> And as the tempest gathers in the pit
> Let the bright beams then scatter it.[113]

What is then secured is more than good order: it is an atmosphere of *amour courtois* in which sensitive, gallant endeavour can flourish under the tutelage of the ladies. Here is George Powell's view, from the prologue to *Alphonso King of Naples* (1690) of the influence shed by the ladies:

> Bright ladies then, whose rays throughout the pit
> Do influence all around with love and wit,
> Oh tune their judgments e'er my fate be known,
> 'Tis in your power to make my case their own.[114]

'Influence' here suggests a muse rather than a critical arbiter: women must not dictate to the state rules of conduct, but suffer themselves to inspire better endeavour through the brightness and silent perfection of their characters. They were the model for the conscientious playwright. William Davenant had his prologue to *The Rivals* (1664) announce,

> Ladies, our author does by me declare
> Your characters are still his chiefest care;
> That what he does present to public view,
> He'd have as excellent as he thinks you.

---

[112] Wycherley, *The Plain Dealer*, II. i. 455–81. For the impropriety of grimacing, see *The Art of Complaisance*, pp. 32 and 42.

[113] John Bankes, Prologue, *The Rival Kings* (1677).

[114] For variations on the theme, see Prologue, *Wits Led by the Nose* (1681); John Corye, Prologue, *The Generous Enemies* (1672). Betterton, Prologue, *The Prophetess*, mocks (in a time of war) the chivalric ethic upheld by such talk.

It would be callous and ungentlemanly to spoil the reputations of the ladies by representing them in public as anything but luminously virtuous. To be exemplary was simply to be realistic. Bankes dedicated *The Rival Kings* to Lady Herbert and wrote, 'In our plays you read your own characters, and they are at best what we have gathered from you, who daily act among yourselves in conversation.' The ladies allow themselves to be copied and the drama is made and, presumably, applauded: the paragon of art for royalty's sake.

However, when the model is also the critic, and when the inspiration and the applause derive from principles of virtue, complications are likely to arise. Dramatists who depicted the matchless virtues of women sometimes insisted, on pain of adverse reflection, on the support of the professedly virtuous female audience:

> First ladies I am sent to you, from whom
> Our author hopes a favourable doom,
> As friends to virtue, since 'tas been her end
> Vice to discourage, Virtue recommend;
> You've seen revenged an injured woman's cause,
> And so much justice can't deny applause;
> Felicia too expects you should approve
> A wife's fidelity and tender love;
> Protect her character as you'd be thought
> The bright originals from which 'twas wrought.[115]

Applause is the outward show of virtue where such a play is concerned: the virtuous heroine demands it, and although she requires the 'protection' of the ladies if the play is to succeed her virtue does not depend on it. That of the ladies themselves clearly does. They will be judged by the extent of their approval of the unequivocally virtuous; if they do not approve ostentatiously it may be assumed that Felicia was drawn from other models. It would have been dangerous to find anything else in the play worthy of commendation if it detracted from the visible applause given to the central representative of virtue. Could a woman enjoy publicly the plot or the wit without being thought wanting in the Felician virtues?

If the reading of romances involved a conspiracy of example, filling the vacant leisure hours with something imaginative which could still be used to enforce subjection and moral inferiority, it is not extravagant to see a

---

[115] Catherine Trotter, Prologue, *Fatal Friendship* (1698). See also Settle, Epilogue, *Love and Revenge* (1674), and Henry Smith, Prologue, *The Princess of Parma* (1699).

similar conspiracy at work in the theatre. Drama produced explicitly to satisfy the needs of the ladies—to present them with models of female virtue—could only be applauded as it answered to their declared moral character, and if its heroines were as unremittingly virtuous as Trotter's Felicia, applause was the only option. The dramatists themselves were in unwitting alliance with the legendary gallants who gathered round and ogled ladies in order to observe reflex revulsion or pleasure when a dirty joke was cracked; both groups were in the business of calling forth to public witness a woman's experience of sex, direct or understood.[116] Once the dramatist had protected the character of the ladies by showing off the virtues of the sex, it was up to the ladies to protect their own characters by applauding (no matter how dull, it seems, the rest of the entertainment); so, when a *double entendre* occurred in the theatre, it was up to a woman to make it clear that she understood only the innocent part, however obvious everyone else's enjoyment of the humour. In both cases, a woman was allowed to judge a play only in so far as it reflected her declared moral character, and in so far as it did that the quality of her response could be gauged only by the extent of her embarrassment.

Documentation of female critical activity is, accordingly, depressingly limited. No one can claim that the long-running debate about the bawdy elements of Restoration comedy was ever a distinguished one, and its monotony was effected in the first place by that tenacious equation of applause with declared moral probity. Ladies complain about bawdy words and scenes which submit them to public embarrassment, while dramatists complain that only the dirty-minded could find anything objectionable in their wholesome productions. Each side accuses the other of hypocrisy. Wycherley rails at the women who disliked *The Country Wife* and *The Plain Dealer* by alleging that the same women would accept from other playwrights a dirty joke, 'as cheerfully as from the watermen'; but it is vain for him to suggest that his words in either play have been 'ravished' in their innocence and made guilty of the ladies' own 'naughtiness': he confesses as much in the famous china scene in *The Country Wife*.[117] Thus far the debate merely reflects contemporary thinking about

---

[116] See Ravenscroft, Prologue, *Dame Dobson*; Durfey, Prologue, *The Banditti* (1686); Shadwell, Prologue, *The Royal Shepherdess* (1669); Otway, Prologue, *Friendship in Fashion* (1678).

[117] Wycherley, 'Epistle to my Lady B——', *The Country Wife* (1675), IV. iii. 207–35: Horner promises Mrs Squeamish a china 'roll-wagon' (a phallic-shaped vase), and is challenged by the jealous Lady Fidget to say what he means. He replies that Squeamish has only 'an innocent, literal understanding'.

the wider role of women in polite society: one side holds that strict rules must be observed when talking to ladies, and that equivocation must be avoided in particular; the other considers that the ladies themselves have made such rules redundant by taking over those parts of conversation previously denied them. So, in the theatre, certain ladies and their advocates demand that plays reflect female virtues, whilst their opponents assert that there are none to reflect. In both instances tension arose as extreme formality gave way to extreme liberty. It was with incredulity that Thomas Shadwell, traditionally the ladies' apologist, observed their attendance at plays which, he considered, ought to have been beneath their contempt:

> Good plays from censure here you'll not exempt,
> Yet can like farces, there below contempt,
> Drolls which so coarse, so dull, so bawdy are,
> The dirty rout would damn 'em in a fair:
> Yet gentlemen such stuff will daily see;
> Nay, ladies too, will in the boxes be;
> What is become of former modesty?[118]

In the theatre, the tension between the traditional apologist and the modern cynic gave rise to two utterly opposed but complementary parties; each determined to rescue the ladies from the ranks of the other, each committed to doing so by requiring them to declare publicly the extent of their experience. The contention of the two was bound to continue as tediously as it did as long as both agreed that play-going was, for women, principally the occasion for declaring one's private moral status.

The implications of the debate are further shown in the preference of some dramatists for plots which showed women in a dim light. Here is Wycherley again, in the epistle to Mother Bennet:

some there are who say 'tis the plain dealing of the play, not the obscenity, 'tis taking off the ladies' masks, not offering at their petticoats, which offends 'em. And generally they are not the handsomest or most innocent who are most angry at being discovered.

There were few satisfactions so profound for the Restoration playwright as that of lashing the age to felt effect, even if it meant a loss of revenue.[119] Wycherley is partly celebrating his own dramatic machismo, his ability to

[118] Shadwell, Epilogue, *Psyche* (1675).
[119] Durfey was particularly fond of expounding the dignity of dramatic satire (a useful way of explaining a box-office flop in some cases): Prologue and Epilogue, *The Fool's Preferment* (1688); Prologue and Epilogue, *Bussy d'Ambois* (1691). See also Crowne, Preface,

score direct satirical hits against a corrupt town.[120] However noble that achievement, it is directly related to the less exalted art of the *double entendre* —even, in the environment of the playhouse, inseparable from it. A satirical hit was significant nowhere more clearly than in the embarrassed recognition of a bawdy joke. That being so, the discomfort occasioned by 'smut' was no trifling matter, since a lewd jest could become, in the hands of the most inept dramatist, a means of scoring points against any woman who happened to be in the theatre. It is idle for Wycherley to suggest, in this seductively concerned sentence from the letter to Mother Bennet, that his satire was directed against the few least worthy:

But those who act as they look ought not to be scandalized at the reprehension of others' faults, lest they tax themselves with 'em, and by too delicate and quick an apprehension not only make that obscene which I mean innocent, but that satire on all which was intended only on those who deserved it.

Given the peculiar condition and pressures of the playhouse, 'satire' could not be confined as easily as Wycherley claims. The bawdy jest pointed a satirical finger at all who succumbed to it, and a woman might appreciate very well the particularity of the dramatic satire and yet remain subject to the no less insistent satire of the auditorium and its routines, forever prying for signs of self-betrayal.

Wycherley's chief satirical target in *The Plain Dealer* itself, the character of Olivia, witnesses the extent of those pressures as they affected individual women. A representative of the 'nice, coy women of honour' who protested about *The Country Wife*, she contends that to remain composed and passive at a 'filthy play' is to compromise one's honour, since it is to publish calm acceptance. Instead it is necessary to indulge in what Eliza (a dubious apologist for her sex) calls 'honour and artificial modesty', which may be derided, like natural blushes, for betraying a want of true modesty. Olivia is further mocked for proposing that the offended patron should stay away from the theatre for the duration of the play in question—a reasonable enough proposal, surely, for anyone seriously concerned about such things. Olivia's is the least adequate voice of protest imaginable—her own imagination is monstrously inventive—but she nevertheless articulates a serious argument about the position of women in the Restoration playhouse. What options did a woman have which

The Married Beau (1694); George Granville, Preface, *The She-Gallants* (1695); Congreve, 'To the Right Honourable Charles Montague', *The Double Dealer* (1693).

[120] For the soubriquet 'Manly Wycherley' see James L. Smith, Introduction to *The Plain Dealer* (London, 1979), p. xxi.

would free her from censure? Eliza argues by misleading similes, and can only propose what the least liberal courtesy author might have suggested: 'the truly modest ... say least and are least exceptious', which was no solution at all when offence was genuinely felt, and which still allowed for the spontaneous blush; worse manners, as Allestree knew, than the things which ought to occasion it, and the infallible sign of private guilt rather than outraged modesty.[121]

Wycherley's own imperatives are hardly more helpful in explaining what the genuinely offended woman could do to avoid ridicule. His chief complaint in the letter to Mother Bennet is that female fashion, in the shape of the mask, has made it impossible to distinguish a modest woman from a promiscuous one: why should the dramatist go out of his way to make the distinction when women themselves, by dressing alike, do not bother? We need only turn to a celebrated passage from Cibber's *Apology* to understand the absurdity of that charge as it applies to women who went to the theatre, and to see some light at the end of the long, dark tunnel of contention between female apologists and female detractors. At the outset, Cibber's account threatens to make one further contribution to that tiresome debate, but shows ultimately the distinction of that bare minimum of historical latitude, more than sixty years after the scandal of *The Country Wife*, which commentators of the Restoration period usually failed to observe:

I remember the ladies were then decently afraid of venturing barefaced to a new comedy, 'till they had been assured they might do it without the risque of an insult to their modesty; or, if their curiosity were too strong for their patience, they took care, at least, to save appearances, and rarely came upon the first days of acting, but in masks ... which custom, however, had so many ill consequences attending it, that it has been abolished these many years.[122]

This appears initially to cancel out Wycherley's case, tit for tat; modesty wins the day over its doubters, and Wycherley is shown to recommend only passive acceptance of the offensive. Such would have been the case of the apologist. Cibber (for once) is wiser. He sees that motives and effects were mixed, that some women acted out of good intentions and some did

---

[121] *The Plain Dealer*, II. i. 455–530.

[122] Colley Cibber, *An Apology for the Life of Mr Colley Cibber, Comedian*, ed. B. S. Fone (Ann Arbor, 1968), 147. The *Apology* was first published in 1741; Queen Anne prohibited the wearing of masks in the theatre in 1704. Discussion of the different uses of the mask may be found below, in ch. 3. J. L. Styan, *Restoration Comedy in Performance* (Cambridge, 1986), 112–13, comments on the cosmetic origins of the mask, but says little about the different reasons for wearing it.

not, that the conspiracy of the theatre against the truly modest was achieved in collaboration with those who merely professed modesty. He does not see a wider range of critical activity among the female audience. He does, however, envisage a wider range of motives for going to the theatre than so many other commentators and polemicists in an age which struggled to inure itself to the challenging by women of traditional moral imperatives in conversation, theatre-going, and other features of fashionable life, and in its struggle resorted for analysis of its women to two eternally contending stereotypes. The crisis of general esteem reported at the beginning of this chapter is reflected, for the female patron of the Restoration Stage, in a crisis of misrepresentation, with all its invidious pressures in the plays, prologues, and auditorium; pressures exerted no less by the traditional apologists than by the modern detractors. For her student, it is a crisis of reliable evidence. What may be learned of her characteristic critical activities beyond the moral self-scrutiny alleged in the evidence adduced so far will be the subject of the last part of this chapter.

III

The time given so far to the question of women's education will have been wasted if it is not already clear that women must have been concerned with a great many things apart from their blushes when they went to the theatre. Some of these must have involved critical discourse unrelated to the moral considerations so often invoked. It is scarcely conceivable, for instance, that romances, so widely read by women and so often plundered for stage plays, should not have occasioned comment in the theatre about the shaping of scenes, the aptness of the dialogue, or the success of the casting.[123] Older educational prerogatives may have insisted that it was pre-eminently a girl's business to blush and learn to analyse her blushing, and the playhouse may have been well-equipped to second that insistence, but some critical activities involved a freer response.

The popularity of musical entertainment in the theatre reflected the

---

[123] For borrowings from romances, see Herbert Wynford Hill, *La Calpranede's Romances and the Restoration Drama*, 3 vols. (Nevada, 1910–11); Allardyce Nicoll, *A History of Restoration Drama*, 3rd edn. (Cambridge, 1940), 86–7; Jerome W. Schweiter, 'Dryden's Use of Scudery's *Almahide*', *Modern Language Notes*, 54, 190–2. Elizabeth Pepys disliked Dryden's *An Evening's Love* because it was 'taken wholly' from *L'Illustre Bassa* (*Diary*, 20 June 1668). For comment on casting the title role of Southerne's *Oroonoko*, after Behn's novel, see Anthony Aston, *A Brief Supplement to the Life of Mr Colley Cibber* in Cibber's *Apology*, ed. R. W. Lowe, 2 vols. (London, 1889), ii. 313.

level of private interest among 'people of quality' in general and 'ladies' in particular.[124] Responses to it could be more interesting than North's account of ceaseless salon warbling suggests; North himself admits as much when he pokes fun at the characteristic expression of delight when a new piece is heard: '*This is fine*'.[125] 'Fine things' were the scraps of poetry and proverbs, maxim and song, which women spent time in learning and admiring, and which held their place in the vocabulary of the theatre audience. 'We are fond of fine things (as the ladies call 'em)', wrote Charles Gildon, while Jeremy Collier, quoting blasphemous passages from Dryden, asked, 'Are these the fine things Mr Dryden says the ladies call on him for?'[126] They were valued not merely as mementoes of an enjoyable evening, but as living constituents of a personal (though fashionable) vocabulary. Mental jottings from tragedy could readily be parodied:

I took delight when he was with me, to repeat often those words in *Sophonisba*; 'The forts impregnable, break up your siege, there's one for you too mighty entered in';[127]

while poetry and song provided Millamant with the means to slight suitors, encourage lovers, and infuriate rivals. 'Love's but the frailty of the mind' is the song she 'would have learned yesterday', in all probability by rote; it is a way of slighting Mrs Marwood (one of the 'inferior beauties' of the song), and it is typical of her that she should not deign to perform it herself but leave it to be sung by Mrs Hodgson 'that is in the next room'. This was partly a deft trick for the benefit of Anne Bracegirdle, who first played Millamant, and who evidently could not sing as well as Mrs Hodgson, yet who could, with Congreve's assistance, still appear completely to advantage in the part, disingenuously urging her rival to hear the song, 'not that there's any great matter in it'.[128] The audience's awareness of the civilizing but representing grace of Millamant's deployment of that particular set of fine things cannot but have gone with an ironic recognition of the limitations of its performance, whether by more or less mercurial beings.

[124] *A Comparison of the Two Stages*, p. 22; John Downes, *Roscius Anglicanus* (London, 1708), 38. [125] *Roger North on Music*, p. 21.
[126] Gildon, Preface, *Phaeton* (1698); Collier, *A Short View*, p. 9. Gildon discusses the popularity of Seneca for fine things; Behn's Lady Knowell spent her serious hours reading Tacitus, Seneca, and Plutarch, (*Sir Patient Fancy*, I. i.), which authors also appear in Mr Bayes's book of 'Drama Common places' (George Villiers, Duke of Buckingham, *The Rehearsal*, I. i. 110, in *Burlesque Plays of the Eighteenth Century*, ed. Simon Trussler (Oxford, 1969), 9).
[127] *Letters of Love and Gallantry*, 2 vols. (London, 1693), i. 62.
[128] *The Way of the World*, III, 329-44.

The appreciation of fine things, in which music and poetry could meet to enhance conversation, is plainly related to the literary habits advocated by critics of the fashionable world; by Hannah Woolley, for one, for whom the value of plays lay in their 'excellent precepts', 'sundry great examples for caution', and 'notable passages'. No doubt Woolley would have regarded the cult of fine things as an abuse of a valuable tool of instruction, just as the blush, ancient sign of innocence, was now held to signify guilt and ill-breeding—another area in which women were not so much forsaking traditional roles as rejecting their moralistic implications. It might tentatively be offered that whatever the emphasis given to accomplishments in the education of the gentlewoman, it was still the older prerogatives of instruction and example which gave shape to women's interest in music, literature, and the theatre. Some broadening of opportunity there may have been in the period in question, but the forms in which new opportunities could be pursued remained unaltered.

That conclusion is strengthened by a consideration of women's appreciation of dramatic poetry, of which Thomas Shadwell was the foremost critic. Twenty years stand between the prologues of *The Sullen Lovers* and *The Squire of Alsatia*, yet their author remained convinced of the damaging effects of the heroic couplet on the sensibilities of his female audience. Before the earlier play he warned the ladies that they would find,

> No kind romantic lovers in his play,
> To sigh and whine out passion, such as may
> Charm waiting women with heroic chime,
> And still resolve to live and die in rhyme;

while the later prologue criticizes the sacrifice of sense to sound in so much contemporary dramatic verse:

> No princess frowns, no hero rants and whines,
> Nor his weak sense embroiders with strong lines.

Such stuff, Shadwell urges, should be left to the chambermaids. Strong lines and heroic chime appear to look forward to a happy retirement between the leaves of a commonplace book, yet there is evidence that serious discussion of the place of rhyme in a drama was not confined to the circles represented, for instance, by Dryden's *Essay of Dramatick Poesy*. Like Dryden and his company of friends, Katherine Phillips had a professional interest in the subject, and there is no reason to assume that the attention she gives to a rival translation of Corneille's *Pompée* was false to the general run of literate female spectators any more than was the conversation of Lisideius, Eugenius, Crites, and Neander to the majority of educated men in the audience:

What chiefly disgusts me is, that the sense most commonly languishes through three or four lines, and then ends in the middle of the fifth: for I am of opinion, that the sense ought always to be confined to the couplet, otherwise the lines must needs be spiritless and dull.[129]

It is perfectly precise and well-tuned appreciation which engaged faculties more discerning than any Shadwell was aware of, and the proliferation of commonplace books, amateur versifying and sung poetry argues strongly that such faculties were by no means rare.[130] No doubt for some the pleasure of the couplet was all in the inebriating chime; no doubt many succumbed to its capacity, in the words of Wycherley's Mr Novel, for allowing 'a *double entendre* to pass with the ladies for soft, tender, and moving passion';[131] but the fact remains that those coarse responses were the foundation for finer ones. That they offered ground for cultivation is important; it allows us to see beyond the trance of dull acquiescence envisaged by Shadwell. Such appreciation was a matter for the theatre as well as the closet. Among actors, a musical delivery was favoured in tragedy and a colloquial in comedy, while Thomas Betterton, so often the hero of tragedy, had a voice which was, according to Cibber, 'Low and grumbling . . . yet he could tune it to an artful climax, which enforced universal attention, even from the fops and orange-girls.' When he spoke in 'flowing numbers', 'the multitude no more desired sense to them than our musical connoisseurs think it essential in the celebrated airs of an Italian opera'.[132] Such gifts were not the admiration of the ladies alone, but the ladies were unusually well qualified to appreciate them. It was not only the hint of a fine phrase or a well-turned verse, but the artfulness of the delivery. It is hard not to detect here the influence of that most time-honoured and domestic of female accomplishments, the well-trained speaking voice, valued by some for aesthetic reasons and by others for political ones. If the cultivation of this faculty gave shape to imaginative

[129] Katherine Phillips, *Letters from Orinda to Poliarchus* (London, 1705), 178–9. Her *Pompey* was performed in Dublin in February 1663; that of 'Certain persons of honour' (thought by Nicoll to include Sedley, Buckhurst, and William Waller) at Lincoln's-Inn-Fields in 1664.

[130] Elstob, pp. iv–v.

[131] *The Plain Dealer*, II, i. 479–80.

[132] *Apology*, pp. 82–3, 64–5. Further comment on declamatory style may be found in Charles Gildon, *The Life of Mr Thomas Betterton* (London, 1710).

and critical energies, it also condemned them, at a time when the rules of dramatic criticism were being so thoroughly pondered, to a trivial want of breadth. The constricting effects of the older educational prerogatives are once again evident; however their potential use may have expanded, they remained inherently limiting.

Where are we to turn for evidence of a distinctively female appreciation of plays which is not encumbered by moral prejudice or triviality, and which measures up to the growing sophistication of dramatic criticism? At the risk of sounding absurd, something like a real grasp of the principles of contemporary critical thought is evident in an activity which was widespread among women theatre-goers, and which at first appears not to embody but to prohibit discriminating criticism: that of weeping. Women often, it seems, wept at the theatre, and they usually provoked the scorn of onlookers when they did so.[133] Even so, discriminating tears there were; it was part of the latest ideas about dramatic design to encourage them. Consider the thoughts of Dryden and his friends on the subject. In the *Essay of Dramatick Poesy* the character of Neander, enumerating the faults of contemporary French drama, cites its tendency to depict passion in speeches of great length and solemnity: a 'long sober shower' which gives the passions of the audience 'leisure to run out . . . without troubling the current'. The English drama, he argues, develops such feelings by 'short speeches and replies', which are 'more apt to move the passions and beget concernment'; its mimetic representation of the bursts and starts of those feelings in its characters produces a more lively and unexpected quality of response in its audience. It is true that the purpose of such a representation is to awaken a more complete kind of emotional indulgence, but that indulgence is valued only in so far as it contributes to the more satisfying variety of response initiated, Neander claims, by the English manner:

Grief and passion are like floods raised in little brooks by sudden rain; they are quickly up and if the concernment be poured unexpectedly in upon us, it overflows us; but a long sober shower gives them leisure to run out . . .[134]

The surprise, the overwhelming onset of emotion, can only be achieved in the varied rhythm not simply of the 'mixed' form (that is, a mixture of tragic and comic scenes) but also of the multi-plotted tragedies favoured

---

[133] See Motteux, 'An Epistolary Essay to Mr *Dryden* upon his *Cleomenes,*' *The Gentleman's Journal*, May 1692, pp. 17–18; Otway, Prologue, *Don Carlos* (1676); Downes, p. 38; Lyrick, in Farquhar's *Love and a Bottle* (1699), laughs 'to see the ladies cry' at a play (IV. i.).

[134] *Essay of Dramatick Poesy*, pp. 34–5.

by the English. It was no maudlin orchestration of grief to which the sensitive were submitted, but a studied patterning of different responses which checked indulgence here and permitted it there.

The affective potential of this conception is treated interestingly in a correspondence between two playwrights, Catherine Trotter and William Congreve. Trotter asked Congreve's advice about the plot of her play, *The Revolution of Sweden* (1706); in reply Congreve expressed courteous admiration and made one important suggestion which reconciled fully (and typically) the emotive demands of Neander with those of intellectual dexterity and surprise set out by Dryden himself in his delightful preface to *Oedipus* (1678):

Custom likewise has obtained, that we must form an under-plot of second persons, which must be depending on the first, and their by-walks must be like those in a labyrinth, which all of 'em lead into the great parterre.

Here, in a similar vein, is Congreve:

One thing would have a very beautiful effect in the catastrophe, if it were possible to manage it thro' the play: & that is to have the audience kept in ignorance, as long as the husband (which sure they may as well be) who Fredage really is, till after her death.[135]

The plot is the affective link between protagonist and audience; his surprises and starts of feeling are theirs too. The amended catastrophe would be the product of careful, involved attention, and could not be appreciated, Congreve suggests, without consistent attention to the artfulness of the plot in withholding and then disclosing its substance. Such a plot would invite emotional indulgence to the same degree and at the same moment as it would command critical respect; the 'beauty' of a catastrophe so achieved is a perfection of art which embraces the cerebral and the affective with equal readiness. These may appear to be exalted words, but they describe at least the potential of the form as envisaged by a senior professional: there was something to be achieved beyond a hopeless capitulation to tears, even if tears were part of the result. When Peter Motteux proclaimed that his most recent production, *Beauty in Distress* (1698), had had 'the honour of forcing tears from the fairest eyes', he was proud to have elicited a response to which the fair beholders were not usually prone; the fairest eyes were those of the court patrons who required a certain amount of rational persuasion to set them off. Clearly it

[135] Congreve, 'To Catherine Trotter', *The Mourning Bride, Poems and Miscellanies*, ed. Bonamy Dobree (Oxford, 1928), 528–30. Congreve's letter of advice is dated 2 Nov. 1703; the play was not performed until Feb. 1706.

was the kind of response which could be cultivated with rational understanding of the possibilities of intricate plotting. To weep could, to that extent, be to make a judgement from within the canons of the age's best literary criticism; in its distinctive way it puts women on an equal footing with amateur critics like Pepys, who could re-read a play a number of times and find the 'design' growing on him as he began to appreciate its dramatic propriety.[136] The fact that women often wept at less sophisticated things does not compromise the value of the act any more than the drunken pretensions to critical acumen of the gallants compromise the grace of a Sedley; rather, it enforces it.

Reference to the wider play of critical principles in the playhouse brings discussion to a close in the very moment of extending its scope; the effect not of an intricate design but of the limits of the subject. It is hard not to concede (even in the absence of direct evidence) that women must have exercised their critical faculties in the same ways and using the same terms as many of their male counterparts in the audience, however they may have been disadvantaged in doing so. It is important to identify distinctively female interpretations of terms such as 'plot', 'design', and even 'wit' along the lines examined hitherto, but to do so without giving ground to the less specialized applications of those terms would be to ignore the simple practicalities of theatre-talk and theatre-going. Already it should be clear that going to the theatre and discussing it were activities very often pursued in mixed company between people who adopted the same concerns and, to an extent, the same critical language. The distinctive pressures which the playhouse enforced on women were real enough, but the extent of their application can hardly be judged until some account is given of the different circumstances in which different women attended the theatre and talked about it. Recent scholarship in the field of the Restoration Audience, no doubt from the need to counter bad generalizations, has sought to define the character of the audience in terms of its individual members rather than by assessing patterns of collective behaviour.[137] Our aim now is to see, the female audience being in question, how those two approaches may serve each other.

[136] Witness his growing admiration for Samuel Tuke's *The Adventures of Five Hours* (1663): *Diary*, 8 and 17 Jan. 1663; 31 May 1663: 'And after dinner, up and read part of the new play of *The Five houres adventures*; which though I have seen it twice, yet I never did admire or understand it enough—it being a play of the greatest plot that ever I expect to see.'

[137] Harold Love debates with Andrew S. Bear on the relevance of sociological approaches: Bear, 'Criticism and Social Change: The Case of Restoration Drama', *Komos*, 2 (1969), 23–31; Love, 'Bear's Case Laid Open: Or, a Timely Warning to Literary Sociologists', *Komos*, 2 (1969), 72–80.

2

ELIZABETH PEPYS,
PLAY-GOER

THE theatrical and literary tastes of Elizabeth Pepys have received almost no attention from commentators on the Restoration theatre audience. Those few who have gone into print on the subject of 'the ladies' have virtually ignored her, yet hers is the best-documented case we have of a Restoration woman who went regularly to the theatre. It seems at best misguided, and at worst evasive, to offer a judgement of the position of women in the audience without giving some attention to the chief factual evidence.

The most conscientious critic so far has been Peter Holland, who devotes unprecedented space—a single page—to Elizabeth's theatre-going.[1] Holland concentrates on one year of the *Diary*, 1668, when Pepys was emerging from the years of thrift and self-castigation in which he had been unable to go to a play as often as he would have liked. He counts the number of visits made by Pepys with and without his wife and her maid, and produces some interesting but confessedly partial statistics.[2] He also indicates briefly some of the arrangements which the couple made to visit the theatre separately and together. In view of the dearth of comment, this is valuable work, but it is still the least that can be done. What is needed is not only a comprehensive analysis of Elizabeth's theatre-going, but some account of her opinions of what she saw. That, it is intended, will be the more valuable for being seen in the light of those general characteristics of women play-goers which have already been examined; for that purpose

---

[1] Peter Holland, *The Ornament of Action* (Cambridge, 1979), 11. Allan Richard Botica, 'Audience, Playhouse and Play in Restoration Theatre 1660–1710', D.Phil. thesis (Oxford, 1985), pp. 104 and 107 makes passing reference to the Pepyses' joint and separate theatre trips. The most valuable contribution of all has been that of the Latham–Mathews edition of the *Diary*, whose index (vol. xi) lists the dates of all such visits.

[2] From 1 Jan. to 31 Aug. Pepys went to the theatre 73 times; for 33 of those visits Elizabeth was away in the country. Of the 40 occasions when she might have accompanied her husband, she did so on 32, 13 times with Deborah Willet and another 10 with Willet and Mary Mercer. Willet, a mere lady's maid, therefore enjoyed 23 outings to the theatre in the space of eight months. Among more affluent families the figure is likely to have been substantially greater.

some attention must be given to Elizabeth's reading habits and accomplishments.

To approach these questions is to realize at once why they have been neglected for so long. That Pepys recorded his own birthday in his diary every year but one and his wife's not at all may be said to put the matter in a nutshell. Sincere affection most often takes the form of sentimental *Arnolpherie*, as here, on 4 Nov. 1662:

Lay long with pleasure, talking with my wife—in whom I never had greater content, blessed be God, than now; she continuing with the same care and thrift and innocence (so long as I keep her from occasions of being otherwise) as ever she was in her life.

Pepys appears the epitome of the jealous bourgeois of town comedies, while Elizabeth remained, her husband's suspicions notwithstanding, the reverse of the type of the bourgeois, patient and faithful to the last in spite of the most overt philandering by her husband.[3] This was no typical subordination of wife to husband, but an aggravated case. Elizabeth married at fifteen without money or connections, her husband a man of conspicuous ability who had prospects in the metropolis. She recommended herself not by her vigour or her independence of mind, but by her beauty and modesty; remarkable and comforting for Pepys on the whole, but sometimes a little hard on his conscience.[4] In the matter of basic arithmetic, she was even her husband's pupil.[5]

Education saw to the difference in learning; in the Pepyses' case there were differences of temperament to widen the gap. Occasionally Pepys's weariness with Elizabeth's intellectual limitations came to be identified with a greater dissatisfaction:

I find my wife troubled still at my checking her last night in the coach in her long stories out of *Grand Cyrus*, which she would tell, though nothing to the purpose nor in any good manner. This she took unkindly, and I think I was to blame endeed—but she doth find, with reason, that in the company of Pierce—Knipp— or other women that I love, I do not value her, or mind her as I ought.[6]

His remorse at the reflex act of contempt towards her is typical in that it tells us something about her interests but a good deal more about the selfishness of his. The crucial question now presents itself: if from a thoroughly reasonable and devoted husband one could expect little more

---

[3] A list of occasions when Elizabeth incurred Pepys's suspicions (it is a long one) may be found in the *Diary*, ed. Latham and Mathews, xi. 214.

[4] For details of Elizabeth's background and courtship, Richard Ollard, *Pepys*, 2nd edn. (Oxford 1984), 40–2.

[5] *Diary*, 21 Oct. 1663, 1 Nov. 1663.   [6] *Diary*, 12 May 1666.

than a delineation of modest womanly attributes, what can be expected from Pepys? There is some evidence of qualifications and accomplishments which will help to disentangle Elizabeth's interests and opinions from those of her husband, even though some of those were, like arithmetic, sponsored by him. His encouragement of her first steps in singing produced satisfaction, despair, and argument in equal measure, and a sort of haphazard proficiency was the result.[7] She could also, under the guidance of the court player Thomas Greeting, pick out tunes on the flageolet; she often 'piped' with Pepys, and he engaged another court musician, Gregory, to teach her the viol.[8] Such attempts at accomplishment (which also included dancing and painting) diversified an otherwise dull life of toil and loneliness; they had to take their place among menial household activities which took up a lot of time, sometimes by her husband's design.[9] Opportunities for self-cultivation were, for the wife even of a professional man of respectable income, irregular and sometimes scarce; when they did arise they could be encouraged through fear of idleness or mischief.

Elizabeth's status on the fringes of true accomplishment is confirmed by her understanding of French, the result not of a lady's education but of French parentage. Pepys looked on with approval as she interpreted for Lady Sandwich and her new French maid; she later felt qualified by status and ability to ask for one herself.[10] Her facility extended to her reading. When Pepys drew up his will on March 17th 1660 he left his wife 'all that I have in the world but my books, which I gave to my brother John, except my French books, which my wife is to have'. Elsewhere the *Diary* suggests that the taste in French books of husband and wife was markedly different. Pepys's consisted largely of technical and religious literature, as well as political works; Elizabeth's not surprisingly (but not exclusively, either), centred on romances.[11] Nevertheless, it was natural in a household where

---

[7] Diary, 1 Oct. 1661, 27 Apr. 1666, 7 Feb. 1667.

[8] *Diary*, 28 Feb. 1667, 20 May 1667, 13 Aug. 1668. The flageolet was a French instrument of the end-blown flute type; fashionable but of limited resources, and not favoured by serious composers. For 'piping and singing' and learning the viol, *Diary*, 4 and 27 June 1667; 20 Nov. 1666.

[9] For dancing and painting, *Diary*, 28 Sept. 1666, 9 May 1665; for Pepys's displeasure with the amount of time taken up by accomplishments, 3 May 1666, 14 June 1663; for her accusation (and his admission) that he kept the house dirty in order to keep her occupied, 27 Aug. 1663.

[10] *Diary*, 15 Nov. 1660, 19 Dec. 1664. For Elizabeth's parentage, Ollard, p. 40.

[11] There is a checklist of Pepys's French books in the Latham–Mathews edition, xi. 23–9. Elizabeth's favourite romances seem to have been *Le Grand Cyrus* (8 Dec. 1660, 12 May

books were often read that a certain amount of common ground should have been found. That is not to say, moreover, that the common ground was achieved by Elizabeth's bending to her husband's wishes—rather the reverse. In reading above all things Pepys was able to appreciate his wife's accomplishments in a disinterested way:

> My wife and I spent a good deal of time of this evening in reading Du Bartas's *Imposture* and other parts, which my wife of late hath taken up to read, and is very fine as anything I meet with.[12]

On another occasion he found her reading something more technical: 'a little book concerning speech in general, a translation out of French, and a most excellent piece as ever I read'.[13] Perhaps the tone indicates surprise at the enlivening of her interest (on 5 May 1669 he commended La Calpranede's preface to *Cassandra* while attributing her commendation of it to its having been recommended by a suspected suitor, Sheeres); her intelligent curiosity stands, nevertheless. She was sufficiently intimate with her reading to make use of it as her husband's temper prompted:

> vexed with my wife's having looked out a letter in Sir Ph. Sidny' about jealousy for me to read, which she industriously and maliciously caused me to do; and the truth is, my conscience told me it was most proper for me, and therefore was touched at it.[14]

On the whole, however, reading was a pleasure which the couple shared. They read to each other, in sickness out of charity and in health out of mirth; it was possible in the Pepys household to read Chaucer for an hour after supper to the assembled family, 'with great pleasure'.[15]

Elizabeth evidently came across a variety of literature in spite of the obvious encumbrances. In its variety her reading exceeded the moral prescriptions of the courtesy authors, and even when it fell within their guidelines her experiences do not resemble the ones usually described.

166) and *Polixandre*, by Marin de Gomberville (31 Jan. 1660). She had her own collection of books: 17 Oct. 1660, 16 Oct. 1668.

[12] *Diary*, 2 Nov. 1662. The work is Guillaume du Bartas, *La Semaine* (Paris, 1578); the *Imposture* deals with the fall of man.

[13] *Diary*, 6 Dec. 1668. The book is *A Philosophical Discourse Concerning Speech* (London, 1668); a translation of L. G. de Cordemoy, *Discours physique de la parole* (Paris, 1668).

[14] *Diary*, 2 Jan. 1665.

[15] *Diary*, 21 Nov. 1666. Elizabeth read to Pepys when he was ill and to save his eyes on ever sixty occasions from 1 Sept. 1667. Their joint reading, in times of health, took in poetry, biography, history, journals, a book of heraldry, plays, and scientific works. *Diary*, 23 Aug. 1663, 22 Dec. 1662, 26 Oct. 1660, 10 Apr. 1664, 30 Jan. 1669, 25 Dec. 1667, 6 Sept. 1667, 23 Sept. 1664.

Romances, for example, do not appear to have encouraged her either to apply herself more vigorously to her domestic duties or to ignore them. It is true that Pepys bought her romances because they absorbed the vacant hours, but we would be sure to know, given the fuss caused by her desire to take up painting and dancing, if they distracted her from work.[16] Consider the episode of telling 'long stories out of *Grand Cyrus*'. Like the others, this was an immense volume in which the narrative was continually interrupted with formal *récits* to explain some feature of the past life of one of the characters; it was both unified, in the sense that all the different *récits* were connected to the main story, and monstrously diverse, since the principle of unity observed allowed for any number of intrigues and liaisons prior to the main one, as long as they involved one of the protagonists.[17] In the latter sense the romance was primarily a work for the leisurely reader; its multitude of different tales meant that it could be picked up and dipped into as the inclination arose, without any particular anxiety about the loss of the story-line. A work like *Le Grand Cyrus* was perhaps more like an encyclopaedia than a novel, offering infinite self-contained variations upon themes of love and honour. Apparently it was this quality which recommended it to Elizabeth Pepys, and which lodged it so firmly and uninspiringly in her mind. The fabric of many of the stories contained in the book seem always to have been present to her imagination; threads of fancy to which, her husband observed, she attached no special purpose (whereas her knowledge of the *Arcadia* shows that she was able to point out moral significance when required). They were anecdotal rather than exemplary; curiosities to be contemplated and related with solipsistic pleasure.

It follows that she should have shown little enthusiasm for plays which drew directly on romances which she had read. She denounced Dryden's *An Evening's Love*, which dramatized some incidents from *L'Illustre Bassa*, a novel she evidently knew very well.[18] It might be objected here that she disliked the play because she suspected unacknowledged plagiarism; but we are told that the borrowing was admitted. This in turn raises a crucial point: was she merely being sullen in criticizing the borrowing even where the author owned up to it;[19] or did she find simply that the performance

[16] *Diary*, 23 and 24 Feb. 1668.

[17] For further comment on the structure of romances of the period, Paul Salzman, *English Prose Fiction, 1558–1700* (Oxford, 1985), 187–90.   [18] *Diary*, 20 June 1668.

[19] Pepys records, 'my wife tells me [the play] is wholly (which he confesses a little in the epilogue) taken out of the *Illustr. Bassa*'. The epilogue to the play does not mention the novel by name, but explains how hard-pressed dramatists were forced to borrow from 'French plots'.

added nothing to her appreciation of the source material? The difference is important, particularly when evidence is so thinly and obscurely spread. We know that Elizabeth could read plays with pleasure and see the same plays with more;[20] in this case all the usual kinds of ornament were available—musical accompaniment, painted scenery, and so on—apart from the pleasures of the first day's audiences. None of this, however, could diminish the thought that the play had been 'taken wholly' from known (though loved) territory. It may say something for her appreciation of the situation, moreover, that she not only accompanied her husband to the second performance of the play, but looked up the relevant passages of the source book; this perhaps indicates a willingness to try her judgement rather than a doped weakening of resolve. Part of the impetus to do so may have been provided by the obvious popularity of the play with the majority of its first audience.[21] Was there a general acceptance of the principle of such plagiarism, or was the book simply not known to the generality of the audience? We cannot tell, but it is probable that Dryden himself disliked the play as much as Elizabeth; as the bookseller Herringman informed Pepys, he thought it 'but a fifth rate play'.[22] Her experience of the play may, in short, lead us to despair of finding a representative of majority opinion among the female audience, but it should also warn us of the folly of assuming that there might be such a one in the first place.

What, then, of her experience of other plays? How does that conform to the conventions established so far? The sheer variety of plays which Elizabeth saw defies instant judgement, and is plainly a fundamental consideration which all those who have spoken of and for 'the ladies' have ignored. In the space of nearly ten years she is known to have gone to the theatre almost two hundred times, to see the work of up to sixty-five dramatists. The range of names is broad. She saw plays by all the major playwrights of 'the former age': Shakespeare, Jonson, Marlowe, Webster, Middleton, Kyd, Dekker, Chapman, Massinger, and Beaumont and Fletcher;[23] many by the Caroline dramatists, Shirley, Brome, Caryll, Habington, and Glapthorne; as well as the work, in comedy and tragedy,

[20] *Diary*, 15 Nov. 1661, 27 Dec. 1662, 23 Sept. 1664.
[21] *Diary*, 19 June 1668.
[22] *Diary*, 22 June 1668.
[23] She saw unadapted Shakespeare at least six times: 1 Henry IV twice, and one performance each of *Hamlet*, *Othello*, *Twelfth Night*, and *Romeo and Juliet*. The Davenant versions were more often seen: she saw eight performances of *Macbeth*, four of *The Tempest*, and two of *Henry VIII*. She also saw two performances of John Lacy's *Sawney the Scot*, a version of *The Taming of the Shrew*.

of all the major figures of contemporary drama—Dryden, Davenant, Etherege, Shadwell, Sedley, the Howards, and the Earl of Orrery. The list suggests particular favourites less strongly than it does an unmitigated enthusiasm for the stage, although among the plays which she saw often or expressed a special desire to see were *Bartholomew Fair*, *The Bondman*, *Macbeth*, *The Tempest*, *The Siege of Rhodes*, and an anonymous version of Corneille's *Heraclius*.[24] Given the range of plays which she took in, this brief list offers little by way of a characteristic taste.

The central difficulty, as before, is in making out a well-defined picture of the woman through the mist of her husband's cajoling and self-infatuation. It would be easy to claim, on the evidence of reading habits, that there must have been some distinction between the taste in play-going of the Pepyses, but it would be less easy to define a distinction so achieved. For all the studiousness of Pepys's reading, the less sophisticated forms of theatre seemed often to attract him most. Once, with Elizabeth and her companion, Mary Mercer, he saw 'the latter end' of Sir Robert Howard's *The Surprizall*, 'wherein was no great matter I thought, by what I saw. Thence away to *Polchinelli*, and there had three times more sport than at the play.'[25]

It was consistently the qualities of performance, of lively spectacle, music, and human ingenuity, which were paramount on the minds of the Pepyses when they went to the theatre. If any distinction is to be made between their enjoyment, it is, perhaps, an obvious one. Pepys was sometimes given to recording his admiration of the more literary accomplishments of the performance—its wit or fine passages—where there is no record of his wife's having so admired it.[26] When, for example, there was an outing to Bartholomew Fair and Elizabeth decided all of a sudden to see the play rather than the real thing, the particular attraction was the 'puppet scene'. Pepys appreciated her judgement in his distinctive way: 'and it is an excellent play; the more I see it, the more I love the wit of it'.[27] He owns her enthusiasm straightforwardly but says nothing of her opinion; his own—which, as far as we can tell, is based on more sophisticated principles—takes precedence. The same pattern is evident in most of the entries which record joint visits. *Romeo and Juliet* Pepys found so

[24] *Diary*, 4 Sept. 1668, 7 Jan. 1668, 19 Apr. 1667, 16 Oct. 1667, 7 Nov. 1667, 4 Nov. 1661, 15 Nov. 1661, 27 Dec. 1662, 23 Sept. 1664, 4 Sept. 1668.
[25] *Diary*, 8 Apr. 1667. *Polchinelli*, an Italian puppet-play, was being acted at Moorfields.
[26] See his judgements of Porter's *The Villain*, 26 Dec. 1662; Orrery's *Mustapha*, 5 Jan. 1667; *The Tempest*, 3 Feb. 1668; and *Catiline*, 19 Dec. 1668.
[27] *Diary*, 4 Sept. 1668.

ill-rehearsed that he resolved 'no more to go to the first time of acting', although he does not tell us whether Elizabeth was party to the resolution; *A Midsummer Night's Dream* he had never seen before nor ever would again, it being 'the most insipid ridiculous play that I ever saw in my life', and again his wife's intentions are not mentioned. Most striking of all, after reflecting on their joint admiration of Betterton and his intended, Mrs Saunderson, in *The Duchess of Malfi*, he complacently observed how strange it was to see 'how easily my mind do revert to its former practice of loving plays'.[28] When Elizabeth is credited with having some kind of opinion, it both precedes the play and conforms entirely to Pepys's: 'we made no long stay at dinner; *Heraclius* being acted, my wife and I have a mighty mind to see it'. Thereafter the entry follows the usual pattern, with a declaration that 'the play hath one very good passage well managed in it'.[29] That said, there is certainly implicit in the entry a pleasure in theatre-going which is acknowledged to be shared and discriminating; a similar pleasure may be found in the report of 23 May 1662, which tells of how Pepys and his wife 'slunk away' after dinner at Lord Sandwich's house 'to the Opera, where we saw *Wit in a Constable*'. The feeling is not really compromised by the subsequent and tiresomely typical judgement that it was 'so silly a play [as] I ever saw I think in my life'.[30]

If it is difficult to discern very much of Elizabeth's enthusiasms and aversions through those of her husband, there is comfort in the thought that one of the reasons for the difficulty offers up an interesting and presumably representative fact. Veblen's theory of middle-class leisure has it that the wife must render her husband the conspicuous leisure which his work prevents him from enjoying, and to that theory some limitations, the present subject being in question, have already been established. Another becomes clear in the pattern of Elizabeth's theatre-going, and how it was made possible in the first place. She went to the theatre at her husband's expense; her precious hours of freedom from the house he was so keen she should inhabit depended on his prosperity and generosity, neither of which was particularly stable. Where they faltered her liberty was severely curtailed, and she might complain bitterly of his selfishness at times of professed restraint. An important statistic needs to be mentioned here, one that questions the conclusions which Peter Holland has drawn from his analysis of the couple's play-going in the year 1668. Holland argues, from

[28] *Diary*, 1 Mar. 1662, 29 Sept. 1662, 30 Sept. 1662.
[29] *Diary*, 8 Mar. 1664. The translator in this case is not known; Lodowick Carlell produced a version of the same play in 1671.
[30] Written by Henry Galpthorne, published in 1640.

a count of thirty-two joint visits out of a possible forty, that going to
the theatre was an amicable, ordinary arrangement between them, yet the
very phrasing of the argument—'out of a *possible* forty'—betrays the
inherent tension of the arrangement: Elizabeth could scarcely afford to go
without her husband. Now consider the balance of their visits to the
theatre throughout the whole period covered by the diary: for Elizabeth's
one hundred and ninety-eight visits her husband, for all his vows and
guilty pangs, made three hundred and eighty-two, nearly twice her total.
Even when he did take her she felt the effects of his selfishness—on six
occasions he reports his fear that his wife might notice him glancing
subversively round the auditorium at other women—and even during the
time in which, by Holland's account, the Pepyses went to the theatre in a
balm of mutual satisfaction, Elizabeth had occasion to complain of her
want of money and liberty.[31] Statistical analysis bears out her complaints,
and Pepys himself could rarely listen without private assent.[32] Her
presence was in some respects an obstacle to pleasure.

The restrictions on Elizabeth's theatre-going were, at least, only
financial and circumstantial rather than moral. Accordingly, she might
benefit from the generosity of friends, to her husband's surprise and
occasional shame:

To the King's House, and by and by comes Mr Lowder and his wife and mine,
and into a box, forsooth, neither of them being dressed, which I am almost
ashamed of.[33]

When finance and his mood permitted, she could go on her own or with
her maid. Here again there are problems with the evidence. Elizabeth's
private theatre-going took in at least one play, *Bussy d'Ambois*, which there
is no evidence of Pepys having seen; but, very much as before, a visit to a
play without him is often marked only by a record of the mere fact,
without mention of the play, let alone her appreciation of it.[34] At least we
can be sure that these individual trips did not cause anxiety of the kind we
might suppose from reading the prologues and epilogues; one evening
Pepys waited anxiously for his wife to return from a play not because he

[31] *Diary*, 25 Nov. 1668, 9 Dec. 1668, 19 Dec. 1668, 1 Jan. 1669, 20 Jan. 1669, 2 Feb. 1669;
for Elizabeth's complaints, 12 Jan. 1668.
[32] *Diary*, 27 Aug. 1663, 24 Oct. 1663, 28 Apr. 1667.
[33] *Diary*, 25 Mar. 1667. She was also treated, on various occasions, by Pepys's father,
brother, by Sir William Penn, and by the Sandwich family.
[34] For *Bussy d'Ambois*, *Diary*, 30 Dec. 1661: Elizabeth went with Sir William Penn and
his children. For other visits without Pepys, 3 Aug. 1663, 30 Sept. 1664, 17 Oct. 1664,
6 Dec. 1666, 17 Dec. 1666; 16 Feb. 1667, 6 June 1667, 25 Sept. 1667.

imagined that she might have been seduced by some rake about town but for the more prosaic fact of its having been late, 'and she having her necklace of pearl on, and none but Mercer with her'.[35] So little further worry did such occasions cause that Pepys, when he found his wife at the theatre with someone else, could see his own part in the conventional cuckolding drama and mock his jealousy:

After the play done, I into the pit and there find my wife and W. Hewer, and Sheeres got to them; which, so jealous is my nature, did trouble me, though my judgment tells me there is no hurt in it.[36]

To that extent Elizabeth was free to go to the theatre; free from the strictures of a frankly jealous husband, free from the 'time-wasters and other nuisances' who, according even to recent work in the field, plagued attractive women in the playhouse.[37] It is a freedom which is witnessed in the occasional agreements between husband and wife to meet inside the theatre. For the première of Etherege's *She Would if She Could*, Elizabeth got a place in the pit before the rush, while Pepys took his place among the '1000 people put back that could not have room in the pit', and had to go to the middle gallery instead; his only worry was that he could not see or hear properly.[38]

The implication is that it was not unusual for the Pepyses to sit apart at the same performance, and that, indeed, was the case. On 28 November 1667 Pepys was even driven to report that he had been 'To the King's Playhouse, and there sat my wife'; that was not, perhaps, as strange an experience as the entry suggests.[39] It was not, at any rate, exceptional for the two to separate: sometimes Pepys wanted simply to enjoy fully the pleasures of the company and opinions of friends; at other times a separate visit was a cordial social arrangement:

at noon resolve with Sir W. Penn to go see *The Tempest* . . . And so my wife and girl and W. Hewer by themselfe, and Sir W. Penn and I afterwards by ourselfs, and forced to sit in the side Balcone over against the Musique-Room.[40]

---

[35] *Diary*, 17 Dec. 1666.   [36] *Diary*, 16 Apr. 1669.
[37] The phrase is Emmet Avery's, from 'The Restoration Audience'.
[38] *Diary*, 6 Feb. 1668. Other such meetings were arranged on 15 Nov. 1661, 14 Oct. 1667, and 10 Sept. 1668. On none of these occasions did Elizabeth wait alone: for the Etherege première she was accompanied by Mercer, Willet, and a cousin, Betty Turner; at other times by Captain Ferrers, Mademoiselle La Blanc, Pepys's brother, and Will Hewer.
[39] Among many examples, see *Diary*, 28 May 1663, 16 Dec. 1661, 8 Jan. 1663, 1 May 1667, 2 Oct. 1667, 23 Jan. 1667.
[40] *Diary*, 7 Nov. 1667. On 24 Jan. 1668 Pepys found 'my wife and Deb, and saw many fine ladies; and sat by Collonell Reames, who understands and loves a play as well as I, and I

Today such an arrangement might appear unusual, even suspicious, yet in such an age and such an environment it was adopted without fuss. Even if Pepys was enamoured of it because he preferred the (apparently) more informed interest of someone like Colonel Reames, the fact of his wife's partial independence stands; as does the fact that joint attendance, regardless of what happened when they arrived, remained the most convenient of all arrangements.

Elizabeth's sallies to the theatre without her husband were not unaccompanied. Nothing portentous should be deduced from that; it was unusual for Pepys to go entirely on his own, and it is still unusual today.[41] Where the company of friends or family was wanting, that of a maid or lady's companion was an obvious alternative; obvious but for the drawback that it involved twice the outlay. The prosperous later years of the *Diary* show Deborah Willet being treated freely to theatre-trips: from 2 October 1667 until 1 October 1668 she was taken to forty-one performances, often when both master and mistress were going, and on thirteen occasions with Mary Mercer (the lady's companion) in attendance too; this compared with the twenty-four performances which Mercer saw from September 1664 to October 1668.[42] Their predecessors had had to content themselves with accompanying their mistress to church or on a walk round St. James's Park; the maids Ashwell and Barker, and Jane, the wife of Pepys's servant Thomas Edwards, were treated to only one theatre outing each.[43] This was designed to better the lot of neither maid nor mistress, and Elizabeth complained bitterly in the early years of the *Diary* that Pepys's financial strictures were depriving her of the company which would not only enliven the perishing hours of boredom but provide her with the means of going out more often.[44] As far as Pepys was concerned, the expense of providing the means was simply likely to generate further expense in the employment.

As money became more readily available the couple and their servants could settle into a more congenial routine of theatre-going, but it is

love him for it'. This may indicate neglect of his wife in favour of Reames, who could offer, in Pepys's view, more informed comment.

[41] *Diary*, 30 Oct. 1660: 'I went to the Cockpit all alone . . .'.

[42] When household visits were arranged it was normal to sit in the pit, at 2*s*. 6*d*. each. *Diary*, 6 Feb. 1668.

[43] *Diary*, 22 Apr. 1663 (here Pepys specifically laments the expense of the trip), 9 Apr. 1667, 20 Sept. 1667. This last has the air of a special treat: 'my wife and I to walk in the garden, she having been at the same play with Jane, in the 18*d*. seat, to show Jane the play.'

[44] *Diary*, 18 Dec. 1662.

significant that on none of the thirteen occasions when both Mercer and Willet attended was Pepys himself absent; his wife's visits still depended on his. It appears, moreover, that Elizabeth was either not free or not inclined to go solely in Willet's company. Of the girl's forty-one visits with her mistress Pepys arranged to go with them on all but two occasions.[45] A maid was certainly not, whatever Elizabeth's ambitions, the means to independence. It made scarcely any difference to her opportunities for enjoying the stage without her husband.

Once in the theatre there were matters of decorum to be observed where servants were concerned. This is not the place to reflect on Pepys's legion indiscretions with Deborah Willet, but one feature of his infatuation with her sheds light on the proprieties of a household trip to a play:

But here, before the play begun, my wife began to complain to me of Willet's confidence in sitting cheek by jowl by us, which was a poor thing; but I perceive she is already jealous of my kindness to her . . .[46]

Pepys's own complaining of his wife's snobbish want of generosity credits the existence of conventions to which she was appealing—and it was only the girl's fourth outing to a play with them—even though he ultimately traces it to other causes. Only an indulgent master like Pepys would suffer such intimacy when the whole family was out. This contrasts with Elizabeth's more companionable attitude on the few occasions when she went alone with a maid or servant: with Willet, when she thought to spy on her truant husband, or with Jane Edwards, to whom she 'showed' James Howard's *All Mistaken*. On the latter occasion economy led the two to the '18d. seat' or middle gallery, no other prudential consideration being necessary.

When not accompanied by husband or household, Elizabeth could sometimes depend on others for company. The diary records fifteen such visits, and there may well have been more.[47] Her most frequent companion was Elizabeth Pearse, the wife of a distinguished naval surgeon; others included Frances Clarke, whose husband was physician-in-ordinary to the King's person, and the two Joyce wives, who were

[45] For the exceptions, *Diary*, 26 Mar. 1668 (he met his wife and Willet by accident, thinking to have gone alone), and 19 June 1668, when, for the première of *An Evening's Love*, Elizabeth went with Willet, 'thinking to spy [Pepys] there'.

[46] *Diary*, 15 Oct. 1667.

[47] *Diary*, 23 Apr. 1669: Elizabeth told of a recent theatre trip only under the pressure of 'a little angry talk'.

Pepys's cousins.[48] Outings with these companions have different characteristics; what many of them have in common is an exclusively female constituency. Elizabeth saw Shirley's *The Court Secret* ('the worst [play] that ever she saw in her life') in the company of Mrs Clarke and Mrs Pearse, with whom she had dined; on a day when her husband saw Fletcher and Massinger's *The Sea Voyage* with all the court in attendance at the King's playhouse, she went to the Duke's Theatre, probably to see *Sir Martin Mar-All*, with Pepys's aunt and Kate Joyce; and when Pepys found her at the première of Davenant's *The Man's the Master* she was with Willet, Mrs Pearse, Mrs Corbett, and Elizabeth Turner, the wife of one of Pepys's colleagues.[49] There was clearly no thought that these visits should have occasioned anything but the enjoyment of a play in friendly society, and however rare their occurrence in the diary years, their unexceptionable geniality indicates that others better off were more familiar with the practice than Elizabeth. The fact, too, that her most regular companions were women whose husbands were acquainted with Pepys professionally suggests that his work, and the acquaintance which went with it, were not as detrimental to his wife's social interest as might have been thought; Mrs Pearse in particular was a regular companion at home and about town. In such a context friendship could be developed without anxiety on Pepys's part. For one outing to the theatre dinner had to be shortened so that Elizabeth could collect her friend to go and see the new play, which entertainment was, even to Pepys's suspicious mind, to be welcomed rather than shunned.[50]

Other occasions suggest other motives. In two instances there is an attractive, though almost accidental, resemblance to the habits described in *The Theory of the Leisure Class*: Pepys was too busy to go to the theatre, so he left his wife to go with someone else.[51] Such an arrangement was very

---

[48] For Elizabeth Pearse, *Diary*, 16 Feb. 1667 and 31 Oct. 1667; for Pearse and Clarke together, 3 Aug. 1660 and 18 Aug. 1664; for Kate and Mary Joyce, 30 Sept. 1664 and 25 Sept. 1667. See also, for visits with her brother-in-law Thomas, 6 Dec. 1666 and 31 Aug. 1663; with Mrs Andrews and company, 26 Dec. 1666; with Mr Cooke and Mercer, 17 Dec. 1666; with Lady Jemimah Mountagu, 17 Oct. 1664; with Mary Batelier and her 'sweetheart', 23 Apr. 1669. For biographical details of her companions, *Diary*, ed. Latham and Mathews, x.

[49] *Diary*, 18 Aug. 1664, 25 Sept. 1667, 26 Mar. 1668. Elizabeth Turner's husband Thomas was Purveyor of Petty Provisions at the Navy Office and Clerk to the Comptroller at the same office at this time.

[50] *Diary*, 16 Feb. 1667. The play has not been identified.

[51] *Diary*, 31 Aug. 1663, 6 June 1667. On the former occasion Elizabeth was taken by Pepys's brother Thomas, on the latter by his father.

much the exception rather than the rule. When Elizabeth was treated to a play by someone other than her husband, as she was by Anthony Lowther and his wife, Pepys was likely to be there too, or at some other pleasure.[52] The fact so often mentioned here, that Elizabeth found it difficult to go to the theatre without her husband, carries a corollary which, if justice is done to the subject, can be ignored no longer: given her frequent attendance in his company, what did she make of it? What pleasures did they share? Something of joint pleasure has already been hinted at in their stealing away from an engagement to see *Heraclius*, and there is more to convince one that joint attendance was something other than a mere convenience. Going to a play was, to begin with, a pleasure which each could cultivate in the other. In the entry for the day following their separate visits to *The Sea Voyage* and *Sir Martin Mar-All*, Pepys records, 'With my wife abroad to the King's playhouse, to show her yesterday's new play, which I like as I did yesterday.'[53] The emphasis, as usual, is on the validity of his own judgement, but it remains the case that Elizabeth was taken not out of charity or a spirit of instruction, but because he thought she would enjoy the play. Another instance of the same case occurred on 26 September 1661: 'With my wife by coach to the theatre, to show her *King and No King*, it being very well done.' Elizabeth had behaved similarly in 'showing' *All Mistaken* to Jane Edwards. Pepys's justification for showing Elizabeth *A King and No King*, lay, it seems, in the quality of its production, and here, above all, we have grounds for pin-pointing the nature of Elizabeth's interest while acknowledging that it coincided in certain respects with that of her husband.

It is the final word on the non-literary character of the Pepyses' enjoyment of the stage that it should have had so much to do with the qualities not simply of production, but more particularly of the performers themselves. After a 'silly play', Fletcher's *The Humorous Lieutenant*, both enjoyed much more being taken behind the scenes with Mrs Pearse and her party to meet 'Nelly, a most pretty woman', whom they both kissed in their delight.[54] This was scant acclaim, however, compared with what they gave the age's leading actor, Thomas Betterton; Elizabeth went so far as to name her dog after him. On 30 September 1662 they found *The Duchess of Malfi* well performed, 'but Baterton [and Mrs Saunderson] to admiration'; while on 25 November 1668 it was, without him, 'but a sorry play'. His acting of Hamlet gave 'fresh reason never to think enough of

52 *Diary*, 25 Mar. 1667, 31 Oct. 1667.
53 *Diary*, 26 Sept. 1667.
54 *Diary*, 23 Jan. 1667.

Baterton', and after one performance of Massinger's *The Bondman* he was 'called by us both the best actor in the world'.[55] One of his greatest roles was, for both of them, Macbeth; in this case Elizabeth's judgement may be seen to operate independently of her husband's:

I away to the Duke of York's House, thinking, as we appointed, to meet my wife there, but she was not; and more, I was vexed to see Young (who is but a bad actor at best) act Macbeth in the room of Baterton, who poor man is sick. But Lord, what a prejudice it wrought in me against the whole play, and everybody else agreed in disliking this fellow. Thence home, and there find my wife gone home; because of this fellow's acting of the part, she went out of the house again.[56]

This is not to suggest that their enthusiasm for the actor was drunkenly partial or that it precluded other kinds of appreciation. A further visit to *Macbeth* prompted the following: 'we still like [the play] mightily, though mighty short of the content we used to have when Baterton acted, who is still sick'.[57] The quality of the play was still evident, in spite of the lamentable Young. It was equally clear that even Betterton's skill could not lend interest to an indifferent piece: 'To a play of my Lord Orrery's called *Mustapha*, which, being not good, made Betterton's part ... but ordinary too'; and when the Duke's House mounted a really bad play such as Thomas St Serfe's *Tarugo's Wiles* the Pepyses could take pleasure (for once) in their favourite actor's having been too ill to take part. It was, wrote Pepys, at once recalling and forgetting the famous tribute he had paid to *A Midsummer Night's Dream*, 'the most ridiculous insipid play that ever I saw in my life, and glad we were that Baterton had no part in it'.[58] When Betterton was the subject the diarist was willing as nowhere else to accord his wife the dignity of noting her opinion. Yet what a tribute is there to the elusiveness of the diary when we scan it for evidence of Elizabeth Pepys's peculiar interest in the stage; nothing was so widespread among female spectators as profound admiration for the age's leading actor, a man uniquely capable, according to Cibber, of silencing the very orange-sellers into rapt attention.[59]

[55] For Elizabeth's dog, *Shorthand Letters of Samuel Pepys*, transcribed and edited by Edwin Chappell (Cambridge, 1933), 22. Betterton's roles, *Diary*, 28 May 1663, 4 Nov. 1661. In *The Duchess of Malfi* he played Ferdinand and his intended, Mrs Saunderson, the Duchess.

[56] *Diary*, 16 Oct. 1667.

[57] *Diary*, 6 Nov. 1667.

[58] Boyle's *Mustapha*, 3 Apr. 1665; *Tarugo's Wiles*, 15 Oct. 1667; *A Midsummer Night's Dream*, 29 Sept. 1662.

[59] Colley Cibber, *An Apology for the Life of Mr Colley Cibber, Comedian*, ed. B. S. Fone (Ann Arbor, 1968).

In a case such as that of Elizabeth Pepys it is often easier to expound the difficulties of analysis rather than to analyse. It is time now, the problem of the case being plain, to justify the present analysis with some consideration of its relevance to the remainder of this study. How, precisely, does the record of Elizabeth's reading and theatre-going help us to understand other female patrons of the Restoration Stage?

Perhaps its most useful feature is the account it takes of the Pepyses' social mobility. Elizabeth's theatre-going having depended so much on the fortunes and inclination of her husband, and those fortunes having risen so markedly during the years of the diary, she really represents two social classes rather than one. In the early years she is tied to housework for want of sufficient servants and means to go out, while her husband is embarrassed by his inability to pay in order to make her leisure hours more enlivening. Later on, some anxieties persist, but it is possible to go to the theatre regularly, attended sometimes by two servants. In that respect her case has shown in detail the workings of economic pressure which allowed some women to go to the theatre and prevented others from doing so; it has also shown how the total female audience could be swollen significantly by the presence of maids and companions, whom it was apparently normal for affluent families to treat to a play in the afternoon. It should be plain, too, that Elizabeth, even when accompanied only by female friends or servants, did not have to worry about going into any part of the theatre; she could take Jane Edwards into the middle gallery or wait for her husband in the pit as readily as she could allow herself to be treated to a box by Mr Lowther.

If there is significant variety in the pattern of Elizabeth's attendance, so is there in the plays she saw and the books she read. The latter may be more easily accommodated to the conventional prescriptions of the courtesy authors; her principal reading was, after all, the lengthy French romances, even if she did not appear to read them after the conventional fashion. For plays, however, her taste was far broader, if not universal, and it seems to have developed in depth as the years of the diary passed. On 6 December 1666 Pepys remarked of his wife's reaction to an unnamed play, 'My wife not pleased with the play, but thinks that it is because she is grown more criticall than she used to be. But my brother, she says, is mightily taken with it.' Favourite plays and authors could still be cherished and seen repeatedly and discussed with Pepys himself, but it must be concluded that the theatre offered too great a variety of delights to be confined either to the prescriptions of the courtesy authors or to the assumptions of the modern critics.

3

WOMEN IN THE
PLAYHOUSE

MY FIRST chapter ended with the promise that, the female audience being in question, the statistical method of analysis would be tested against the sociological. Naturally, the female audience *being* in question, the sparest factual analysis may require the attention of the theorist no less than that of the scholar. Consider the following statistics: of the four hundred or more names of people whom we know to have attended the Restoration theatres, no more than eighty belong to women; that in a city which contained thirteen women for every ten men.[1] It is possible, of course, that we shall need neither theory nor a great deal of scholarship to explain the imbalance; common sense may take their place. We know that a number of women went disguised to the theatre, that there were sufficient reasons for doing so to account for women of all classes, and that a mask and an accomplished manner could be very difficult to penetrate.[2]

We know, too, that there were compelling reasons for some women to stay away from the theatre altogether; and there is, moreover, no evidence that the diaries, letters, and other documents which supply our eighty names were vitiated by the shortcomings of the prologues and epilogues in reporting the presence of women in the theatre. Might not the statistical imbalance be explained by the absence of some and the fashionable stealth of others?

Partly, perhaps; but scholarship and theory have their claims as well. The Restoration audience was, as all recent commentators have shown,

[1] Allan Richard Botica, 'Audience, Playhouse and Play in Restoration Theatre, 1660–1710', D.Phil. thesis (Oxford, 1985), Introduction, p. viii, gives the figure of 'more than four hundred'; I include in my count of identifiable female spectators the Maids of Honour mentioned in lists of performances given to royalty, PRO, L.C.5/141–51 (edited extracts in A. Nicoll, *A History of Restoration Drama*, 3rd edn. (Cambridge, 1940), pp. 305–14), and named in selected eds. of Edward Chamberlayne, *Angliae Notitia* (London, 1669–77) and CSPD: Charles II. The ratio of women to men is in Gregory King, *Natural and Political Observations* (1696), reprinted in George Chalmers, *An Estimate of the Comparative Strength of Great Britain* (London, 1804), 39.

[2] See Pepys, *Diary*, 18 Feb. 1667, for Sir Charles Sedley's attempts to identify a pair of masked ladies at the theatre.

largely 'respectable'; the idea that vizards took up 'half the Pit, and all the Galleries' was a humorous invention for raillery's sake.[3] Equally, a trend in social intercourse appears to be partly responsible for the preponderance of men's names in the list of four hundred; it has been one of E. L. Avery's distinctive contributions to the field to show how many professional men went to the theatre together, as Pepys did, and a good many of those four hundred names belong to the professional (and therefore male) acquaintance of the predominantly male diarists and correspondents given to meeting them at the theatre, often, as we have seen, to the exclusion of women. There are, naturally, limits to the case—for the last four years of the *Diary*, Elizabeth Pepys accompanied her husband on two out of every three visits to the theatre, and for the first four, on less than one in three— but it is extensive enough to account partly for the statistical discrepancy. Women may often have escaped mention not necessarily because they did not go to the theatre but because the attention of the chief chroniclers was directed elsewhere.

A further peculiarity of the statistical evidence requires little explanation, but needs to be stated nevertheless. Over half of our eighty named ladies were titled: a reflection not of the true proportion of nobility or gentry, but of the disproportionate interest of the major sources in the behaviour of the eminent.[4] However obvious its implications, the possession of such a fact at least raises two of the central questions of this chapter, even if it does so while warning us of the perils in attempting to answer them: in what numbers were women of different classes represented, and what, precisely, was the ratio of women to men in the theatre audience? They are at once the most basic questions in this whole study and the most difficult to answer. It is prudent to tackle them initially by examining in more detail the nature of the difficulty.

If we turn for assistance to the journals written by some of the many foreign travellers who visited London in the late seventeenth century, we may find a less intoxicated account of the theatre audience than the one given by some more closely associated with it, but (at least in the case of Samuel de Sorbière's *Relation*) it is at the cost of a visible appreciation in the difficulties of numerical calculation:

---

[3] John Crowne, Epilogue, *Darius* (1688). For respectable patrons, see Emmet L. Avery, 'The Restoration Audience' *Philology Quarterly*, 45 (1966); Harold Love, 'The Myth of the Restoration Audience', *Komos*, 1 (1968); Botica, 89–107.

[4] See e.g. Pepys on the pleasures of looking at Lady Castlemaine at the theatre: *Diary*, 23 July 1661; 27 Aug. 1661; 1 Feb. 1664; 3 Apr. 1665; 5 May 1668; 21 Dec. 1668.

La Comédie est bien plus divertissante, et plus commode aux entretiens. Les meilleures places sont celles du parterre, où les hommes et les femmes sont assis pesle-mesle, chacun avec ceux de sa bande.[5]

The pit was the favoured place, for view as for society, and it does not appear to have observed social or sexual distinctions—no bright ladies in boxes shedding benign rays over a male-dominated pit. There was simply a confusion of men and women such as to give the lie to any simple proportioning of representation according to the capacities of pit, box, and galleries. Sorbière's countryman, Balthasar de Monconys, noticed a similar confusion at the Theatre Royal in Bridges Street:

Tous les bancs du parterre ou toutes les personnes de condition se mettent aussi, sont rangez en amphithéâtre . . .;[6]

again the English playhouse seemed remarkable for its gregariousness, its freedom from established social and sexual territories so often invoked in the prologues and epilogues.

Even where social discrimination is allowed, it is of little help in determining the sexual balance of the audience. An Italian traveller of the late 1660s, Count Lorenzo Magalotti, found that the people of quality tended to sit in the boxes rather than the pit; even there, however, confusion reigned:

The theatre is nearly of a circular form, surrounded, in the inside, by boxes separated from each other, and divided into several rows of seats, for the greater accommodation of the ladies and gentlemen, who, in conformity with the freedom of the country, sit together indiscriminately; a large space being left on the ground floor for the rest of the audience.[7]

We know from another traveller, Brunet, that there were fourteen of those boxes, and that they held approximately twenty people each, but even with that information we are left guessing about the ratio of men to women.[8]

Still more disconcerting is a second observation of Magalotti's, made eight days after the one above. Heywood's *Love's Mistress* was, he wrote,

[5] Samuel de Sorbière, *Relation d'un voyage en Angleterre* (Paris, 1664), 166–7.

[6] Balthasar de Monconys, *Journal des voyages de Monsieur de Monconys*, 2nd edn. (Lyons, 1666), 25–6. Surprise was also occasioned by there being something to sit on; the *parterres* of the Parisian theatres were for standing only. See John Lough, *Paris Theatre Audiences in the Seventeenth and Eighteenth Centuries* (London, 1957).

[7] Lorenzo Magalotti, *The Travels of Cosmo the Third Grand Duke of Tuscany, Through England* (London, 1821) 25 Apr. 1669.

[8] François Brunet, 'Voyage d'Angleterre' (1676): BL Add.MS 35177.

'highly agreeable . . . for its novelty and ingenuity; and all parts of it were likewise equally praised by the ladies and gentlemen, who crowded in great numbers to the theatre to fill the boxes, with which it is entirely surrounded, and the pit, and to enjoy the performance . . .'[9]

The obvious discrepancy between this and the former account—on the one hand the fine people keep to their boxes, on the other they crowd into the pit—suggests that it was a matter of chance or occasion how the pattern of spectators within the theatre resolved itself. To that most basic question, what was the ratio of men to women in the audience, we must, it seems, reply with a further question: *which* audience?

There are many indications not only that the arrangement of any given (or individual) audience was subject to change, but that there were different kinds of audience which varied in social and sexual composition as circumstances demanded.[10] It is not only a matter of the brief, single day's changes which require our attention—the New Year opera for the 'citizens' or the influx of Members of Parliament during the recess—but the more substantial intervals when the character of the audience could change so markedly as to affect the kind of entertainment offered.[11] When he produced *The Old Troop* in 1672 John Lacy envisaged a 'vacation audience' of people with no ear for poetry and a great liking for slapstick: Dryden wrote 'to th'Tearmes', when the fashionable world had returned from the country, and he 'to th'long vacations', when only those with business and a minimum of leisure would be there to watch. Even within the space of a few days' run the composition, social and sexual, of the audience could change significantly. John Crowne doubted the value of embellishing plays with 'rich trappings' when the fashionable people were likely to ignore them after the first day and turn them over to 'Citizens and their Wives'.[12] Events less regular than the vacations might result in drastic changes, numerically and critically, in the audience: the outbreak of war, for instance. During the Third Dutch War and its aftermath Dryden, Crowne, and John Leanerd all lamented the absence of 'our gallants', gone off to fight, and joked that those women who usually did business with them in the theatres now went elsewhere for custom; Wycherley urged

---

[9] Magalotti, 3 May 1669.

[10] For complaints about the movement of spectators around the auditorium, see Shadwell, Prologue, *The Woman Captain* (1679); Wright, Prologue, *The Female Vertuosoes*; Farquhar, Epilogue, *The Constant Couple* (1699); Davenant, Prologue and Epilogue, *The Man's the Master* (1668).

[11] For Christmas and New Year's Day operas, see Pepys, *Diary*, 27 Dec. 1662; 1 Jan. 1663. For 'Parliament men', 2 Nov. 1667.

[12] Crowne, Epilogue, *Henry VI* (1681).

that 'Men o'th'Exchange' to step into the breach and learn gallantry and judicious criticism.[13] This is not mere raillery. The Army Lists show that over seven hundred new commissions were given during the Third Dutch War; in 1678, when war with the French seemed imminent, more than eight hundred. It is not only a question of numbers. When war drew away men who led opinion, as it did in 1666, voices might be heard which otherwise languished in silence and doubt.[14]

It is clear that the size of the female audience cannot be understood simply by looking at the attendance figures for different parts of the auditorium, even though such figures are available in more or less reliable estimates.[15] That is to say that the number of women in the audience, and the ratio of women to men, cannot be calculated without extensive reference to the different patterns of attendance; such reference is not evasive, but prudent. The best course, therefore, is to examine the different theatre-going habits of as many different women as possible. The case of Elizabeth Pepys has revealed something of the freedom with which a middle-class woman could go to a play; let us now test that case against the full range of female patrons of the stage.

It is with the most privileged that we shall begin. The best-documented case after Elizabeth Pepys also happens to be the least typical. In her patronage of the stage Lady Penelope Morley was unusually privileged; she had at her disposal not only her late husband's estate but his shares in the Theatre Royal, which, she clearly felt, entitled her to frequent the place without payment.[16] Hers is a case of theatre-going without

[13] Dryden, Prologue, *Marriage à-la-Mode* (1671); Crowne, Prologue, *Charles the Eighth* (1671); John Leanerd, Prologue, *The Counterfeits* (1678); Wycherley, Epilogue, *The Gentleman Dancing-Master* (1672). Similar thoughts were uttered at the time of the Low Countries Campaign by William Mountfort, Prologue, *Greenwich Park* (1691) and Shadwell, Epilogue, *Bury Fair*. Bodleian Library, Ballard MS 33, f. 102, records surprise at beaux being seen in the theatre during the hostilities of 1697.

[14] *English Army Lists and Commission Registers, 1660–1714*, ed. Charles Dalton, 6 vols. (London, 1892–4), i. 120–55. Both Buckingham and Rochester, cited in Dennis's list of leading wits who secured the success of *The Plain Dealer*, fought in the Second Dutch War. In June 1672 Wycherley himself enlisted in the Duke of Buckingham's regiment, as did Buckhurst (another on Dennis's list) and the dramatist Henry Higden.

[15] See T. L., Letter, *The Theatrical and Monthly Inquisitor and Monthly Mirror*, July 1816, pp. 25–6; Leslie Hotson, *The Commonwealth and Restoration Stage* (Cambridge, Mass., 1928), 288; Edward A. Langhans, 'New Restoration Theatre Accounts', *Theatre Notebook*, 17 (1963), 118–34; Judith Milhous, 'The Duke's Company's Profits, 1674–1677', *Theatre Notebook*, 32 (1978), 76–87; and P. Sawyer, 'The Seating Capacity and Maximum Receipts of Lincoln's-Inn-Fields Theatre', *Notes and Queries* 199 (1954), 290.

[16] See Hotson, *The Commonwealth and Restoration Stage*: for details of the transfer of Sir Thomas Morley's shares in July 1693, pp. 306–7; for the schedule of performances she

economic restraint. Nevertheless, the schedule which she presented to the patentees of the theatre in 1701 reveals patterns which are likely to have been observed by some of the less privileged. The document records visits made between 6 November 1696 and 9 June 1701. She attended one hundred and seven performances at the Theatre Royal in that time, and saw thirty-seven in the first five months of 1701; in December 1700 and January 1701 she went to no fewer than twenty-two performances. In two especially concentrated bouts, she saw Cibber's *Love Makes a Man* five times in the space of nine days in December 1700, and in May 1697 went to the theatre on four consecutive evenings. On all but three of those one hundred and seven occasions she sat in a box, presumably in the interests of treating friends at the expense of the playhouse or being extremely well attended; on the three outstanding ones she went into the pit, to see three very different kinds of play: initially for the Dryden/Davenant version of *The Tempest*, then for the once controversial Shadwell play, *The Lancashire Witches*,[17] and finally for the rakish-cum-reformation Vanbrugh comedy, *The Relapse*. She saw the first two of those plays within three days of each other, which hardly suggests that the initial foray into the lower house had been an unpleasant experience. Of other plays her choice, disappointingly, was much as the conventional wisdom about the ladies might lead us to expect. Big operatic productions loom large: *King Arthur* six times, *The Island Princess*, *The Tempest*, and *The Indian Queen* three times each. Southerne's *Oroonoko*, which one observer dubbed 'the Favourite of the Ladies', she saw three times.[18] She also had a taste for the so-called 'new mode' in comedy, and for the successes of earlier years in pathetic tragedy: five visits each were made to Farquhar's *The Constant Couple*, Cibber's *Love Makes a Man*, and to plays by Otway and by Lee. She did, however, like Elizabeth Pepys, have a taste for drama of the former age (although it was nothing like as well represented in the 1690s as it had been in the 1660s), taking in seven performances of plays by Jonson; and, more surprisingly, she also had a stomach for one performance each of *The Plain Dealer* and *The London Cuckolds*, both of which had excited female opposition in previous years which was well catalogued in the printed editions and, presumably, in popular memory.

attended (presented to the patentees of the Theatre Royal for her reimbursement), pp. 377–9.

[17] The play first appeared in September 1681, during the Popish Plot Crisis, and was thought to be full of 'dangerous Reflections'. For its passage through opposition and censorship see Shadwell's 'To the Reader', which introduces the play.

[18] For *Oroonoko* see *A Comparison Between the Two Stages*, p. 19.

Of the social character of Lady Penelope's visits there is little to be said. The schedule shows that from November 1696 to June 1700 she saw fifty-two performances, forty-seven of them in company (she also claimed for the cost of entertaining); whereas in the really concentrated period of play-going, from June 1700 to June 1701, when she saw fifty-five performances, she was accompanied on only ten occasions. Her enthusiasm for the theatre clearly out-stripped her field of acquaintance, however keen she may have been, like Pepys, to 'show' favourite productions to company; a responsibility which, as a non-paying shareholder, she can scarcely have been unwilling to assume.

Except for its almost boundless frequency, there is nothing particularly surprising about Lady Penelope Morley's attendance at the theatre; she sat in a box nearly every time because it was the best seat and she did not have to pay for it, and she saw almost precisely the repertoire of plays which one would expect from reading the conventional accounts of the likes and dislikes of 'ladies'. Close inspection of her schedule with the relevant pages of *The London Stage* to hand does, however, lend a measure of support to what will already have been inferred from Cibber's account of the introduction of the vizard-mask into the theatre: that ladies tended not to go to completely new plays without some assurance of their propriety, whether in the form of advance intelligence of the subject or of the reputation of the author.[19] Lady Penelope Morley saw fewer than half of the première productions given at the Theatre Royal during the time covered by her schedule; and the ones she did see were what might be termed 'safe bets': a handful of plays by George Powell, a confessed advocate of the ladies, the two sentimental comedies by Farquhar and Cibber, and some dramatic operas.[20] Such figures must be treated warily; Elizabeth Pepys, after all, could not accompany her husband to the theatre for nearly three months in 1668 simply because she was away in the country. Nevertheless, the regularity of Lady Penelope's theatre-going, and the facility of it, do rather suggest that she deliberately avoided some first day peformances. It was not, moreover, only first days which she missed, but entire first runs; they were likely to be short, and there must have been times when intelligence of a new play could not travel with

---

[19] *The London Stage 1660–1800*, 11 vols. (Carbondale, Ill., 1960–8). *Part I: 1660–1700*, ed. William van Lennep (1965).

[20] She saw 13 out of a possible 31 premières at the Theatre Royal during the time indicated. For Powell's advocacy of the ladies, see his Prologue to *Alphonso, King of Naples* (1691). The operas were Motteux, *The Island Princess* (1698); Durfey, *Cinthia and Endimion* (1696). One of the Powell premières was also an opera, *Brutus of Alba* (1696).

sufficient speed or accuracy. If it was as common for women to stay away from the first day as Cibber implies, the large number of plays which were not revived at all may well have passed by a significant section of the female audience; a play such as Southerne's *The Wives Excuse, or cuckolds make themselves* (1691), which had the misfortune to combine an unusually well reasoned defence of a woman's right to defy all suitors with a title which promised other things, may simply, in its one or two day run, not have been seen by those patrons on whose support its author had counted.

Again there are qualifications to be made: just because Lady Penelope Morley was able to see all plays at the Theatre Royal without charge does not mean that she would have wanted to; and to claim that her only reason for staying away from a new play was to protect her modesty is to fall under the misapprehension of certain dramatists that women cared about nothing else when they went to the theatre. Such doubts are not merely destructive; they should help us to be more exact. Consider the exceptions to the alleged rule of first day abstinence: Elizabeth Pepys went to the first performance of *An Evening's Love* only to prompt her husband, who went the day after, to reflect on its smuttiness; on another occasion dinner was interrupted so that she could go to a first day with Mrs Pearse. Some more eminent ladies made as big a show as possible out of attending a first performance: Rochester begged the 'ladies of maturer ages' not to crowd the fronts of boxes at new plays to be admired by young sparks; the Earl of Dorset offered the same advice to the Countess of Dorchester.[21] Clearly some women were not sufficiently conspicuous in the fashionable world to have to worry about being seen at a new and surprisingly smutty play; while others found their own occasions to be conspicuous, regardless of the need of some (those represented by Wycherley's Olivia, for instance) to absent themselves. For these latter (middle-aged) ladies, the poets contended that they had nothing to lose by letting slip a blush or two; it was a sign of unabated energy rather than guilt.

The equation should now be obvious. It was only those women who in the first place were conspicuous for no other reason than that they desired it who had to worry about remaining inconspicuous when circumstances were not in their favour; when a new play or a revival of a known lewd play was offered. Hannah Woolley gives us a sketch of a morning in the

[21] John Wilmot, Earl of Rochester, 'Prologue spoken by Mrs Cook the second day', *Valentinian* (1684); Charles Sackville, Earl of Dorset, 'On the Countess of Dorchester', in William J. Cameron, ed., *Poems on Affairs of State*, 7 vols. (New Haven and London, 1971), v. 385. The Countess of Dorchester was Catherine Sedley, the daughter of the poet. See also *The Modern World Disrob'd* (London, 1708), 37–8: 'The *Toping* Lady'.

life of a lady of fashion which shows very clearly what the determined exhibitionist had to consider when she contemplated spending the afternoon at the playhouse. The fastidious interplay of rumour, reputation, and self-display suggests a world remote indeed from that of Elizabeth Pepys:

Many of our Sex are to blame, who have no sooner ting'd their Faces artificially, than some Attendant is dispatcht to know what Plays are to be acted that day; my Lady approveth of one which she is resolved to see, that she may be seen; being in the Pit or Box, she minds not how little she observeth in it, as how much to be observed at it.[22]

Being seen is the principal consideration, and it determines the eventual choice of both play and seat: the former on the grounds both of the quality of company likely to be attracted, and of the suitability of the play as an occasion for self-exhibition. One could not be seen, as Wycherley's Olivia has testified, at a play whose reputation for bawdy was likely to enhance one's own. The reputation of the play and the playwright were intricately involved with those of their potential patrons who declared themselves most openly at the theatre. Woolley's archetypal fashionable lady tends to make up her mind about a play before she sees it; her attendant is there only to supply the names. To go at all was an act of critical approval, according to Woolley the only act of criticism of the entire day. The play became an out-size 'fine thing' which could be owned and treasured for the freedom it allowed one to be demonstrative in the theatre. So we see that those peculiar moral imperatives examined in the first chapter of this study, which had it that a woman's public character depended so much on her attending and applauding a particular kind of play, could bear only on the demonstrative. For those women, much of the important critical activity had to take place before the event; and failing a printed copy or the recommendation of disinterested critics, rumour and the reputation of the author were bound to play their part, however untrustworthy.[23] Aphra Behn's experience with *The Luckey Chance* has shown just how misleading

---

[22] *The Gentlewoman's Companion* (London, 1675), 35–6.

[23] The opportunities for picking up casual gossip about plays and the theatre, even outside the kind of *salon* depicted in *The Plain Dealer*, II. i., were prodigious. Their extent is witnessed in Pepys's conversations with his shoemaker and bookseller: *Diary*, 24 Sept. 1662, 22 July 1663, 17 Aug. 1664, 13 Feb. 1667, and 22 June 1668; and in *Remarques on the Humours and Conversations . . . of the Town*, p. 62: 'Ev'ry one [is a critic] that has Money to Buy, or Leisure and Patience enough for to Read; even from the Groom to the Lord, from the Prentice to the Alderman, from the Chambermaid to the Countess, from the little Miss in the Nursery, to the grave matron in her Closet . . .'

such sources of information could be. Such was the framework of doubts in which Lady Penelope Morley, a woman conspicuous only, perhaps, for the regularity with which she was able to occupy the most expensive seats in the house, had to make up her mind about a new play.[24]

If it was a minority of women who were demonstrative at the theatre, and if the occasional need to become inconspicuous was suffered only by the minority, the uses and artifices of demonstratives itself were yet many. To look at the options available will not, as will become clear, be to exclude from discussion the role of more passive spectators like Elizabeth Pepys. For variety of artifice, the inventory of glances and attitudes drawn up by Steele's Lady Brumpton is precise and localized, but it still represents only a fraction of the possibilities available:

What pleasure 'twill be when my lady *Brumpton's* footman's call'd (who kept a place for that very purpose) to make a suddain Insurrection of Fine Wigs in the Pit, and Side-Boxes. Then with a pretty sorrow in one's Face, and a willing Blush for being star'd at, one ventures to look round and Bow, to one of one's own Quality, Thus: (*Very Derectly*.) . . . To one that writes Lampoons, Thus: (*Fearfully*.) To one who really loves, Thus: (*Looking down*.) To one's Woman Acquaintance, from Box to Box, Thus: (*With looks differently Familiar*.) And when one has done one's part, observe the Actors do theirs, but with my mind fixt not on those I look at, but those that look at me.[25]

The actor's notation is Lady Brumpton's as it is Steele's, and it is finely honed in its directions both for expression ('a willing Blush') and location: a flexible means of asserting status and amorous inclination in a place where social and sexual claims on one's attention were strongly localized.

For much of the time this could be carried on at the level of the routine ogling so often mentioned in accounts of the theatre audience, although even there an exact understanding of the disposition of audience and auditorium was a pre-condition of success.[26] Aphra Behn's Diana was a

[24] The expense of the boxes (4s.) made them highly conspicuous to the socially ambitious: see Pepys *Diary*, 25 Mar. 1667, 19 Jan. 1661, 5 May 1668, 7 Nov. 1667.
[25] Richard Steele, *The Funeral* (1701) I. ii.
[26] Shadwell, Epilogue, *The Lancashire Witches*: 'The City neither likes us nor our Wit, / They say their Wives learn ogling in the Pit, / They'r from the Boxes taught to make Advances, / To answer stolen Sighs and naughty Glances.' See also Lee, Epilogue, *Gloriana* (1676); Vanbrugh, *Aesop Part II* (1697), II. i.; Crowne, Epilogue, *Darius*. 'The Cunning Wanton' in *The Modern World Disrob'd*, 30, has mastered all glances including 'the Side-Box Squint'. The side-boxes were traditionally the places from which beaux ogled the ladies facing them and in the pit (see *The Country Gentleman's Vade Mecum*, 32), although the Royal Box, when occupied by King Charles and his brother, could be used for the same purpose; see Pepys, *Diary*, 21 Dec. 1668.

skilful practitioner when it came to her principal activity in the theatre
(and the vividness of her appreciation commands some belief in her
representativeness), that of winning new admirers:

> I never go abroad, bit I gain new Conquests. Happy's the Man that can approach
> nearest the Side-box where I sit at a Play, to look at me; but if I deign to smile on
> him, Lord, how the overjoyed Creature returns it with a Bow low as the very
> benches; then rising, shakes his Ears, looks round with Pride, to see who took
> notice how much he was in favour with Mrs. *Dy*.[27]

The location and behaviour are perfectly suited to the unobtrusively
public nature of the event; the play between the pit and the boxes nearest
to the stage is both conspicuous and capable of being ignored ('to see who
took notice . . .'). The pleasure of watching and gathering information was,
to the rest of the audience, a selective one which could readily be foregone
in favour of the play proper or more significant liaisons elsewhere in the
theatre; it was not necessarily a nuisance.

Some degree of propaganda is implicit in these efforts even of the not
especially distinguished to draw attention to themselves in the playhouse;
they became a way of declaring one's power over other conspicuous
members of the audience. It is not surprising, therefore, to find that the
most conspicuous women of all had the most refined and noticeable line
in exhibitionism; their conquests and humiliations were matter for intense
gossip and speculation to a far wider range of theatre-goers. For example,
the Pepyses' interest in the career of Lady Castlemaine never waned, and it
was ably sustained by her often highly dramatic appearances at the
playhouse. Sometimes it was enough that she should simply be there:

> My wife and I to the theatre, and there saw *The Jovial Crew*, where the King,
> Duke and Duchess, and Madam Palmer were; and my wife, to her great content,
> had a full sight of them all the while.[28]

Such sights were compensation enough for a poor play, and the content
was not only Elizabeth's. There is not a single stage performance, not even
by a favourite or friendly actress, which receives the detailed attention
which Pepys gave to the foibles of the royal mistresses. He was once
spellbound as Lady Castlemaine ('without whom all is nothing') called for
a patch to suppress a rising pimple by her mouth.[29] It was a fascination

---

[27] Aphra Behn, *The City-Heiress* (1683), II. ii.
[28] *Diary*, 27 Aug. 1661 (Palmer was her husband's name); 3 Apr. 1665: 'All the pleasure
of the play was the King and Lady Castlemaine were there.'
[29] *Diary*, 5 May 1668; 15 Nov. 1666.

which he shared with friends; the naval surgeon James Pearse could report to him in loving detail how the same lady had placed herself next to the royal box as the King arrived for *The Indian Queen*, then leaned over his guests to whisper with him, and finally removed herself to sit at his right hand, to the evident embarrassment of King and audience alike.[30] Pearse swore that she did it only to 'show the world that she is not out of favour yet—as was believed'. Zempoalla herself could hardly have been more demonstrative, nor her audience more attentive. It was not only Lady Castlemaine who indulged in such tricks. The scandal of the Duke of York's pursuit of Lady Chesterfield, reported in somewhat forgiving terms by Pepys, resulted in the innocent lady being sent away to the Peak District; four days after her departure, the Duke and his Duchess were sufficiently sensitive about the affair to indulge, for the spectators' benefit rather than their own, in 'some impertinent, and . . . unnatural dalliances' at the Cockpit Theatre.[31]

Behaviour of this kind was only possible (or useful) given two conditions: the attentiveness of the spectators and their familiarity with the private life of the person being attended to. In the case of Pepys's regard for Lady Castlemaine, there is no doubt of either. The noble lady often did not have to construct a performance to attract the attention of her admirer; the revealing accidentals of her behaviour were sufficient:

it vexed me to see Moll Davis, in the box over the King's and my Lady Castlemaine's, look down upon the King and he up to her; and so did my Lady Castlemaine once, to see who it was; but when she saw Moll Davis, she looked fire.[32]

It was an intriguing performance which could scarcely have been improved by study, and its strength was in the intimacy of detail disclosed: an addition to the existing knowledge of Lady Castlemaine's lying in, dining out, and falling from favour, gained from observation and a variety of acquaintance.[33] The playhouse, with its high concentration of the fashionable and professional, proved the ideal theatre for the alternate joys and woes of the eminent to be acted and appreciated. When the Queen arrived from Portugal in May 1662, Lady Castlemaine was found to be 'a

[30] *Diary*, 1 Feb. 1664.
[31] *Diary*, 3 Nov. 1662, 1 Jan. 1663, 5 Jan. 1663. The full story is told in Hamilton, *Memoirs*, pp. 188–93.
[32] *Diary*, 21 Dec. 1668.
[33] *Diary*, 22 Sept. 1663; 21 Mar. 1665; 13 Apr. 1662; 13 Oct. 1663; 13 June 1663; 13 July 1660. Pepys's chief source of information was Lord Sandwich, at this time Master of the Great Wardrobe.

most disconsolate creature', looking 'dejectedly' at a play, 'slighted by people already'.[34] It was obviously not only the Pepyses who were aware of her position; others perceived it and acted accordingly. Not everyone was party to rumour, although Pepys confessed great surprise when he found someone in the playhouse who did not recognize the great lady; and on another occasion, during a puppet-play at Bartholomew Fair, he wondered at her courage in going out to so public a place, the risk of abuse being great, only to find that the 'silly people do not know what work she makes'—not to know why she should be thought ill of was a crime indeed to one who belonged (here, somewhat complacently) to the *cognoscenti*.[35]

The political activity of that particular eminent lady in the playhouse caused an answering activity in the rest of the audience. Pepys twice noticed a woman who, the image of Lady Castlemaine, flitted wantonly about the pit in rude imitation of her ladyship's own freedom with the opposite sex: she sat next to him, was 'acquainted with every fine fellow, and called them by their name', and 'before the end of the play, frisked to another place'.[36] Criticism of her exhibitionism at the theatre reached the presses, again in the form of an impersonation; in this case, it seems, of her speaking voice:

on Shrove-Tuesday last, splendidly did we appear upon the Theatre at W.H. being to amazement wonderfully deck'd with jewels and diamonds, which the (abhorr'd and to be undone) subjects of this Kingdom have payed for.[37]

Whatever the unchecked admiration of the Pepyses and their friends (it is they who are mocked as well as the Countess), it is clear that the theatre was not free from the resentments and political reflections which surfaced about town.

One did not have to be politically active to excite such attention; the vicissitudes of the less daring were of little less interest and renown. Steele's Lady Brumpton expected everyone to know about her recent bereavement, and the following rather ordinary incident, reported by Pepys, speaks of a wealth of private information absorbed and acted upon

---

[34] *Diary*, 21 May 1662.

[35] *Diary*, 7 Mar. 1664, 30 Aug. 1667.

[36] *Diary*, 4 Feb. 1667; 21 Dec. 1668.

[37] *The Gracious Answer of the most Illustrious Lady of Pleasure the Countess of Castlemaine to the Poor-Whores Petition* (London, 1668); a mock reply to a mock appeal following the pulling down of City brothels by apprentices on 24 Mar. 1668, *The Poor-Whores Petition to the most splendid, illustrious, serene, and eminent lady of pleasure, the Countess of Castlemayne*. 'W.H.' in the extract quoted must indicate Whitehall. See also Pepys, *Diary*, 24 Mar. and 5 Apr. 1668; and, for the political character of the riot, *Diary*, ed. Latham and Mathews, ix. 129, n. 2.

by the majority of spectators, to the extent that the simplest play of the face by one of the protagonists could excite wry speculation:

Here I saw Lord Rochester and his Lady, Mrs. Mallett, who after all this ado hath married him; and, as I hear some say in the pit, it is a great act of charity, for he hath no estate. But it was pleasant to see how everybody rose up when my Lord Jo. Butler, the Duke of Ormond's son, came into the pit toward the end of the play, who was a servant to Mrs. Mallett, and now smiled upon her, and she on him.[38]

The familiar tone refers the known past to the intricate game of the present: 'all this ado' goes back to Rochester's attempt two years before to abduct his future wife.[39] The settlement now being plain, the husband's position is made to seem precarious by his wife's favouring publicly a former (and known) suitor, a favour which everyone could watch and, it seems, contribute to.

If such behaviour could become a source of information and even propaganda, it also became, inevitably, a pattern for imitation. In a famous instance, Lady Mary Cromwell was seen to put on a vizard-mask as the theatre began to fill up, and to keep it on throughout the play; it had, according to Pepys, become 'a great fashion among the ladies', to the extent that he had, on the same day, to go 'to the Exchange, to buy things with my Wife; among others, a vizard for herself'.[40] It was a ritual which the intimacy of the playhouse encouraged, and in which Pepys acquiesced rather unwillingly, disdaining the products of fashion while observing them with helpful acuteness;[41] his wife might admire Mrs Stewart for having her hair 'done up with puffs', but he could not but dissent, attributing her admiration to a hankering after the latest fashion as exhibited in the playhouse.[42] There was more to it than that; the rewards

[38] *Diary*, 4 Feb. 1667.

[39] The episode, and its consequences for Rochester, are recounted in the *Diary*, 28 May 1665. Pepys knew that Elizabeth Mallett's fortune was £2,500 per year; he was also able to inform Lady Sandwich that Rochester had been arrested at Uxbridge and sent to the Tower. Further details may be found in the *Diary*, ed. Latham and Mathews, vi. 110, n. 3.

[40] *Diary*, 12 June 1663.

[41] An early instance of the effect of playhouse design is Davenant, Prologue, *The First Dayes of Entertainment at Rutland House*, in *The Dramatick Works of Sir William D'Avenant*, ed. James Maidment and W. D. Logan, 5 vols. (Edinburgh, 1874), iii. 197: That half are freely by the other faced / And we are shrewdly jealous that you come / Not merely to hear us, or see the room, / But rather meet here to be met, I mean / Each would see all, and would of all be seen.

[42] *Diary*, 4 Feb. 1667. The fashion mentioned was for artificial rolls of hair, worn as a supplement rather than a substitute. In spite of his disdain Pepys twice recorded his shame at seeing his wife under-dressed at a play: 8 May 1663, 25 Mar. 1667.

of exhibitionism fell to all who participated in it, whether by acting or simply admiring. For the protagonists it was an opportunity to enhance their popular reputations while admiring one another; for the mere onlookers, to study at close quarters the foibles of the great—an informal school of manners and fashionable gossip, so to speak.

This view of the audience differs in important respects from that of one of the most influential scholars in the field, Emmet Avery. Avery's case is that the troublesome elements so often referred to in the prologues and epilogues were minorities, nuisances against whom the wit of prologues could be directed with the support of the decent majority of spectators. It is not the numerical proportions of this which need to be questioned; it is the disposition of the majority on whom, Avery argues, the dramatists could so confidently count. It is Pepys, according to Avery, who is the type of the professional, decent spectator;[43] yet it was Pepys who so relished the distracting games of the fashionable world, and Pepys who noticed more about the foibles of the royal mistresses than about the (one would have thought) no less inviting qualities of the star actresses. The minority of nuisances and the majority of dependables were in that sense rather more in collaboration than Avery's argument implies, and it was not only those who, like Pepys, were interested in the intricacies of court and town gossip who collaborated. The fashionable audience could be a remote but enthralling spectacle to many highly inconspicuous theatre-goers on whom no dramatist could call for support. Thomas Betterton's Mrs Brittle, for instance, is the type of city-wife who went to the theatre simply to wonder at the antics of the fashionable patrons:

'Tis the pleasant'st Thing in the World to see A Flock of Wild Gallants fluttering about two or three Ladies in Vizard-Masks, and then talk to 'em so wantonly, and so loud, that they put the very Players out of countenance—'tis a better entertainment than any part of the play.[44]

The Pepyses' interest in both play and audience was more sophisticated, but it still provided, no less than Mrs Brittle's preference for refined hooliganism, the context of admiring curiosity in which the diversions

[43] Emmet L. Avery, 'The Restoration Audience', *Philological Quarterly*, 45 (1966), 57: 'nearly everyone in the Navy Office attended the theatre, sometimes frequently . . . Had we another Pepys in the inner circles of the army, the law, the clergy, or the medical profession, we might hope to find an equally large group of professional men who formed a substantial portion of the audience'. This last is true, as Botica, pp. 89–108, has shown; it is the character of their appreciation which Avery mistakes.

[44] Thomas Betterton, *The Amorous Widow* (1670), II. i. A similar situation is described in Crowne, *The English Friar* (1690), II, iii.

and histrionics of the conspicuous could flourish. If there was, as seems certain, a well-disposed majority of decent spectators on whom the dramatists could so confidently call for support, it was a majority whose allegiance might readily be transferred to those 'time-wasters and other nuisances' who drew so much attention.

This symbiotic relationship between the conspicuous exhibitionists and their inconspicuous admirers certainly gained strength from the relationship of boxes to pit in the theatre. The political scheming of Lady Castlemaine and the intimate disclosures of Lady Rochester were published from the boxes, raised above the pit and framed, suitably enough, with their own miniature proscenium arches. That does not mean that exhibitionists were confined to the boxes and their admirers to the pit. Hannah Woolley's extrovert lady could be admired equally in the pit and the boxes, and the conversations and meaning glances to which Pepys, Shadwell, and others draw our attention generally took place between different and equally conspicuous areas of the theatre; from box to box, or box to pit. Nevertheless, the boxes were always conspicuous in so far as they were thought of as the territory of the quality. *The Country Gentleman's Vade Mecum*, which is as close to a factual account of the theatre audience as anything the age produced, warns that the boxes were for royalty, persons of quality, and ladies and gentlemen of the highest rank, 'unless some Fools, that have more Money than Wit, or perhaps more Impudence than both, crowd in among 'em'.[45] The fact that instances of such impudence were sometimes referred to with derision may indicate the severity of the restraint, something of which is clear in Pepys's own surprise at seeing his wife under-dressed in a box and, indeed, in his general attitude towards people who occupied seats above their station and income.[46]

It is also true that much of the evidence of the prologues and epilogues suggests that the boxes were the more conspicuous for being the exclusive territory not merely of the fine people, but of the ladies of quality.[47] There is some more reliable evidence to support this: that of another French traveller, Henri Misson, who remarked that the first row of boxes was

---

[45] ?Stacy, *The Country Gentleman's Vade Mecum* (London, 1699) 38.

[46] Lee, Prologue, *Gloriana* (1676); Rawlins, *Tom Essence* (1677), IV. i.; Durfey, Prologue, *The Fool's Preferment* (1688). For Pepys on 'prentices and mean people in the pit at 2s. 6d.', 1 Jan. 1668.

[47] John Bankes, Prologue, *The Rival Kings* (1677); John Corye, Epilogue, *The Generous Enemies* (1672); Durfey, Prologue, *The Banditti* (1686); Trotter, Prologue, *Fatal Friendship* (1698); Francis Manning, Epilogue, *The Generous Choice* (1700).

'taken up by Persons of the best Quality, among whom are generally very few men'; and, a little after our period, of the Scots traveller John Macky, who noted that:

> on the 1st *Row* of *Boxes* sit all the Ladies of Quality; in the second the Citizens' Wives & Daughters . . . so that between the Acts you may be diverted by viewing the Beauties of the Audience,

in which latter respect the theatre of Macky differed little from that of Pepys.[48] Pepys himself makes a suggestive contribution when he records, with the assurance of one pointing out a known landmark, 'We sat under the boxes and saw the fine ladies'; although it was a landmark capable of being transplanted elsewhere: on another day he sat 'in the pit among the company of fine ladies'.[49] Such evidence, with its manifest contradictions, may be used only to show how the pattern of female attendance could change from day to day; the prologues and epilogues, for the reasons given, cannot be trusted to report accurately, while the travellers took in only a small sample of the range of possible audiences. Our safest bet is the frankly contradictory Pepys. That said, it is of no less interest to us to know that 'the fine ladies' sometimes went to the theatre *en masse*, and that they sometimes sat in the pit and sometimes in the boxes, than it would be if we knew that they always filled the boxes alone, as the prologues appear to suggest. Further evidence that the 'fine ladies' did attend spasmodically and in large numbers may be found in Woolley's sketch of the typical lady of fashion, who chooses her play according to the kind of company it is likely to attract; if she is to be seen to full advantage, by as many of her peers as possible, it is important for her to go at the same time as other women of the same class (even Lady Penelope Morley, unimpeded by financial or social considerations, did not go every night; some choices had to be made).[50]

---

[48] Henri Misson, *M. Misson's Memoirs and Observations*, trans. John Ozell (London, 1719) 219–20. The journal was written in 1676. See also Giovanni Torriano, *Mescolanze dolce di varie historiette* (London, 1673), 126, where the pit is said to be the best place for looking upon the ladies in their boxes. John Macky, *A Journey Through England in Familiar Letters*, 2 vols. (London, 1714), i. 109–10.

[49] *Diary*, 3 Dec. 1668, 31 Jan. 1661.

[50] Advance information about the company took different forms. The eponymous hero of Crowne's *Sir Courtly Nice* (1685) was able to guess by the *kind* of play: 'comedies . . . are so ill-bred and sawcy with Quality, and always cramm'd with our odious Sex'. Peregrine Bertie, writing to the Countess of Rutland, could be more precise: 'Thursday was acted *Mithridates* for the Queen and Goodman played. Today is *Othello*. The Jenkins ladies will be there'. 'Peregrine Bertie to the Countess of Rutland, Feb. 6th 1685/6', HMC 12th Report, Appendix V, Rutland MSS, ii, 104.

Needless to say, publicity was not the only aim of titled ladies who sat in the boxes; it is plain that many women desired little more from the experience than the charm of a small and relatively private party, which it was the peculiar facility of the boxes to encourage.[51] A letter from Lady Mary Bertie to her niece, Katherine Noel, records an outing to the first part of *The Conquest of Granada*, and it indicates the relaxed, unostentatious congeniality of such gatherings:

My brother Norreys tooke a box and carryed my Lady Rochester and his mistresse and all us to, and on Tuesday wee are to goe see the second part of it which is then the first time acted.[52]

The mistress could be carried along too without exception; in the next sentence Lady Mary writes, 'I am suere you would be with us if wishes could bring you.' The theatre, and the pleasure of the box (it has the air of formal treat) were there neither for display nor to harass the moral dignity of the family. Three months later Lady Mary reported another visit, this time in exclusively female company: 'with my lady Rochester and my lady Bettey Howard and Mrs Lee at a play.'[53] It is not clear where the four ladies sat; the fact that a box was mentioned before may indicate that it was exceptional even for Lady Mary to sit in one, a treat reserved for formal outings. These visits confirm what the experience of Elizabeth Pepys has already suggested: that it was perfectly acceptable for parties of women to go to the theatre. The two cases also show that such parties were not the prerogative of one social class; the Ladies Howard, Rochester, and Bertie were no more free to go than Elizabeth and Kate Joyce, the tallow-chandler's wife. Complications of engagement were more likely the higher one's circle, but the freedom to attend was, money apart, uniform.[54] Nor were these parties socially exclusive. Elizabeth Pepys sat with Lady Fox in her 'pew', and she and her husband were engaged to take Lord Sandwich's daughters to see *Bartholomew Fair*, where they seated themselves 'close by the King, the Duke of York, and Madame Palmer'.[55] To the

[51] For James Howard's *The English monsieur* on 7 Apr. 1668 Pepys sat 'for privacy sake in an upper box'; such choices must have been available regularly for the affluent.
[52] 'Lady Mary Bertie to her niece Kathern Noel at Exton, Jan 2/71/2' HMC Rutland, II. 22.
[53] HMC Rutland, II, 23.
[54] For the complications which an over-stocked social calendar might present to the theatre-goer, Alice Hatton, *Hatton Correspondence*, ed. Edward Maunde Thompson, Camden Society, NS 23, 2 vols. (Westminster, 1878), i. 245.
[55] *Diary*, 15 Feb. 1669; 7 Sept. 1661. Lady Fox's husband, Sir Stephen, was Clerk of the Green Cloth, and had a box at his disposal. Pepys's comment is interesting; the play was his

same play Pepys took a group of Navy Office wives—Lady Batten, Mrs Allen, and Mrs Thompson—and any gathering of fine ladies was certain to be attended by a number of waiting-women.[56] Bright stars often mingled with lesser luminaries.

Formal parties did not necessarily entail the taking of a box. The pit could be used without disturbance, and it is possible that even for the visit of the Sandwich daughters to *Bartholomew Fair* mentioned above no special arrangement was made; they seated themselves 'close by the King', but that may have meant a place on the upper benches of the pit, which, as other reports show, was a good place for overhearing the conversation.[57] Pepys felt no compunction about leaving his wife in the pit while he retired to a box with Sir William Penn, and he knew that family visits were scarcely out of the ordinary; there was no reason for him to regard the box as the only proper place for his patron's children.[58]

So far we have seen that the boxes, although they were the centre of much of the activity of the 'time-wasters and other nuisances' whose significance modern criticism has learned to diminish, regularly housed more modest patrons who desired either privacy or a strictly limited circle of company. What, then, of the character of the pit and its bearing on

favourite, *The Adventures of Five Hours*: 'but I sat so far, I could not hear well, nor was there any pretty women that I did see but my wife, who sat in my Lady Foxe's pew with her'. The boxes, and their ladies, could be a more convenient and accessible entertainment if one was unlucky in a seat.

[56] *Diary*, 27 June 1661. Pepys was not nervous of the sensitivity of his companions to *risqué* language; on the eighth of the month he had seen the same production and found it 'much too profane and abusive'. For biographical details of Lady Batten and others, see *Diary*, ed. Latham and Mathews, x. For maids, Elizabeth Pepys's going with both Mercer and Willet is some indication of what the affluent could afford; see also, for Lady Castlemaine's maids, *Diary*, 5 May 1668.

[57] *Diary*, 1 May 1667.

[58] *Diary*, 10 Aug. 1661, 1 Apr. 1663 (further visits with the Sandwich daughters, Jemimah and Paulina); 30 Dec. 1661, 19 May 1662, 22 May 1662 (Sir William Penn and his children); 30 Dec. 1668 ('We happened to sit by Mr Andrews our neighbour and his wife, who talked so fondly to his little boy'). Sir Edward Dering also took his children: see his *Notebook*, BL Add.MS 33892 f. 598. See also R. Jordan, 'Some Restoration Playgoers', *Theatre Notebook* 35 (1981) 51-7. Jordan found that the account books of the MP for East Horsley, Sir John Nicholas, show that he often took his son, daughter, and niece to the theatre, as well as his wife, sister, and the son of his friend, Sir Francis Compton. The last visit recorded was made when the eldest child was thirteen, while Sir John's niece, Mary Cholmley, was only six upon her first visit. The whole family went on a day when *The Country Wife* was being acted; which theatre is not known. When the whole family went he secured a box; when alone or with male company (including his own son and Sir Francis Compton's) he sat in the pit.

women's attendance at the playhouse? Already we have seen that it held
no dangers for Elizabeth Pepys and her maids, in spite of the suspicions of
her husband; it held none, either, for Lady Penelope Morley or for the fine
ladies among whom Pepys sat. The traditional account of flocks of vizard-
maskers pestered by noisy thugs and gallants would appear to have little
credibility. Perhaps its most telling antagonist is the Pepys who found
himself in the actresses' tiring-room, suddenly confronted by the kind of
behaviour which, it seems, he hardly ever encountered elsewhere, and
certainly not in the playhouse:

> To the King's House, where going in for Knipp, the play being done, I did see
> Beck Marshall come dressed, off the stage, and look mighty fine, and pretty, and
> noble; and also Nell, in her boys' clothes, mighty pretty. But Lord! their
> confidence! and how many men do hover about them as soon as they come off
> the stage, and how confident they are in their talk![59]

The unpleasantness of the experience was not only in the breaking of the
illusion of nobility. It is as if he had never before encountered such
uninhibited flirtation, and it is hard to believe that he would have
frequented the pit as he did—let alone leave his wife there—if it boasted
that kind of behaviour as often as some would have one think. He was not,
it should be said, in spite of his ample affections for the opposite sex, a man
to let go by suitable adjectives when describing their freer representatives.
There is no reason to suppose that he would have neglected to remark
upon lubricity or even skittishness had they been in evidence, as they were
in the instances of Lady Castlemaine's double, Nell Gwyn in *déshabillé*,
and the Duchess of York.

   Nevertheless, there are contradictions in the reliable evidence which it
would be unwise (not to say dishonest) to ignore. Henri Misson reported
that the pit contained: 'Men of Quality, particularly the younger sort,
some ladies of Reputation and Vertue, and abundance of Damsels that
hunt for Prey.'[60] At least this shows that women like Elizabeth Pepys were
not put off by the presence of the more traditional type of female patron,
even if it does suggest that they were, if only on occasion, outnumbered by
them. The literature of the vizard-mask contains similar contradictions.
We have seen how Cibber's well-known account of its inception describes
both the innocent intentions of its first wearers and the undesirable
practices of its last, and Pepys's *Diary* offers a slightly more detailed but
broadly similar history. When Pepys bought his wife her first mask he was

[59] *Diary*, 7 May 1668. Also 5 Oct. 1667.
[60] *M. Misson's Memoirs*, p. 219.

unaware even of what Cibber took to be its initial function; it was bought simply to gratify a taste for fashion. It was not long, however, before the ill consequences which Cibber lamented came to the diarist's attention. The richness of the moment concerned demands a long quotation:

to the King's to *The Mayds Tragedy*; but vexed all the while with two talking ladies and Sir Ch.Sidly, yet pleased to hear their discourse, he being a stranger; and one of the ladies would, and did, sit with her mask on all the play; and being exceedingly witty as ever I heard woman, did talk most pleasantly with him; but was, I believe, a virtuous woman and of quality. He would fain know who she was, but she would not tell. Yet did give him many pleasant hints of her knowledge of him, by that means setting his brains at work to find out who she was; and did give him leave to use all means to find out who she was but pulling off her mask. He was mighty witty; and she also making sport with him very inoffensively, that a more pleasant rencontre I never heard. But by that means lost the pleasure of the play wholly, to which now and then Sir Ch.Sidlys exceptions against both words and pronouncing was very pretty.[61]

This is another important contribution to the 'time-wasters and nuisances' debate; in spite of losing the pleasure of the play, Pepys was obviously delighted by the free and tantalizing play of wit which the mask could provoke, although he was careful to note that the masked woman was 'virtuous' and made sport 'inoffensively'. Evidently the less virtuous already found the disguise convenient to their purposes in the theatre, even if a man such as Pepys—or Sedley himself—found it easy to distinguish the frivolities of good breeding from the exigencies of professional practice. Even so, it was only one of the women who wore her mask, and it seems to have surprised Pepys that she wore it for the duration of the whole play. Once again Pepys provides us with satisfyingly inconsistent information: it is clear on the one hand that there were women who wore masks to the theatre with the intention of picking men up, on the other that the mask could occasion quite innocent and even civilized activity, and that in doing so it did not necessarily constitute a threat to the good order of the playhouse. Elizabeth Pepys, we have seen, bought a mask because it was fashionable; Congreve's Millamant might use one to play elaborate (but innocent) games of deception with her future husband, rather like the 'talking lady' who so tantalized Sir Charles Sedley; and the author of a collection of fashionable letters saw a play masked merely to be sociable:

[61] *Diary*, 18 Feb. 1667.

In the beginning of last Summer when I was endeavouring to divert my Love, and Grief, I went with a Lady to see a Play: she was not in a humour to dress, and wou'd needs have me go *Incognito*.[62]

The mask concealed more than the decayed face of the prostitute or the healthier features of a fashionable woman who could afford to be seen neither at a *risqué* play nor about a liaison;[63] it also concealed a variety of innocent intentions, and that it did conceal them was, of course, the difficulty which its wearers faced. By the time Shadwell wrote *A True Widow* in 1678 the mask, whatever the intentions of its bearer, was taken as a sign of licentious intent. The game was no longer to discover whether a woman was sufficiently experienced to understand a smutty joke; her experience (or, at least, intention) was taken as read, and she had simply to be identified:

1ST MAN. What, not a word? all over in disguise: silence for your folly, and a vizard for your ill face.

2ND MAN. Gad! some whore, I warrant you, or chambermaid in her lady's old clothes.

3RD MAN. She must be a woman of quality; she has right point.

4TH MAN. Faith! she earns all the clothes on her back by lying on it; some punk lately out of keeping, her livery not quite worn out.

ISABELLA. I deserve this by coming in a Masque . . .[64]

Isabella's pursuers have a number of different ideas about her origins, but they all assume that she is there for a single purpose. Her own contribution to the exchange does, however, show that it was not her being in the pit which caused such a flurry of speculation, but her being masked; it is in the nature of a sign such as the mask that those who did not adopt it could remain free from trouble. The jealous Pinchwive plainly thought so too. No fool he, but 'a cunning rogue that understands the town', he fails to thwart Horner through inferior calculation rather than innocence; he sees straight away the dangers of attempting to conceal his wife in the obvious way: 'a mask makes people but the more inquisitive,' he asserts:

if we should meet with Horner, he would be sure to take acquaintance with us, must wish her joy, kiss her, talk to her, leer upon her, and the devil and all. No, I'll not use her to a mask, 'tis dangerous.[65]

---

[62] *Letters of Love and Gallantry*, 107-8. *The Way of the World*, IV, i. 205-14.

[63] For prostitutes and the mask, Dryden, 'Prologue and Epilogue to the King and Queen', *Poems and Fables*, pp. 294-6: 'Fine Love no doubt, but e'er two days are o'er ye, / The Surgeon will be told a wofull story. / Let Vizard Masque her naked Face expose / On pain of being thought to want a Nose.'

[64] *A True Widow*, IV. i.   [65] *The Country Wife*, III. i. For Dorilant's approval, I. i.

Much safer not to tempt advances like that by remaining bare-faced and attentive in one of the quieter parts of the auditorium. Pinchwife himself took Margery to the eighteen-penny (or middle) gallery 'that she might not be seen', a tactic which gained the approval of Dorilant; while Stacy's *Vade Mecum* affirms that in the most turbulent house it was possible to enjoy a play without danger, interruption, or undue expense:

> your best way is to fix yourself in some advantageous part of the pit, where with the least disturbance and interruption, you may not only observe the actions and behaviour of the actors, but likewise hear every individual part distinctly.[66]

There one could enjoy, as Pepys did, the plot and design of the play. Even in a spirit of raillery, when the presence of nuisances was greatly exaggerated, Dryden could sanction such a view of the pit:

> Here's good accommodation in the pit;
> The grave demurely in the midst may sit,
> And so the hot burgundians on the side
> Ply Vizard-Masque, and o'er the Benches stride.[67]

A charmed circle in the middle of the house, where the roaring devils would not enter. Even allowing for a maximum of disturbance, it appears to have been possible to sit in the pit bare-faced, demure, and attentive.

It is plain, then, that the pit could accommodate a wide variety of women. Indeed, the majority of those women theatre-goers whose names we know all seem to have sat in the pit from time to time; the exceptions were principally court luminaries, for whom it would doubtless have been improperly familiar to enjoy a play in such mixed company. 'Fine ladies' were to be seen there on occasion; fashionable women who wished to be seen might sit there; a regular patron such as Lady Penelope Morley could choose to descend from the boxes for a small number of entirely different plays; Elizabeth Pepys, her friends, maids, and companions might watch from the pit with the daughter of one of her husband's colleagues, or secure a place there for her husband if she happened to arrive early. Misson's 'Damsels that hunt for Prey' there may have been; but neither did their hunt disturb the modest nor their masks necessarily disclose their real intentions. In the pit the titled mixed with the wives of the professional, the fashionable exhibitionist demanded the attention of the middle-class lady's maid, and the modest felt safe enough to do without a

[66] Stacy, pp. 49–50.
[67] Dryden, 'Prologue for the Women, when they Acted at the Old Theatre in Lincoln's-Inn-Fields', *Poems and Fables*, p. 312.

male escort. It was, to use Sorbière's term, a 'pesle-mesle' not only of ladies and gentlemen, but of ladies of different social classes who also had very different ideas about how best to enjoy the theatre.

In striking confirmation of this view appears a woman whom the prologue writers would have put down as a 'city-wife' and therefore one who came to the theatre only to imitate the bad habits of her betters.[68] Deborah Willet's Aunt Hunt is one of the few known women who qualifies immediately for the dubious distinction of that title (another is Pepys's cousin, Kate Joyce, who married a tallow-chandler), yet she also appears to have been qualified for some of the more flattering ones on offer:

> my wife and I to the Duke of York's playhouse and there saw, the first time acted, *The Queene of Arragon*, an old Blackfriars play but an admirable one, so good that I am astonished at it and wonder where it hathe lain asleep all this while, that I have never heard of it before. Here met W. Batelier and Mrs Hunt, Deb's aunt, and saw her home; a very witty woman and one that knew this play, and understands a play mighty well. Left her at home in Jewen Street.[69]

Jewen Street was in the heart of the city, just off Aldersgate. The play, by William Habington, had been chosen for the Duke of York's birthday five days before the special satisfaction of 'the ladies'.[70] In that respect *The Queen of Arragon* was a 'ladies play', although known and appreciated by one apparently ill-fitted to the task. Here, then, is a 'city-wife' meeting and chatting with a professional man and showing close knowledge of an obscure play and of plays in general. It is certainly an episode which defies the usual classifications, but it would be unwise to regard it as typical; Pepys was, after all, little less surprised by the woman's knowledge and discrimination than by the quality of the play which they had just seen. Her example is at once encouraging and dispiriting for anyone trying to rescue the Restoration Audience in general, and its female constituents in particular, from the myths which represent them so poorly. One's

---

[68] Manning, Epilogue, *The Generous Choice*; Dilke, Prologue, *The Lover's Luck* (1696); *The Rambling Rakes* (London, 1679), 49; ?Aphra Behn, Epilogue, *The Debauchee* (1677); Behn, *The Second Part of the Rover* (1680), ii, i.; Cibber, Prologue, *Love's Last Shift* (1696); and Motteux, Prologue to Pix, *The Innocent Mistress* (1687). It was also customary to joke about the sobriety of the female city audience: see Crowne, Prologue, *Charles VIII* (1671); Mary Manley, Prologue, *The Lost Lover* (1696); Thomas Porter, Prologue, *The French Conjurer* (1677); and Congreve, Prologue to Powell's *A Very Good Wife* (1693).

[69] *Diary*, 19 Oct. 1668. The play was published in 1640; for a discussion of its blend of platonic intensities' with political significance, Martin Butler, *Theatre and Crisis* (Cambridge, 1985).

[70] HMC 12th Report, Appendix VII, Fleming MSS, p. 59.

instinctive response is to claim her as evidence of a highly literate and discerning presence which has nothing to do with the familiar categories of ladies and city-wives, or, indeed, with the representatives of the genteel and professional classes whose presence has been noted; proper inspection of the evidence, however, argues that we must appreciate what Pepys himself was so struck with: surprise that he should have come across so able a woman in such unlikely circumstances. Mrs Hunt should be welcomed into any picture of the Restoration Audience, but it would be sentimental to assume, at least on the evidence of Pepys, that she could be thought typical of any part of it.

Of her social peers the evidence is by turns limited and untrustworthy. The Pepyses' near-neighbour, Mary Batelier, was a linen-draper at the Royal Exchange; she and her brother William, a wine merchant, were regular companions of the Pepyses, although they went to the theatre with them on only a few occasions (perhaps enough to reinforce, nevertheless, the sense of free social intercourse given by the meeting with Mrs Hunt). Mary and her 'sweetheart' once treated Elizabeth to a subversive trip to the Nursery Theatre; the Pepyses once took her to the puppet-play, *Polchinelli*.[71] Only three trips were made to the main theatres, a surprisingly small number given the intimacy of their acquaintance; explanation would be a matter of mere speculation, since we are told nothing of the occasions but the simple fact of attendance.[72] Beyond that, we have only a smattering of names with which to represent this middling female audience: another neighbour, Mrs Andrews the merchant's wife; and two Lord Mayor's daughters—Pepys's cousin Jane Turner, and Mary Browne, who was to become John Evelyn's wife.[73] So much for the limitations; now for the untrustworthiness.

The two chief myths of the city-wife, of sobriety on the one hand and lubricity on the other, have already been mentioned; another may be more reliable for staying clear of obvious aspersions. In 1714 John Macky referred to the upper row of boxes as the territory of 'the Citizens' Wives and Daughters', and in Stacy it is the middle gallery 'where the Citizens' Wives and Daughters, together with the *Abigails*, Servingmen, Journeymen and Apprentices, commonly take their Places'.[74] Motteux's epilogue

---

[71] *Diary*, 23 Apr. 1669; 29 Aug. 1666.

[72] *Diary*, 6 Sept. 1667; 31 Aug. 1668 10 Sept. 1668. The plays were *Hamlet*, *Heraclius* and Fletcher and Rowley's *The Maid in the Mill*.

[73] *Diary*, 30 Dec. 1668, 21 Apr. 1668, 7 May 1668; for Mary Evelyn's appreciation of *The Conquest of Granada* see *The Diary and Correspondence of John Evelyn*, iv. 177.

[74] *The Country Gentleman's Vade Mecum*, pp. 38-9.

to Mary Pix's *The Innocent Mistress* also refers to the tendency of the citizens' wives to attend with their daughters, but this time they are said to have gone into the pit, a habit which was also observed by Aphra Behn in her prologue to *The False Count* (1682). None of these accounts is implausible from the point of view of location; the safety of the pit has already been established, and we know that Elizabeth Pepys went with Jane Edwards to the middle gallery. Even Pinchwife thought it a safe place, and Misson noticed only 'ordinary people' there.[75] There should be no objection, therefore, to the suggestion that many ordinary, respectable women sat in the middle gallery, whatever the horrors depicted by certain playwrights.[76] The real difficulty of such evidence is that it is almost impossible to know whom the poets meant when they referred to 'city-wives'; the term is broad enough to admit a thoroughly confusing variety of women. In which of the usual categories, for example, are we to place Elizabeth Pepys if not in that of 'city-wife'? Does she belong there with Hester Andrews, Mary Batelier, Mrs Hunt, and Aphra Behn's Lady Fulbank, the wife of a cautious banker?[77] The answer is that she does, and that the category is almost meaningless: it describes simply a large yet unobtrusive contingent of women, many of them the wives of men who themselves could not be defined by the usual terms of classification. It is a striking fact that in describing the theatre-going habits of 'citizens' and their wives (so despised by Pepys when they crowded into the pit[78]) the prologues and epilogues often described perfectly accurately the habits of Pepys and his circle: there is the same emphasis on family visits; the same desire to secure a good seat for viewing rather than for being viewed; the same unalarmed readiness to sit in the middle gallery. Even the grotesque caricature of the 'cit' proudly taking his place in a box more accurately reflects Pepys's mentality than any of the others on offer; this in spite of the fact that he recognized better than anyone an upwardly mobile citizen when he saw one, at any rate in the playhouse.[79] Allan Botica has argued

[75] *M. Misson's Memoirs*, p. 220.

[76] Rochester, 'Prologue ... to be spoken by Mrs Barry', *Valentinian* (1681); Crowne, Prologue, *The Destruction of Jerusalem, Part II* (1677); Behn, Prologue, *The Forc'd Marriage* (1670): Thomas Jevon, Epistle, *The Devil of a Wife* (1685); Congreve, Epilogue, *The Double Dealer* (1693).

[77] In *The Luckey Chance*.

[78] *Diary*, 1 Jan. 1668; 27 Dec. 1662.

[79] As well as the repeated tales of wives and daughters, see Shadwell, Epilogue, *The Lancashire Witches*: 'The Citt, who with his Wife and hopeful Son, would come to a Merry Play'; this accords exactly with the visit of the Andrews family on 30 Dec. 1668. Motteux, Epilogue to Able Boyer, *Achilles* (1700): 'Your City-Fry ... Who came by Three to sit on

convincingly that seventeenth century models of social description failed to accommodate (like many others since) the 'middling sort of people' of London, those, like the Pepyses, of gentle tastes and aspirations who were determined to enjoy the delights of the capital.[80] This failure is evident in the representation of middle-class men as upstarts, and of middle-class women either as sober matrons or as adultresses in search of a little genteel fornication. Such terms had little to do with those women who went to the theatre whom we know to have been 'city-wives' in the residential sense, not to mention those, like Elizabeth Pepys, Elizabeth Pearse, Jane Turner, and Mary Evelyn, to whom they applied by default. This is one area where the obscuring jocularity of the prologues and epilogues must stand condemned by the few individual 'city-wives' or 'ordinary women' who have been mentioned, and the individuals, whatever their manifest unusualness (as in Mrs Hunt's case) be taken as broadly representative. If the prologues say that 'citizens' wives' and their daughters took up a lot of room in the pit and middle gallery, we must assume that it was really people like Mrs Pepys and Mrs Pearse, as well as Miss Batelier and Mrs Andrews, who did so; not merely the people who, Pepys tells us, packed the place only at Christmas.

Those particular problems of definition apply only to the middle range of female spectators; the upper and lower categories, 'ladies' and 'vizards', however they may have been confused for other reasons, maintained a high profile. In fact, there is more information about the way prostitutes behaved in the playhouse than about the nebulous breed of city-wives. We know how they went about approaching their potential customers; we know how they got into the theatre without paying; we even know many of their names (or at least their flamboyant pseudonyms[81]) and can hazard a fair guess at their total number.[82] The interests of the theatrical and the oldest profession often seemed, to the delight of the mildest ironist, oddly

the First Row'; cf. *Diary*, 8 Jan. 1663; 6 Feb. 1668; 16 Dec. 1661. See also *Diary*, 20 Sept. 1667; 19 Oct. 1667; 16 Apr. 1669.

[80] Botica, pp. 43–8.

[81] *The Wand'ring Whore* (London, 1661), pp. 11–15, contains lists of bawds, hectors, pickpockets, and whores. Among the latter are the colourful names of Ursula Bunny, The Queen of Morocco, Toothless Betty, Pockey Pug-Nasty, Butter and Eggs, and 'Sugar C——'. Wives of bricklayers and paviors also appear; one Mrs Brooks, of Dog-and-Bitch Yard, was opposite Deb Willet's Aunt Hunt on Jewen Street. On non-working days, these too might be 'city-wives'.

[82] Roger Thompson, *Unfit for Modest Ears: A Study of Pornography in the Seventeenth Century* (London and Basingstoke 1979), 232–42, reports that the SPCK black list in 1695 ran to over seven hundred names.

intertwined; nothing was so likely to concentrate custom as a rich and lasting theatrical success, and in times of theatrical hardship, such as the worst months of the Polish Plot Crisis, the prostitutes were pitied for suffering economic deprivation along with the players.[83] One woman was enterprising enough to open house next door to a theatre.[84]

The dramatists made great play of the presence of prostitutes in the theatre, but there is much to suggest that they were not nearly as widespread as may be supposed.[85] Stacy, for example, admitted the presence of whores who bantered with young men, but he also suggests that much of the preliminary activity normally associated with the prostitutes themselves was conducted by a *Procurer* whose 'chief place of *Rendezvous*' was the Playhouse, 'the change she never fails to be upon'.[86] It was her task there to 'put off her Dammag'd Commodities', which were to be found (and Stacy is perfectly precise about this) not in the theatre itself, but at her house '*in Bow-Street in Covent-Garden*', whither the knowing and unsuspecting alike were bidden to retire after the play for supper. It was, from the prostitutes' point of view, mere economic sense that it should have been so; although it was possible to avoid paying to get into the theatre, the managements were under pressure to enforce payment, and it seems probable that on most of the occasions when prostitutes entered the pit they could expect to have a proportion of their likely earnings removed by the door-keeper.[87] That can hardly have been an encouragement.

There are further indications that numbers in the playhouse itself were limited. Both are straightforward except for the obvious difficulty of distinguishing, in the evidence presented, a masked prostitute from any other masked woman.[88] The first is the fact that 'gallants' were said to go

[83] Crowne, Prologue, *Henry VI* (1681).

[84] *The Wand'ring Whore*, p. 15, lists 'Mrs Mails by the *Curtain Play-house*', i.e. the Nursery Theatre in Holywell Place, just off the Curtain.

[85] For a list of references to whores and maskers in prologues and epilogues, Montague Summers, *The Restoration Theatre* (London, 1934), 85–91.

[86] *The Country Gentleman's Vade Mecum*, pp. 43–4. The initial encounter is said to have involved a quoting of scripture and a prattling in bawdy, to see what might 'well agree with [the] Palate'.

[87] Edward Ward, *The London Spy* (London, 1700) quoted in Hotson, pp. 289–90, on ladies in the park who 'began to flow as fast into the walks, as whores into the Eighteen-Penny Gallery, at the third act'. PRO, L.C. 7/1 contains a variety of orders to enforce payment at the playhouses; see eg. the entry dated 7 Dec. 1663.

[88] The word 'vizard' is most often used (according to *OED*, first used to describe a woman rather than a mask or face as late as 1652), and is as effective a mask as any it signified; the older word, 'punk' (1596 in *OED*), could be used for greater precision, as in

to the upper gallery between the acts in order to banter and do business with prostitutes;[89] if that was so there cannot have been any (at least on those occasions) in the pit, which is where the same gallants spent most of their time. The second has already been quoted: the delight of Betterton's Mrs Brittle in the sight of 'a Flock of Wild Gallants fluttering about two or three Ladies in Vizard-Masks', a pattern which is repeated in the encounter of Isabella and the four gentlemen from Shadwell's *A True Widow*, and again, with the addition of a little ingenuity, in a Joseph Haynes prologue:

> the *Gallery Nymphs* . . . who t'each Play,
> Like *Weavers* with unlawfull *Engines*, come
> And manage *twenty Shuttles* with one *Loom*.[90]

Obviously the estimated ratio cannot be admitted as evidence; proverbial smartness and metrical smoothness produced it. We can, however, admit the pattern of behaviour it describes and adduce it as proof, along with the financial considerations and the willingness of the Pepyses to sit in the middle gallery, that even at the rowdiest performance the number of 'punks' (or 'maskers' with the same intentions) might be minimal. Moreover, those who were there might simply be in transit between other places where custom was to be found. An imaginary 'town miss' declared that she sauntered around Covent Garden waiting for a 'kind coxcomb' to appear, but 'if I miss my expectation there, I whip up to the last two acts of the play, and seldom fail to sup at the *Dog* or the *Horse-shooe*'.[91] Such mobility made obvious professional sense and meant that 'punks' were in all likelihood a fleeting as well as a numerically insignificant presence in the theatres, whatever the jocular attempts of some playwrights to bind them into a 'faction'.[92]

Thomas Duffett, *New Poems, Songs, Prologues and Epilogues* (London, 1676), 80, and Lee, Prologue, *Gloriana*.

[89] Shadwell, Prologue, *The Woman Captain*, on gallants ascending 'for dangerous intrigues to th'Gallery'; Dryden, 'Prologue and Epilogue to King and Queen'.

[90] Joseph Haynes, 'Prologue to the Northern Lass', in Autrey Nell Wiley, *Rare Prologues and Epilogues* (London, 1940), 204. See also Dryden, 'Prologue and Epilogue to the King and Queen', and Crowne, Epilogue, *Sir Courtly Nice*: 'Our Galleries were finely used of late, / Where roosting Masques sat Cackling for a Mate; / They came not to see the Plays, but Act their own, / And had throng'd audiences when we had none.'

[91] *The Town-Misses Catechism* (London, 1703), 3-5.

[92] There is some evidence that the number of prostitutes in the theatre increased towards the end of the century. James Wright, (London, 1699), 3, reports that 'Quarrels and abuses' caused by whores kept some 'civil people' away from the theatre. It was only five

Set against the usual formulae of ladies in boxes, maskers in the pit, and city-wives and whores in the gallery, the full picture of Restoration women in the playhouse appears rich indeed. It includes Duchesses, royal mistresses, the wives of the aristocracy, and members of their households; the wives, daughters, sisters, and nieces of Members of Parliament, playwrights,[93] professional men, craftsmen, merchants, and shopkeepers; a large contingent of lady's companions and maidservants; as well as that conspicuous minority of women of all classes who, whether to trick a lord, tout for custom, or simply appear fashionable, disguised themselves at the theatre. To the list must be added, for the sake of completeness, actresses and orange-sellers.[94] Their style of attendance seems little less broad: the boxes were there for display, for luxury, or private company; the galleries for economy and, occasionally, for business; and the pit for society and the spectacle of the stage and its most eminent patrons. There is, furthermore, no indication that the unexceptional, inconspicuous majority needed to attend with a male escort any more than they had to worry about the damaging effects of a new play upon their reputations.[95] It was for those who felt entitled to be conspicuous to retreat from view, behind a mask or away from the playhouse altogether, when embarrassment and self-betrayal threatened.

years after this that women were forbidden to wear masks in the playhouse. For details of the prohibition, J. L. Styan, *Restoration Comedy in Performance* (Cambridge, 1986), 113, and Summers, pp. 90–1. For 'factions', Congreve, Epilogue, *The Double Dealer*; Crowne, Epilogue, *Darius*; Trotter, Prologue, *Fatal Friendship*. See also *The Town-Misses Declaration and Apology* (London, 1675), 7, which jokes that poets stole repartee from whores.

[93] HMC Rutland, II. 22: Lady Mary Bertie's companions at the theatre are said to include Lady Rochester and 'Lady Betty Howard', who was Dryden's wife.

[94] For Nell Gwyn's play-going, see William van Lennep, 'Nell Gwyn's Playgoing at the King's Expense', *Harvard Library Bulletin*, 4 (1950), pp. 405–8; and Pepys, *Diary*, 7 Jan. 1669. For 'Orange Moll' and her successors, Thomas Phillips and his wife, see Hotson, pp. 291–3; there were up to six vendors in the theatre.

[95] Occasional violent disturbances could, of course, prevent many people from attending, as during the years of the Popish Plot scandal. See 'The Dowager Countess of Sunderland to Henry Sidney, 6 Jan. 1679/80', in *The London Stage*, i. 284.

4

WOMEN AT COURT
AND PATRONAGE OF
THE STAGE

I

WHEN the Duchess of Newcastle visited London in the spring of 1667, Pepys and 'almost all' went to catch a glimpse of her in the strange black and silver coach. '100 boys and girls' ran after her, and everyone wondered at her dress and entourage, making her 'whole story . . . a romance, and all she doth . . . romantic'.[1] Not the least extraordinary of her actions was to go to the Duke's Theatre to see her husband's play, *The Humorous Lovers* ('the most ridiculous thing that ever was wrote', according to Pepys), and afterwards to make 'her respect to the players from her box . . . and give them thanks'.[2] One would not have thought such behaviour, in an age of fulsome dedicatory epistles and apparently regular royal patronage, so very odd; yet it was a gesture which characterized the Duchess no less individually than her passion for philosophy and fancy-dress. It was she and her husband alone, Shadwell was to claim four years later, who gave real support to aspiring literary talent; and the base from which support was offered was not the Court, not London, but the country seat at Welbeck.[3] Pepys was right to be struck by her applause for the players; they were not likely to receive such encouragement from anyone in permanent residence.

It has long been a commonplace of theatre history that the Restoration Stage lost the support of the Court and had to turn to other, perhaps less discriminating patrons.[4] The sparest survey can hardly avoid mentioning

[1] *Diary*, 1 May 1667, 10 May 1667, 11 Apr. 1667, 26 Apr. 1667. See also Evelyn, *Diary*, 18 Apr. 1667, 27 Apr. 1667. For comment on this visit, Richard W. Goulding, *Margaret Lucas, Duchess of Newcastle* (Lincoln, 1925), 17–21. For the Newcastles' withdrawal from the Court, Douglas Grant, *Margaret the First* (London, 1957), 171–91.

[2] *Diary*, 11 Apr. 1667.

[3] 'Thomas Shadwell to Her Grace the Duchess of Newcastle', *A Congratulatory Folio presented to the Duchess of Newcastle* (London, 1671), 129.

[4] For early evidence of this, *A Letter to A. H. Esq.: Concerning the Stage* (London, 1698), 2–3; John Dennis, 'The Causes of the Decay and Defects of Dramatick Poetry', *Critical Works*, ii. 277.

the fact; until 1682 the two patent companies were named after the King and the Duke of York, and after 1695 they often bore the names of their managers.[5] There are many other such signs. Between 1660 and 1676 only one published play was dedicated to someone who was neither at Court nor immediately associated with it;[6] thereafter publishers, soldiers, theatre-managers, and whores might be honoured with a play.[7] Similarly, in the 1670s, the number of performances at Court given by the patent companies declined drastically, and preference was given, infuriatingly, to French and Italian comedians.[8] There had always been tension between the Court and the professional theatres, whether through the pretensions of the actors or the political daring of some playwrights, and it was a tension which was inimical to true patronage.[9] The most that any playwright could expect who did not enjoy the society of Welbeck was, according to Charles Hopkins, a trifling bauble or sum of money:

> Let other Poets other Patrons chuse,
> Get their best Price, and prostitute their Muse;
> With flattering hopes, and fruitless labour wait,
> And court the slippery Friendship of the Great;
> Some trifling present by my lord is made,
> And then the patron thinks the poet paid.[10]

Hopkins's patron in this case was William Congreve, a man better qualified to advance a reputation than any lord. Frustration with the

---

[5] For instance, 'The Petition of the Players' in Allardyce Nicoll, *A History of Restoration Drama*, 3rd edn. (Cambridge, 1940), 331–41.

[6] The play was Thomas Duffett's *The Spanish Rogue* (1673); its dedicatee Nell Gwyn, to whom Aphra Behn dedicated *The Feign'd Curtezans* in 1679.

[7] See Otway, 'Dedication' (to Bentley, the printer), *The Souldier's Fortune* (1681); John Bancroft, 'Epistle Dedicatory to Captain Richard Savage', *The Tragedy of Sertorius* (1679); Elkanah Settle, 'To Mr Christopher Rich', *Distress'd Innocence* (1690). Botica, pp. 180–4, has a broad but often inaccurate survey of the new breed of dedicatees.

[8] For theatrical events at Court, Eleanor Boswell, *The Restoration Court Stage* (Cambridge, Mass., 1932), 279–93. For foreign companies, see M. Horn-Monval, 'French Troupes in England during the Restoration', *Theatre Notebook*, 7 (1953) pp 81–2; I. K. Fletcher, 'Italian Comedians in England in the Seventeenth Century', *Theatre Notebook*, 8 (1954), pp. 86–91; Sybil Rosenfeld, *Foreign Theatrical Companies in Great Britain in the 17th and 18th Centuries*, Society for Theatre Research Pamphlet Series, No. 4 (London, 1955). *The London Stage*, i. 234, has a report of the players' dislike of the trend: 'it will half break both our houses'.

[9] Pepys, *Diary*, 23 Feb. 1661: 'I see the gallants do begin to be tired with the vanity and pride of the theatre-açtors, who are indeed grown very proud and rich.' For their 'insolence' see 20 Apr. 1667, which also records the censorship of Edward Howard's *The Change of Crowns* for its abuse of the Court (see also 15 and 16 Apr. 1667).

[10] Charles Hopkins, 'To Mr William Congreve', *Boadicea* (1697).

indifference of potential noble patrons prevailed among most dramatists and theatre-people; even where personal protection was not sought, as Shadwell sought it at Welbeck, it was expected that the Court should attend the public playhouses regularly to swell the audience with hangers-on and onlookers. When they did not the financial consequences could be serious.[11] How well the ladies at Court emerged from this situation we shall now consider.

If the best female patron of all was too seldom in London to offer much more than fleeting encouragement to the stage, those who were better placed appear, on the evidence adduced so far, to have taken little more than personal advantage of its proximity. To read Pepys is to know that the lady of the Restoration Court was an object of fascination to the ordinary spectator of the Restoration Stage, and one well disposed to take advantage of the fact, capable of exercising control over the attention of the audience if not over the stage itself. Self-advertisement was only one of the vices of noble patronesses. Political scheming which did not take the form of calculated exhibitionism could be still more of a challenge to the players. In January 1669 Lady Castlemaine bribed Elizabeth Corey, an actress in the King's Company, to play the part of Sempronia in Jonson's *Catiline* in imitation of an enemy at Court, Lady Elizabeth Harvey; it is said that when the line was uttered, 'But what'll you doe with Sempronia?', Lady Castlemaine, wishing on her enemy the fate of her ambassador husband, Sir Daniel, cried out, 'Send her to Constantinople!' The actress was duly imprisoned, then released at Lady Castlemaine's bidding; when the play was given again she repeated the performance only to have oranges flung at her by men hired by Lady Harvey.[12] Another actress, Nell Gwyn, found herself under Lady Castlemaine's protection for a brief time, for undisclosed but probably subversive reasons.[13] Less frankly manipulative was Lady Castlemaine's patronage of certain handsome men of the stage; her

[11] For ample discussion and tabulation, Botica, pp. 174-8.

[12] For Lady Harvey's ambitions and her enmity with Lady Castlemaine see Elizabeth Hamilton, *The Illustrious Lady* (London, 1980), pp. 124-30. In *Catiline*, Sempronia is an ageing courtesan with ambitions to be a stateswoman; the line may be found in *Ben Jonson*, ed. C. H. Herford and Percy and Evelyn Simpson, 11 vols. (Oxford, 1925-52), v. 524, and Lady Castlemaine's response to it in John Harold Wilson, *Nell Gwyn, Royal Mistress* (London, 1952), 76, quoting BL Add.MS. 36916, f. 128. Pepys wrote about the incident on 15 and 16 Jan. 1669. Bodleian Library, North MSS. C. 10, ff. 42-3, shows how Corey added more mannerisms to her role in later showings.

[13] Pepys, *Diary*, 26 Aug. 1667; see also Wilson, *Nell Gwyn*, p. 65. Elizabeth Barry, too, was 'protected'; according to an unidentified letter of Feb. 1699 (quoted in *The London Stage*, i. 507), by Lady Lisburne.

famous affairs with Wycherley, Hart, Goodman, and the muscular rope-dancer, Jacob Hall, made her obvious game for satirists.[14]. The catalogue of sins against disinterested patronage is impressive; application to the epistles dedicating plays to noble women may simply expand it. The number of women honoured with a dedication was pitifully small: fourteen, to be precise.[15] It may be that this bears further witness to the superior power of individual male courtiers to influence public opinion, and therefore to the preference among dramatists for courting their favour rather than that of individual ladies;[16] and it may be, too, that the fact that dedications to women did not follow the changing pattern of dedications in general, but were almost always addressed at least to Duchesses, shows that only a few very distinguished ladies were thought capable of effective action in favour of a play.[17] Something of this is evident in John Bankes's distinction (unique among the prologues and epilogues of the age) between the finest ladies in the theatre:

> To all the shining Sex this Play's addrest,
> But more the *Court*, the *Planets* of the rest;[18]

and, indeed, in Etherege's dedication of *The Man of Mode* to the Duchess of York:

[14] For her first encounters with Wycherley, Dennis, *Critical Works*, ii. 409–10. For Charles Hart, see Pepys, *Diary*, 7 Apr. 1668, and Cibber, *Apology*, ii. 71–5. For Cardell Goodman, see John Oldmixon, *A History of England during the Reign of the Royal House of Stewart*, 3 vols. (London, 1709, ii. 576, and Thomas Davies, *Dramatic Miscellanies*, 3 vols. (London, 1759), iii. 264. For Jacob Hall, Boswell, p. 348; Hamilton. *Memoirs*, p. 112. Tom Brown, *Letters from the Dead to the Living* (London, 1704), 62, speaks of a 'precise Countess that wou'd be scandaliz'd at a *double entendre*' being found 'betwixt a pair of sheets with a well-made footman'; this may allude to the same tale of a brawny lackey used by Marvell in his satire of Lady Castlemaine in *The Last Instructions to a Painter*, in *Complete Poems*, ed. Elizabeth Story Donno (Harmondsworth, 1972), 157–83, which may place her with those averse to bawdy comedy. Further gossip about her affairs with actors may be found in *A Dialogue between the Duchess of C[leveland] and the D[uchess] of P[ortsmouth] at their Meeting in Paris with the Ghost of Jane Shore* (London, 1682); *A Session of Ladyes* (London, 1688); and *The Duchess of C[leveland]'s Memorial* (London, 1708).

[15] These were the Princesses Mary and Anne; the second Duchess of York (Mary d'Este); the Duchesses of Cleveland, Portsmouth, Albemarle, Richmond, Newcastle, Ormond, and Monmouth; Lady Herbert and Lady Elizabeth Delaval; and Nell Gwyn and Mother Bennet. None received more than two plays.

[16] See above, pp. 30–1.

[17] Only two plays were dedicated to women in the 1690s: Congreve's *The Mourning Bride* (1697), to Princess Anne, and the first part of Durfey's *Don Quixote* (1694), to the Duchess of Ormond. This scarcely argues strongly for a powerful 'ladies' faction' during those years.

[18] John Bankes, Prologue, *The Unhappy Favourite* (1681).

all are so ambitious of making their Court to you, that none can be severe to what you are pleas'd to favour.

These considerations apart, the picture drawn by the dedicatory epistles to women is, whatever the obsequiousness expended in making it, scarcely a rosy one. Only a few instances of practical assistance emerge from the thick mess of unction. Lee thanked the Duchess of Richmond for bringing the Queen to the third day of *Theodosius*; Otway the Duchess of Portsmouth for restoring him to political favour during the Popish Plot years; and John Bankes Lady Herbert for her civilizing conversation.[19] These exceptions granted, most of the epistles follow the pattern used so often in the prologues and epilogues, depicting their subjects as inspiring models of beauty and virtue, the bright originals from which the playwright drew his characters. Such language must have amused many beside the Pepyses, who laughed to find Dauncey's biography of Henrietta Maria dedicated to 'that paragon of virtue and beauty, the Duchesse of Albemarle', whom they knew to be otherwise.[20] It is in two parodies of the dedicator's excesses, however, that we find out most about the treacheries of the form and the real activity which lay behind it. In both instances the author is Wycherley.

When Wycherley dedicated his first play, *Love in a Wood* (1671), to the Duchess of Cleveland (formerly Lady Castlemaine), he was a newcomer to the art of the strained compliment who immediately grasped its comic potential. He refers to their affair simply by deploying all the clichés of the medium:

though I cannot lie like [other poets] I am as vain as they and cannot but publicly give your Grace my humble Acknowledgements for the Favours I have received from you.

'Favour' and 'protection' are used with extreme Platonic emphasis in all the dedications cited above, and in few of them is anything said about what favour or what protection was actually bestowed. Wycherley enjoys his joke against his lying predecessors not only by granting a generous

---

[19] Nathaniel Lee, 'Epistle Dedicatory to Her Grace the Duchess of Richmond', *Theodosius* (1680): 'you brought Her Royal Highness just at the exigent Time, whose single Presence, on the Poet's Day, is a subsistence for him all the Year after.' John Downes, *Rocius Anglicanus* (London, 1708), 38, records that the Court ladies attended the play daily. Thomas Otway, 'Epistle Dedicatory to Her Grace the Duchess of Portsmouth', *Venice Preserv'd* (1682); Thomas Wilkes, *A General View of the Stage* (Dublin, 1759), 87, states that Otway received more material help from the Duchess: a present of twenty guineas. John Bankes, 'Epistle Dedicatory to my Lady Herbert', *The Rival Kings* (London, 1677).

[20] *Diary*, 26 Oct. 1660.

double meaning to 'favour' but by then, quite contrary to convention and his own rude insinuation, telling us specifically about the ways in which the Duchess really assisted him: she saw the play 'twice together' and sent for a copy of it, if only to flatter him with her interest. The mockery of the dedicator's art contains its own, double-edged comment on the state of patronage: on the one hand, that so much noise should be made for so little return; on the other, that the favours actually returned in this instance should have been as much a travesty of true patronage as the empty compliments so commonly bandied about. Beyond that, there is a clear view of how desperately poets craved the patronage of the few willing to grant it: Wycherley warns his Duchess that 'civility makes poets as troublesome as charity makes beggars', and that she is sure in the future, having accepted this dedication, to be 'pestered with such scurvy offerings as this—poems, panegyrics and the like'. A similarly bleak report is given, no less obliquely, in the epistle 'To my Lady B——' which precedes *The Plain Dealer*, where, once again, Wycherley reflects on the meanness of noble patronesses while having fun with the conventional terms of adulation:

Though I never had the honour to receive a Favour from you, nay, or be known to you, I take the confidence of an author to write to you.

Such confidence was necessary if the gifts which produced the ironic poise of that sentence were to be kept from languishing in the debtors' prison.

Some reasons for the diminution of responsibility among potential female patrons may be found in the character of their environment, the Restoration Court. Swift thought the Court of Charles I the milieu most beneficial to the interest of women and of civilized conversation. In later years the values which it had upheld were ridiculed: the restraints and ideals embodied in 'platonic' societies had no place in the Restoration Court, but belonged only to memory, popular scorn, and eccentric outsiders like the Duchess of Newcastle and the matchless Orinda.[21] In their place a still older mode of conversational practice again became fashionable, one based on aggression and mutual suspicion. The author of *The Art of Complaisance* observed that:

the two great subjects which make up the Conversation of the Court, are Love and War. If the thoughts of the more brave and active Spirits, are taken up with

[21] For the Duchess's Platonic leanings, Theophilus Cibber, *The Lives of the English Poets*, 3 vols. (London, 1773), ii. 164; for Katherine Phillips, Philip Webster Souers, *The Matchless Orinda* (Cambridge, Mass., 1931), pp. 39–78.

Sieges, ingagements, and the acquisition of Glory, those of the vain effeminate and impertinent, are no less busied in the Conduct of an Amarous Intreague. If chance or any other respect cast you into the Company of one of the latter sort, you must be content to hear him relate his conquest of the lady of some decrepit Knight, in terms as Martial, as an old Soldier would the taking of the best fort in Flanders ... he attacks her, is repulsed, then charges again, and again forced to retreat; once more, supposing her a Fort, he gives the assault, storms and enters ...[22]

Heroic tragedies, not as outdatedly 'platonic' as Mary Evelyn supposed, used the same figure of speech repeatedly; the effect, according to the author of *The Art of Complaisance*, was to enforce admiration of boorish gallantry, whether on stage or in private conversation.[23]

How little the Restoration court owed to the values identified by Swift is further evident in the more celebratory (but no less critical) account of Hamilton's *Memoirs*. The Court of Charles II was 'the seat and fountain of sports, pleasures, enjoyments, and all the polite and magnificent entertainments, which are generally inspir'd by the inclinations of a tender, amorous, and indulgent Prince'. It was a world in which 'the beauties studied to charm, the men to please', with the result that all 'improv'd their talents the best they could', and acquir'd distinction in 'dancing, magnificence, wit, and amours', while maintaining a general want of facility in constancy. The bulk of Hamilton's record suggests, however, that these talents were improved casually and supported negligently. The King's relish for the compositions of the guitarist, Corbetta, is said to have given the instrument 'such a vogue, that every body play'd on it, well or ill; and one was as sure to see a *Guitar* on the *Toilets of the Fair*, as either *Red* or *Patches*', which argues that it was really no more than a cosmetic adornment.[24]

The vogue for casual musical and literary accomplishment, so much alive about town, promoted no less casual liaisons at Court such as that between Teresa Stuart, who had 'a liking for Musick, and some Relish for Singing,' and the Duke of Buckingham, who had 'an agreeable Voice' and

[22] S. C., *The Art of Complaisance* (London, 1673), 63.

[23] See Lee, *Sophonisba*, II. i., and Mithridates, v. i.; Dryden, *The Conquest of Granada*, II. i.: *Abdalla*: When cities are besieged, and treat to yield, / If there appear relievers from the field, / The flag of parley may be taken down, / Till the success of those without is known. / *Lyndaraxa*: Though Abdelmelech has not yet possest, / Yet I have sealed the treaty in my breast. See also Walter Charleton, *The Ephesian Matron* (London, 1659), 46, and George Granville, 'Upon my Lady Hyde's having the Small-pox', in *The Gentleman's Journal*, ed. Peter Motteux, Apr. 1694, 93–5.

[24] Hamilton, pp. 176–7.

flattered the beautiful gossip with printed and sung lampoons, and 'invented and told *Stories*, which made her *die with laughing*'. A similar relationship flowered between Frances Jennings and Rochester, who 'began to spoil her by reading to her all his Composures, as if she had been the best *Critick*';[25] which expresses succinctly the meeting of high compliment and low expectation so floridly demonstrated in the epistles dedicatory. Such encounters consolidated the role of poetry in the vernacular of court opinion. When Lord Chesterfield sent his wife 'to the Peaks' because of the Duke of York's infatuation with her, the whole court was amazed that an Englishman 'could be so uncivil as to be *jealous* of his *Wife*', and a shower of lampoons descended from Rochester, Dorset, Sedley, and Etherege, 'and all the *Wits* then in Vogue'.[26] This ease of contact with poets and poetry provided a young woman at court with the means to a literary education of a sort, and produced in the most worthy the elements of real critical distinction; the Chevalier de Grammont's future bride, Miss Hamilton, was sufficiently well-read and discerning to show what all men at court and about town pretended to, 'an admirable faculty of distinguishing betwixt real and false Wit', a faculty which it was usually the prerogative of a Congreve or an Addison to discover.[27]

Ease of contact with actors and the theatre did not always, as we have seen, prove beneficial to the higher interest of the drama; on occasion, however, it might supply the ladies at court with the means to a finer appreciation of the productions of the stage. The play *Calisto*, commissioned from John Crowne in 1674, was designed for performance by seven young ladies at court—the Princesses Mary and Anne included—with an army of attendants, dancers, and professional actors in support.[28] It is said that the cast was coached by the leading acting couple of the day, the Bettertons.[29] Their employment may reflect not simply the need to make

[25] Hamilton, pp. 233, 241.   [26] Hamilton, pp. 192–5.

[27] Hamilton, pp. 115–16. William Congreve, 'To the Right Honourable Ralph, Earl of Montague', *The Way of the World* ed. Brian Gibbons (London, 1971); Joseph Addison, *The Spectator*, Nos. 61 (10 May 1711), and 62 (11 May 1711), *Selections from* The Tatler *and* The Spectator, ed. Angus Ross (Harmondsworth, 1982), 341–9.

[28] For documents relating to the performance, including a list of those taking part, Boswell, pp. 180–213.

[29] See Philip H. Highfill, Kalman A. Burnim, and Edward A. Langhans, *A Biographical Dictionary of Actors, Actresses, etc. in London, 1660–1800*, 10 vols. (Carbondale and Edwardsville, 1973–84), ii. 80. The compilers were indebted for their facts about preparations for *Calisto*, however, to Edmund Curll's frequently unreliable *A History of the English Stage* (London, 1741). Theophilus Cibber, *The Lives of the English Poets* (London, 1773), iii. 158, claims that Queen Anne settled a pension of £100 on Mary Betterton in remembrance of her services; there is no reliable record of this.

the performance as polished as possible but an abiding belief in the educational possibilities of good acting which the reputation of the professional stage and some of its performers had done nothing to compromise; it is interesting to note that someone as remote from the public theatres as the Duchess of Newcastle should have agreed so fully with someone as close to them as Thomas Betterton that acting had the power to impart grace, spirit, and life to its student however it was abused by those who practised it for other reasons.[30] For the young ladies who took part in *Calisto* this meant that the educational prerogatives were at one with the professional's appreciation of stage technique, and a heightened understanding of the values of performance in the theatre in general cannot but have been the result.

A training in the graceful accomplishments of virtue was not, of course, the only education which young women were likely to receive at Court. On New Year's Day 1663 Pepys commented that 'there is almost nothing but bawdry at Court from top to bottom', while Hamilton tells us all we need to know of the resourcefulness required of the beautiful to combat the advances of the designing, and of the malice practised by the mischievous in guying the unfortunate.[31] The prevailing passion for masquerade extended far beyond the confines of the balls given on special occasions;[32] even Queen Catherine, habitually withdrawn and sober, joined the Duchesses of Richmond and Buckingham in a frolic to 'disguise themselves like country-lasses in red petticoats, wast-cotes, &c. and so goe see the faire', which took place at Audley End.[33] Of greater interest for its bearing on the stage is the no less popular passion for gaming; so prevalent was it that Queen Catherine's room 'at play' could provide Hamilton with an apt similitude expressing crowdedness, while the famous account by Evelyn of the frivolous last days of Charles II evinces the popularity of

[30] Margaret Cavendish, Duchess of Newcastle, 'Fourth Epistle to the Readers', *Playes written by the Thrice Noble, Illustrious and Excellent Princess, The Lady Marchioness of Newcastle* (London, 1662). See also, in the same volume, the play, *Youth's Glory, and Death's Banquet*, pp. 126–7. Identical thoughts are to be found in Charles Gildon, *The Life of Mr. Thomas Betterton* (London, 1710), 18–20; much of the work consists of an 'acting manual' allegedly of Betterton's devising.

[31] See e.g. the wooing of Miss Hamilton by the Duke of Richmond in Hamilton, pp. 135–6; and the trick played on Henrietta Blague and Lady Muskerry in *Memoirs*, pp. 98–9.

[32] A list of 'grand ballets' at Court, some of them to celebrate royal birthdays, may be found in Boswell, pp. 237–8.

[33] *Select Papers chiefly relating to English Antiquities: published from the Originals, in the Possession of John Ives* (London, 1773), 40–1.

card-games among 'greate courtiers and other dissolute persons'.[34] Individuals became famous for the 'tables' they kept: the Duchess of Portsmouth and Cleveland, and Hortensia Mazarin for Basset, for example, in defiance of the prevailing preference for Comet.[35] It is no surprise to find playwrights at first complaining about the attractions of the game and then deriding them. Aphra Behn alleged in 1677 that Basset and Ombre had kept ladies away from the third or benefit day of her last production, while Durfey found to his cost in 1688 that the increased popularity of Basset among ordinary people could not be made fun of without incurring the displeasure of its more distinguished champions:

> some certain very nice persons, especially one, took it so to heart, that dear Basset should be expos'd, that my honest intentions were quite frustrated, and that the piece might be sure to be ruin'd, their Majesties were told, it was so obscene, that it was not fit to be acted.[36]

It was evidently not easy to employ satire against 'the town' without involving the ladies at court; in this instance at least the female audience had more of a corporate identity than Durfey had bargained for. By championing the game of Basset the court ladies no doubt recommended it to the sort of women whom Durfey intended to reprove; thus, by distancing themselves from the stage by their adoption of alternative diversions they actually involved themselves in yet more intimate antagonism with it.

The court may have provided women with a kind of literary education, and it may have offered them limitless opportunities for frivolity and idleness, but it did all those, according to Hamilton, against a background of economic anxiety special to it. We have already found that the reputation of marriage as a bond of affection was in decline; at Court, the King himself wrote to his sister as early as 1664 that 'the passion of love is very much out of fashion in this country, and [that] a handsome face without money has but few gallants, upon the score of marriage'.[37] This was a serious business to the many women who came to Court to make a

---

[34] Hamilton, p. 188. Evelyn, *Diary*, 4 Feb. 1685. Charles was 'toying with his Concubines while about 20 of the greate courtiers and other dissolute persons were at Basset round a large table'.

[35] For Mazarin and Cleveland, see Mary Manley, *The Adventures of Rivella* (London, 1714), 95; for the Duchess of Portsmouth, HMC Rutland, II. 84–5.

[36] Durfey, 'To Lord Morpeth,' *The Fool's Preferment* (1688). Also Aphra Behn, Prologue, *Abdelazer* (1677).

[37] Letter from King Charles to the Duchess of Orleans, quoted in Julia Cartwright, *Madame: A Life of Henrietta, Daughter of Charles I and Duchess of Orleans* (London, 1891), 153.

good match; as St Evremond observed to the boisterous Chevalier de Grammont, 'You will have no Success with such as are unmarry'd: Honourable Designs and Settlements of Land, are what's requir'd here.'[38]

Miss Hamilton herself found how far economic ambitions had replaced sentimental ideals in the matter of courtship; she was wooed first by the Duke of Richmond, 'but tho' he was in Love with her Person, yet he was still more so with her Money', and she naturally resented it that a man of quality, 'who pretended to be in *Love*, should drive a bargain like a *Shopkeeper*'.[39] This situation affected the daughters of the genteel and noble acutely. Dowries were liable, as in the case of the Verney sisters, to have suffered from the effects of sequestration under the Commonwealth; while those who could offer large portions as an enticement faced burgeoning competition from better-endowed middle-class girls.[40] The customary restraints on young women marrying beneath their class naturally made things worse. Pepys's record of a disagreement between Lord and Lady Sandwich shows amply the strength of one man's feeling in the matter:

my Lady saying that she could get a good merchant for her daughter Jem, he answered that he would rather see her with a pedlar's pack at her back, so she married a gentleman, than she should marry a citizen.[41]

Jemimah Sandwich was found a place at Court as Lady of the Wardrobe to the Queen, and eventually a suitable husband, but her good fortune was exceptional.[42] T. H. Hollingsworth has shown that during the Restoration period a steeply rising proportion of the daughters of ducal families remained unmarried, while study of the lists of women retained by the Queen and the Duchess of York reveals an increasing longevity of service among dressers and Maids of Honour, who were sent up as girls and expected to marry as girls.[43] The final word on the subject, which is also

---

[38] Hamilton, p. 105.   [39] Hamilton, pp. 135–6.

[40] *Verney Memoirs*, ii. 361, 365, 480. For a variety of complaints about the high portions of 'city-daughters,' and the inability of the gentry to compete, see Antonia Fraser, *The Weaker Vessel: Woman's Lot in Seventeenth Century England* (London, 1984), 269.

[41] *Diary*, 20 Oct. 1660.

[42] *Diary*, 25 June 1665, 3, 5, 27 July 1665 for details of the settlement.

[43] T. H. Hollingsworth, 'A Demographic Study of the British Ducal Families', in *Population in History*, ed. D. V. Glass and D. E. C. Eversley (Chicago, 1965), 9–10. For women retained at Court, Edward Chamberlayne, *Angliae Notitia* (London, 1669–77); The Calendar of Treasury Papers, iv (1672–5), 752; HMC 8th Report, Appendix, pt I, pp. 278–80. Three out of the six maids of honour to the Queen remained in her service from 1661 to 1668, while during the period 1669–73, which saw the death of the first Duchess of York, the Queen's and the Duchess's maids all remained in service at one court or the other.

the final word on the much-lamented decline in 'platonic' values, goes to Miss Hobart in Hamilton's *Memoirs*:

As for Husbands, this is not the Place to find them. For unless Money or Caprice determine the Match, there is almost no Hope of getting married: Virtue and Beauty in this respect are equally useless here.[44]

To no group would this varied context of pressures and opportunities have been more apparent than to the Maids of Honour. They are the starting-point for discussion of the patronage of particular women at Court because, in the range of activities and qualities which they exhibit, they embody most fully the spirit of 'the ladies' as it has hitherto been identified. There were, until Charles's death, ten Maids of Honour: six served the Queen, and four the Duchess of York. They were in the charge of a governess, or 'Mother to the Maids', and had to be unmarried and of gentle birth to qualify.[45] Resignation was permitted only when a suitable marriage was imminent, although there were notable exceptions: Hobart, for example, some-time Mother of the Duchess's Maids, relinquished her post after it was discovered that she was 'something more fond of the *fair sex* than she appear'd to be'.[46] For the most part, however, the Court was jealous of its Maids of Honour, and strongly resisted the entreaties of women who, like Sarah Jennings's mother, sought to usher them away lest they acquire 'great bellies' before (or instead of) husbands.[47] Hobart warned one of her charges, Miss Temple, that the attitude of most men towards the group was scarcely ingenuous:

They look upon Maids of Honour only as Amusements, placed expressly at Court for their Entertainment, and the more Merit anyone has, the more she is expos'd to their Impertinence.[48]

Such a state of affairs was the more alarming when girls chosen for the office took up their duties at a very early age. Both Margaret Blagge and Sarah Jennings were only twelve when they did so.[49] The duties themselves do not appear to have demanded much. The journal kept by Margaret Blagge, which Evelyn found such edifying reading, indicates a

[44] Hamilton, p. 185.
[45] Details of the hierarchy of appointments and pensions may be found in Chamberlayne, *Angliae Notitia* (1669 edn.) pp. 303–20.
[46] Hamilton, p. 234.
[47] HMC Rutland, II. 32.
[48] Hamilton, p. 186.
[49] *DNB*: Jennings; John Evelyn, *The Life of Mrs Godolphin*, ed. Samuel, Lord Bishop of Oxford (London, 1847), 9–10.

perpetually silent round of attendance, reading, and prayer; while Henry Sidney's diary shows that the responsibilities of the Maids were light indeed compared with what was expected of their counterparts in The Hague.[50] Most of their time seems to have been spent in attending at masked balls and in pursuing activities best described as unofficial. Margaret Blagge chose to leave the Court in order to be a real maid of honour rather than only 'to have a name', and spent most of her days reminding herself of those duties upon which her colleagues improvised so freely (Eveyln reports that she would not 'pass away the tedious hours of attendance' by talking 'among the gallants' or making 'impertinent visits').[51] Abundant leisure was available to all but the scrupulous, and two of the maids, Frances Jennings and Goditha Price, were not above employing it by dressing as orange-sellers and venturing into the pit of the playhouse.[52]

Fortunately, that is not the only record we possess of their interest in the theatre. Documents from the Public Records Office show the amounts owed to the theatres for court performances and for seats at the public playhouses. They reveal that the Maids of Honour frequently attended the King and Queen at plays and had a liking for the racier modern comedies: *The London Cuckolds*, *The Souldier's Fortune*, and *The Man of Mode*.[53] Boxes were reserved for them for at least one performance of each of those plays, in each case some time after the reputation of the plays had been established; and that ignores the strong possibility—bearing in mind their leisure and general freedom of movement—of their making visits independently of their mistresses. There is one interesting omission from the list of plays for which a box was secured: Wycherley's *The Country Wife*, which, it is well known, caused an outcry among 'the ladies' for its 'clandestine obscenity' and its contention that most women are much more afraid of having their sins revealed than of committing them in the first place. The perpetrators of the outcry, hitherto unrecognized by historians of the stage, are identified beyond doubt in the play's successor, *The Plain Dealer*. In his dedication of that play Wycherley complains that

[50] Evelyn, *Life*, pp. 21–4. For their friendship, see also W. G. Hiscock, *John Evelyn and Mrs Godolphin* (London, 1951). Henry Sidney, 'Mr. Sidney to Mr. Hide, The Hague, August 5/15,' *Diary of the Life and Times of Charles the Second by the Honourable Henry Sidney*, ed. R. W. Blencowe, 2 vols. (London, 1843), i. 55.

[51] Evelyn, *Life*, pp. 25–6.

[52] Pepys, *Diary*, 21 Feb. 1665; Hamilton, pp. 215–16.

[53] PRO, L.C. 5/142, p. 81; also 5/145, p. 120. For the popularity of *The Man of Mode* as an imitation of the manners of the Court, La Marquise Campana di Cavelli,' *Les Derniers Stuarts*, 2 vols. (Paris and London, 1871), i. 171.

it, too, 'lost its reputation with the ladies of stricter lives in the playhouse'; not itself very remarkable but for the same ladies being referred to twice in the piece as 'the nice coy women of honour', a conventional phrase manipulated with characteristic ease. We then find the following exchange between Olivia and Eliza in the second act of the play itself:

ELIZA. None rail at the Court but those who cannot get into it or who are ridiculous when they get there, and I shall suspect you were laughed at when you were there or would be a Maid of Honour.

OLIVIA. I a Maid of Honour! To be a Maid of Honour were yet of all things my Aversion![54]

So, by expressing her aversion to the office, Olivia, who abominates 'filthy, obscene, hideous plays', who goes into raptures of disgust on the subject of her creator's previous production, yet who gaily deceives friends and lovers alike, demonstrates unequivocally how she covets it. The point of the satire is unmistakable, however judiciously indirect the means.

If the Maids of Honour were principally responsible for 'crying down' *The Country Wife*, who, precisely, were the Maids of Honour at the time? There are considerable difficulties of identification;[55] these granted, it is still possible to draw up an almost complete list. There is one distinguished name—Sarah Jennings, later first Duchess of Marlborough—and perhaps one other; Anne Killigrew, the poetess to whose memory Dryden was to dedicate his famous lines lamenting the depravities of the stage.[56] The others are less notable: Carey Fraizer, daughter to the King's physician, Sir Alexander Fraizer, and soon to achieve notoriety for her involvement with Sir Car Scroop, a friend of Sedley;[57] Elizabeth Godolphin, Margaret Blagge's future sister-in-law; Henrietta Price, Goditha's younger sister; and Dorothy Howard, her sister Anne, Phillipa Temple, Ann Walker, and Frances Sheldon. Little is known about most of

---

[54] *The Plain Dealer*, II, i. (LL. 97–102 in *Plays*, ed. Holland).

[55] There is no single reliable record of appointments. Chamberlayne prints the names of all those retained by the various royal households; sometimes the names do not change from one edition to the next, thereby contradicting other records (none of them complete) such as the Calendar of State Papers and lists of pensions contained in the Calendar of Treasury Papers. Pepys and Hamilton provide some assistance.

[56] Dryden, 'To the Pious Memory of the Accomplisht Young Lady Mrs. Anne Killigrew . . . An Ode', in *The Poems and Fables of John Dryden*, ed. James Kinsley (Oxford, 1970), 344–50. Records of the appointments of Jennings and Killigrew may be found in *DNB*: Jennings and Killigrew, and in CSPD Charles II, 1673–5, pp. 41, 499, 685. There is no record of the precise date at which Killigrew began her appointment; Wycherley's play opened in January 1675 and it is not certain whether she was then in place.

[57] HMC Rutland, II. 37.

these women, and little more needs to be said of them here; it is remarkable, however, that they were able to drive Wycherley to such bitter antagonism given their youth and negligible influence at Court, where they were, according to Miss Hobart, 'Amusements, placed expressly at Court for [the men's] Entertainment'.

Needless to say, just because the Maids of Honour appear to have formed themselves into a faction to object publicly to *The Country Wife*, we must not regard them as the representatives or *agents provocateurs* of all 'ladies' who found comedies unpalatable. It is true that they visited *The London Cuckolds* at least once, and that the play was 'cried down' by 'some squeamish Females of Renown', but there is no more specific evidence to incriminate them. It seems more likely, indeed, that their action over *The Country Wife* was precipitated by events—or rather, one event—peculiar to the 1670s, which embodied just those ideals mocked by Wycherley's play. That event was Crowne's *Calisto*, performed at Court for the first time on 15 February 1675, just over a month after the appearance of *The Country Wife*. The process of rehearsal and performance, lasting several months, has been researched by Eleanor Boswell;[58] what needs to be done is to discuss the play itself in the context of Crowne's commission to produce something fit for young ladies in the London of the 1670s.

The piece was designed to engage the theatrical interests of the Princesses Mary and Anne, and a number of other young ladies at Court, including the Maids of Honour. Crowne tells us that he was 'confined in the number of persons; I had but seven allowed me, neither more nor less: these seven to be all ladies, only two were to appear in men's habits'.[59] In the interests of variety, Crowne also wrote separate scenes of singing and dancing, in which professional performers appeared, including the filthy beast Horner himself, Charles Hart. Margaret Blagge returned to Court to

[58] Boswell, pp. 179–240.

[59] Crowne, 'To the Reader', *Calisto*; all Crowne's remarks about the play are quoted from this source. A cast-list may be found in Boswell, pp. 201–2. The seven ladies were the Princesses Mary and Anne, Henrietta Wentworth, Lady Anne Fitzroy (the King's daughter by Lady Castlemaine), Mary Mordant, Sarah Jennings, and Margaret Blagge. Carey Fraizer played a nymph. Exclusively female plays at Court by were no means unusual. HMC 12th Report, VII. 70 (12 Apr. 1670): 'their Majesties were diverted with a Comedy acted at St. James's by the little young ladies of the Court'. Lord Fountainhall, *Historical Observes of Memorable Occurrents* (Edinburgh, 1840), 13: the Queen's birthday celebrated by 'the acting of a comedy called *Mithridates, King of Pontus* wheirin Lady Anne, the Duke's daughter, and the ladies of honour were the onlie actors'. Also HMC Rutland, II. 22: 'The Queen is preparing a ball to bee danced in the greate Hall by herself and the Dutchesse of Buckingham, Richmond, Monmouth, Mrs. Berkeley, and Madame Kerwell the French maid of honor. There are no men of quality but the Duke of Monmouth . . .'

act in the play, obviously under duress, and disliked both rehearsing and performing, taking care when off stage to have some pious tome about her to prevent improper conversations.[60] Blagge and the Princesses apart, the young ladies who performed the play were not the innocent things which their youth or Crowne's commission might suggest; as Boswell has shown, one or two reputations were already sufficiently established to make the casting of a play about an advance by Jupiter and an attempted rape by Mercury a mischievous business.

However, at a time when there was outspoken concern about the indecency of some plays, it was clearly the duty of the playwright to provide something fit for royal performers in their royal setting. In the event, the solemnity of Crowne's approach must have amused any dramatist taken to task for offence caused to the ladies. His chosen subject, the advances of Jupiter towards the virgin Calisto in the shape of her leader, the goddess Diana, involved, we know, a scene of attempted rape; and he was very conscious of having to produce 'a clean, decent, and inoffensive play ... so I was engaged in this dilemma, either wholly to deviate from my story, and so my story would be no story, or by keeping to it, write what would be unfit for Princesses and Ladies to speak, and a Court to hear'. It was, whatever cynicism might suggest, a real dilemma; on this occasion, at least, the moral propriety of the entertainment was strictly monitored. Those who observed the rehearsals for *Calisto* imposed a rigorous regime upon its author, making the process of revision correspondingly painful. The first version was rejected ('my arrows, though as fine as I could then in haste turn them, yet were too course') and he was set to paring them down 'to make 'em thin enough to pass through nice and delicate ears'. It was a process in which the interests of 'the ladies' were consistently allowed to prevail over what caused most offence in the playhouses, where impotent outrage or non-attendance was the only recourse for the offended; and it may be indicative of the Court's dissatisfaction with the playhouses that *Calisto* should have been performed so often, to the regular exclusion, we have seen, of the professional companies.[61] It is as if a particular kind of drama, intended for the most

[60] Evelyn, *Life*, pp. 21 and 93–4. Rehearsals for the play took place largely at the Duchess of Monmouth's residence. Evelyn admired her acting of the title role at the rehearsal stage in *Diary*, 15 Dec. 1674.

[61] In the 1670s there were 43 recorded theatrical occasions at Court, compared with 68 in the previous decade. The only repeat performances were of *Calisto* and the plays of the Italian and French comedians, and only seven new plays were seen there (only two of which, Ravenscroft's *The Citizen Turn'd Gentleman* and Otway's *Friendship in Fashion*, were comedies; the remainder were tragedies by Dryden, Lee, and Settle).

delicate ears, was being owned in defiance of what the professional theatre had to offer.

That is not to say that what was offered in *Calisto* was merely a bland celebration of the merits of chastity; far from it. It certainly gives us a yardstick with which to measure what was expected of a dramatist who undertook not to offend 'the ladies', but in doing so it reveals a number of surprises. For a start, the piece might not (or should not) have been very palatable to any mildly discerning spectator who was also loyal to his King. The character of Jupiter is what he is in Molière's *Amphitryon*: an *exposé* of the absolute rights over all subjects, and particularly female ones, of a man who enjoys absolute power. When Jupiter proposes to Mercury his plan to take Diana's shape in order to seduce Calisto, he exclaims, with a Carolean indifference to responsibility,

> I care not what disorders there shall be;
> Let heaven and hell slide into Anarchy.
> All politic cares of every kind
> I'll from my breast remove;
> And will today perplex my mind
> With never a thought but Love;

when challenged he merely vows,

> I cannot err, whate'r my actions be;
> There's no such thing as good or ill to me.[62]

The defiance of Almanzor is joined to the irresponsibility of Charles.

More remarkable, considering the pains to which Crowne was put, is the scene in which Jupiter, in Diana's shape, makes his attempt upon Calisto. The following lines, spoken by a woman (Henrietta Wentworth) to a woman, cannot but have had an ambiguous power to remind many of the absent and disagraced Hobart, and to poke fun in the crudest way at the outdated pretensions of 'Platonicks':

> In my lost heart a strange uncommon flame:
> A kindness I both fear and blush to name;
> Nay, one for which no name I ever knew,
> The passion is to me so strange, so new.[63]

The way the couplets skirt round the nameless passion creates precisely that effect of titillation which one would have supposed Crowne anxious to avoid.

---

[62] *Calisto*, II. i.
[63] *Calisto*, II, i.

Even so, the play does remain for the most part loyal and decent, and the voluble support it gives both to the amorous warmth of Jupiter's Court and the chill chastity of the followers of Diana raises no commanding dissent. The contradictions settle without undue disturbance; even the occasional anti-platonic joke has to give way to the praise showered on Calisto herself (and her actor, Princess Mary):

> No ill can her fair soul invade,
> Her whole composure is for virtue made,
> Her body in so pure a mould is wrought,
> Her very body may a soul be thought.[64]

In the end chastity wins the day, and in particular the chastity of the two princesses. Jupiter has the last word and provides an appropriately self-conscious theatrical image:

> These virgins' consecration nought debars,
> I'll in a full assembly crown 'em stars.[65]

The 'full assembly' is the theatre (both stage and auditorium) as it is the galaxy, and the image unites stage and court; performers and audience belong to the same lustrous assembly and embody the same aspirations towards virtue. The stage metaphor so popular earlier in the century has widened to embrace actors and spectators alike, and to celebrate them. In this particular case the audience played its own part, no less than the dramatist, in ensuring that the performance was played out in the right conditions; a document printed in full by Boswell shows the strict rules governing seating and behaviour set down for the production by the Lord Chamberlain, and enacted whenever it was performed.[66] The play was enjoyed in these conditions repeatedly. Crowne records that he kept working to improve it 'to give some refreshment to the audiences, who

---

[64] *Calisto*, III. iii.

[65] *Calisto*, V. ii. The image is made more vivid by the habitual wearing (by actors and spectators) of expensive jewellery at these occasions. Evelyn, *Life*, p. 98, tells of Margaret Blagge's losing a precious stone lent her by the Duchess of Richmond for *Calisto*. See also HMC 12th Report, VII, p. 70, for a comedy acted by court ladies 'glorious and cover'd with jewels'. BL Add.MSS 36916, f.62, reports that the Crown Jewels themselves were produced for Lady Castlemaine to wear in Katherine Phillips's *Horace*.

[66] L.C. 5/141, p. 549. The pit was to be divided into areas for noblemen, Privy Councillors, their wives and ladies 'of good quality', while 'convenient places' were to be kept for Ladies of the Bedchamber, Maids of Honour and Dressers. The document is an interesting one; for the strict divisions it recommends, almost a photographic negative of the situation in the public theatres (it was presumably drawn up with a view to avoiding the freedom which obtained there).

would have been weary of a better play at the second or third representation, and therefore must needs be weary of it the twentieth or thirtieth, for near so often it has been rehearsed and acted'. The sustained interest which the Court took in the play made it of, for, and about the Court.

In so far as it was about the ladies at Court who performed in it and encouraged it, the play offered, purity of diction apart, a defence of true modesty against the slanders of the loose-tongued. Representative of the latter is the wicked Psecas, so confident in her accusation that she can call in question the chastity of Diana herself:

> Have you not heard of her Endymion?
> Nor of her young Hippolytus who fled
> From every Nymph, in private to her bed?[67]

The grotesque absurdity of the allegation naturally has its moral point, and it is a point which is emphatically reiterated by Diana herself as a rebuke to Psecas's persistant slandering of Calisto:

> And know it is my will,
> You never more presume to touch her fame,
> Nor mention, but with high respect, her name.[68]

It is a world in which a woman's reputation may be defended by divine edict; even though the very casting of the play, which made a goddess of a bastard and referred to known liaisons at Court, must have demonstrated the vanity of supposing that it could be so. Nothing so potently expresses the sterile platonic ambitions of the exercise, or its essentially self-congratulatory purpose. It was in vain that Crowne and those who watched over him sought to insulate the play from the ravages of the public theatres on the courtly female sensibility; its very production by and for the Restoration Court sabotaged its claims to celebrate anything but the (in any case) highly conspicuous virtues of the two princesses. If *Calisto* was planned as a riposte to the values represented by a play such as *The Country Wife*, which had to be 'cried down' by Maids of Honour whom it had offended, the venture proposed little by way of a cogent, or even a sincere alternative.

II

If the Maids of Honour represent the extremes of female patronage at Court, something of the less conspicuous territory in between may be

---

[67] *Calisto*, iv. i.
[68] *Calisto*, iii, iii.

found in the spasmodic attentions of two of the King's mistresses to the stage. Enough has been said to establish that Lady Castlemaine did not always act out of disinterested concern when she went to the theatre or consorted with its employees, but there remains some evidence that she sought to combine the interests of court and stage in such a way as to benefit dramatists. Dryden wrote in his epistle to her which prefaces his first play, *The Wild Gallant* (1663), that she encouraged him in writing the piece and presenting it for performance, and that she sponsored its two performances at Court. Pepys found the first of those occasions a dismal failure which pleased neither King 'nor anybody else', although he was still able, as usual, to take succour from the sight of the play's patroness; unaware, apparently, that she had lent the play her support.[69] *The Wild Gallant* was not in any respect a contentious or controversial play; there is nothing to suggest that enlistment of its author would yield political or any other kind of advantage. For once the hyperbolic thanks rendered by playwright to patron appear to have issued from a genuine sense of indebtedness, and Dryden's gratitude was to out-last the stage life of the play by some years.[70]

A command performance of a new play was one way of assisting a dramatist, even if there is no indication that Lady Castlemaine repeated the experiment (not surprisingly, given the King's and everybody else's displeasure with the play). Another was to engage the performers at an earlier stage in giving 'repetitions' or rehearsals to members of the Court, so that opinions could be sounded and rumour activated before the public opening. Aphra Behn's experience with *The Luckey Chance* shows the importance of this facility, and it may be some indication of the failure of responsibility among women at Court that this report should be so rare:

Wee are in expectation of an opera composed by Mr. Dryden, and set by Grabuche, and so well performed at the repetition that has been made before His Majesty at the Duchess of Portsmouth's, pleaseth mightily . . .[71]

In the event, the new opera, *Albion and Albanius*, suffered two setbacks which no patron could prevent: King Charles, who had liked the piece at the repetition, died a month after seeing it, presumably at the time when

---

[69] *Diary*, 23 Feb. 1663.

[70] Dryden wrote his poem, 'To the Lady Castlemain, upon her encouraging his First Play' (*Poems and Fables*, pp. 153–4), in 1674. It is a conventional panegyric which tells us nothing about the assistance rendered, and which would have amused Wycherley: 'You sit above, and see vain men below / Contend for what you only can bestow'.

[71] HMC Rutland, II, 85. See also, for royal encouragement given to the opera, Dryden, 'To the Marquiss of Halifax', *King Arthur* (London, 1691).

the public opening was scheduled; and when it did finally open it flopped on its sixth day, 'not answering half its charge', as Downes puts it, because of the scare over the Duke of Monmouth's landing.[72] As with Lady Castlemaine's protection of *The Wild Gallant*, the intervention of a lady at Court failed conspicuously; as before, the lady concerned did not repeat the experiment. Another such instance shows clearly the lack of consistency in these attempts to assist an author by organizing public rehearsals for his work. The Duchess of Ormond saw that the first part of Durfey's *Don Quixote* (1694) was rehearsed before 'Nobility and Gentry', which Durfey found 'a happy Presage of [the play's] future good Fortune', for on the third day, 'when the Ladies came . . . there never was at this time of the Year, in the Hemisphere of the Playhouse, so dazzling and numerous a Constellation seen before'.[73] The Duchess of Ormond's help allowed the play to overcome 'the Slander and Prejudice which malicious Criticks had resolv'd upon'; so far so good. When Durfey produced the third part of his *Don Quixote* trilogy, however, there were vigorous complaints that it was offensive; perhaps from those very ladies who had sponsored the first play, judging from Durfey's mortified reaction.[74] Two features of the affair seem particularly striking: the simple failure of understanding between poet and patron, born of the recent tradition of irregular contact and false starts; and the fact that Durfey reserved his most florid praise for the appearance *en masse* of ladies at the third day, as if that, rather than any assistance given with the conception of the play, were now the acme of the poet's expectation of his patron—her power to engineer a big turn-out at the right time, as the Duchess of Richmond did for Lee's *Theodosius* or the Duchess of Portsmouth for the same author's

---

[72] Downes, p. 45. The Duchess's action is interesting given her alleged part in the beating of Dryden in Rose Alley in 1679. See Anthony Wood, *Athenae Oxoniensis*, ed. H. Bliss, 4 vols. (Oxford, 1813), iv. 210 and by Narcissus Luttrell, *A Brief Historical Relation of State Affairs* (Oxford, 1857), i. 130. More recent scholars implicate her and exculpate Rochester: J. H. Wilson, 'Rochester, Dryden, and the Rose-Street Affair', *Review of English Studies*, 15 (1939), 294–301; and V. de Sola Pinto, 'Rochester, Dryden, and the Duchess of Portsmouth', *RES* 16 (1940), 177–8.

[73] Thomas Durfey, 'Epistle Dedicatory to Her Grace the Duchess of Ormond', *The Comical History of Don Quixote* (London, 1694).

[74] Durfey, Preface, *The Comical History of Don Quixote. The Third Part* (London, 1695): 'I must confess when I heard the ladies were prejudic'd about some Actions and Sayings in *Mary* the Buxome's and Sancho's Parts, I was extremely concern'd; not that I was conscious myself I had justly offended . . . but that I should have 'em counted nauseous and indecent, and so disoblige that essential part of the Audience which I have always studied with so much Zeal to divert in all my former Plays with innocent Mirth, Scenes of Decency and Good Manners.'

Sophonisba.[75] John Bankes's praise for the benefits of Lady Herbert's conversation seems to belong to another age; the female patron had now become something of a financial asset.

She might also threaten, if she was as politically active as the Duchess of Portsmouth, to be a financial liability. Her occasional patronage of Dryden and Lee apart, the Duchess's interest in literature and the arts seems to have been minimal; some biographers find no trace of it at all.[76] What interest she had appears to have been largely political. Whether she had any part in encouraging Otway to lampoon her arch enemy, Shaftesbury, in his *Venice Preserv'd*, we do not know; what is certain is that the dramatist dedicated the play to her, thanking her for restoring him to favour at Court.[77] In less politic fashion did the Duchess declare her opposition to another enemy, Elkanah Settle; a Catholic, the Duchess resented Settle's success with his anti-Catholic play, *The Female Prelate* (1679), at the height of the Popish Plot crisis, and made it clear that she and the Court would give it no support:

on Wednesday the Duchess of Portsmouth to disoblige Mr Settle the Poet carried all the Court with her to the Dukes House to see Macbeth.

The play remained a financial success in spite of her gesture;[78] an indication of how little influence the Court had left even when it took concerted action.

Political activity of another kind provides us with one of the few instances of truly active and disinterested patronage among the evidence to hand. In April 1692 Queen Mary decided to prohibit performance of Dryden's penultimate play, *Cleomenes*, because of its alleged reflections on the government; to the disappointment, it seems, of all theatre-goers.[79]

[75] Lee, Epistle Dedicatory, *Theodosius*; for *Sophonisba*, 'To Her Grace the Duchess of Portsmouth', *Sophonisba* (1675).

[76] Henri Forneron, *Louise de Keroualle, Duchess of Portsmouth* (London, 1887). The entry in *DNB* concurs.

[77] In the play, the character Antonio, a senator, represents Shaftesbury; he is an idiotic fetishist. For the Duchess's enmity with Shaftesbury, see Forneron, ch. 6, and David Ogg, *England in the Reign of Charles II* (Oxford, 1984), 537–8.

[78] Newdigate Newsletter, 2 June 1680, quoted in *The London Stage*, i. 287. *The True News*, 4–7 Feb. 1680, reports on abuse of the Duchess's name in the Duke's playhouse. For the success of the play, see George W. Whiting: 'Political Satire in London Stage Plays, 1680–83', *Modern Philology*, 28 (1930), 29–43, and 'The Conditions of the London Theatres, 1679–83', *MP* 25 (1927), 195–206; also Otway, Prologue, *The Souldier's Fortune* (1681). *Domestic Intelligence*, 19 Dec. 1679, records a rival version, 'Acted by scholars of a Latin School in Canon Street'.

[79] Luttrell, *A Brief Historical Relation of State Affairs*, ii. 413. The play concerns the attempted overthrow of the degenerate Ptolemy by the Spartan Cleomenes.

Dryden applied for redress to Laurence Hyde, Earl of Rochester, and his family, to whom he read the play, and his cause was taken up in earnest by Rochester's daughter-in-law, Jane. Rochester himself pleaded for the play before the Queen, while Jane Hyde applied to the Lord Chamberlain; when the prohibition was, by their efforts, relaxed, Jane refused to accept Dryden's offered dedication of the play to her because she did not wish her generosity to be made public.[80] For once the hyperbolic praise with which Dryden thanked his patroness through her father-in-law was justified; a goddess indeed who worked with such stealth and to such potent effect.

It was not only on the occasion of the ban on *Cleomenes*, moreover, that Dryden had cause to pay tribute to the acumen and influence of Jane Hyde. Two years before, in dedicating *Amphitryon* to her father, he expressed both relief and disappointment at the discerning Jane's absence from London during the production:

I have reason to apprehend the sharpness of her judgement, if it were not allay'd with the sweetness of her Nature; and, after all, I fear she may come time enough, to discover a thousand Imperfections in my Play, which might have pass'd on vulgar Understandings. Be pleas'd to use the Authority of a Father over her, on my behalf; enjoyn her to keep her thoughts of *Amphitryon* to her self; or at least not compare him too strictly with Molière's.[81]

He fears good-humouredly that she might exercise the traditional prerogative of the male wit in poisoning the judgement of the less discerning; she was very much not to do with a 'ladies' faction in any of the senses hitherto identified, but capable of making as detailed, independent, and disparaging a comparison of the two versions of the story as Dryden himself. It is therefore doubly interesting to find that Dryden refers in the same dedication to the success which the play enjoyed among other 'Fair Ladies'. He attributes it, with characteristic generosity towards his collaborators, to Purcell's music, 'and particularly to the composition of the *Pastoral Dialogue*, [to which] the numerous Quire of Fair Ladies gave so just an applause on the Third Day'.

If we turn to the piece, a 'Dialogue of Thyrsis and Iris', we find that it is indeed a delight, musically and dramatically witty (and a little *risqué*), and

[80] Dryden, 'To the Right Honourable the Earl of Rochester', *Cleomenes* (1692). Jane Hyde married Henry, Laurence Hyde's eldest son. She and her father-in-law succeeded in getting the play reinstated without cuts; the Lord Chamberlain confessed to the poet that she was 'the most Earnest Solicitress, as well as the Fairest, and that nothing could be refus'd to my Lady Jane'.

[81] Dryden, 'To the Honourable Sir William Levison Gower, Bart.', *Amphitryon* (1690).

that it suggests in its devotees all the hallmarks of that more conventional appreciation which Jane Hyde transcended.[82] An importunate Thyrsis begs to be kissed 'longer / and longer yet and longer', but is urged by the teasingly modest Iris, fearful of placing her trust where it might be betrayed, to *love* her 'longer / And longer yet and longer'. He then requests her pity, asking now to be kissed *kindly*, and she, pleased with his submission and fond courtship, agrees to do so; with the important proviso, naturally, that he will tell no one of the favours he has received from her. Gentleman that he is, Thyrsis consents, and the two sing of the pleasures of love and excitements which each new day will bring. The piece is a delight, but it is scarcely a sign of sophistication among its audience that it should have been so warmly approved; not, at any rate, sophistication of the kind which Jane Hyde possessed, but rather of the sort enjoined upon women by the rote-learning of songs and continual practising of music which their station encouraged. Its conventional thematic appeal—the preserving of the women's reputation and the right attitude of the lover—together with Dryden's hope that Jane Hyde might keep her thoughts about the rest of the play to herself, argues that it was that lady alone who, in Dryden's estimation, had the measure of the play's conception. She was a leader of opinion as Rochester and Buckingham had been.

Whatever the rarity of her intelligence, the example of Jane Hyde and Dryden's respect for her prompts some interesting questions about the response of well-informed women to plays which used material from the French literature which it was considered proper for women to read. We know that Elizabeth Pepys scorned Dryden's *An Evening's Love* for its plagiarism of *L'Illustre Bassa*, and that transposing the events of French romances on to the stage could occasion a variety of critical activity. Jane Hyde's intimate acquaintance with Molière's *Amphitryon* suggests strongly that there must have been serious consideration by those who knew their Molière of, for example, the way Wycherley made use of *L'École des femmes* and *L'École des maris* in *The Country Wife*, or the points of contrast between his *Plain Dealer* and *Le Misanthrope*.[83] Those particular plays are most often associated with the ladies who found them offensive;

---

[82]   The text may be found in Dryden, *Poems and Fables*, pp. 445–6; a recording is available on Henry Purcell, *Theatre Music—Vol. IV*. With Judith Nelson, Martyn Hill, and Christopher Keyte. Directed by Christopher Hogwood. The Academy of Ancient Music (London, DSLO 550, 1978).

[83]   For Wycherley's use of Molière see *Plays*, ed. Holland, pp. 229, 345–6; Norman Suckling, 'Molière and English Restoration Comedy', *Restoration Theatre*, ed. J. R. Brown and B. Harris (London, 1965), 93–107; and John Wilcox, *The Relation of Molière to Restoration Comedy* (New York, 1938), 104–9.

yet Jane Hyde's example shows that we need not assume that all women who saw them were concerned with moral matters to the exclusion of literary ones. The business of borrowing was a familiar one to the theatre-going public, and there is good reason to assume that those most intimately acquainted with the works of one of the most plundered masters of all were well qualified to discuss in detail the achievements of his pupils. Even if the only recorded instance we have of such appreciation is the one given here (and that, according to Dryden, a rare one) it reminds us that there were responses among women to comedies which had nothing to do with outrage or illicit pleasure. Above all, the example of Jane Hyde, sponsor of politically responsible drama, polite critic of irresponsible and counterfeit dramatic practice, and a leader of opinion equal in authority, it appears, to the male wits of earlier decades, embodies the achievement of the few women at Court concerned to cultivate and advance the interest of the stage.

Further understanding of the slackness and inconsistency of patronage among women at Court may be gained by considering the interest shown by the three foremost ladies of the age, the Queens of Charles, James, and William. Once again, the Restoration Court suffers badly by comparison with the Caroline. Henrietta Maria's patronage of the stage had been both private and public; it extended to acting, advising designers, listening to performers, and lending her name to a professional company.[84] At the centre of the Court's interest in drama, she could command regular performances from professional actors and commission work for amateur performance, sometimes influencing its means and ends; where political ends were sought, they were woven intricately into the texture of the drama and not left to the histrionic outburst or calculated pillory.[85] None

[84] For her acting, see CSPD Charles I: 1625–26, p. 273; CSPD Charles I: 1627–28, pp. 88–9; Elizabeth Hamilton, *Henrietta Maria* (London, 1976), 108–15; Quentin Bone, *Henrietta Maria, Queen of the Cavaliers* (London, 1973), 83–4; and Le Comte de Tillières, *Mémoires*, ed. M. C. Hippeau (Paris, 1863), 134–8. For her recommending the use of movable perspective scenery in the French style, see Stephen Orgel and Roy Strong, *Inigo Jones: The Theatre of the Stuart Court*, 2 vols. (Berkeley and Los Angeles, 1973) i. 24–5; and W. A. Jackson and Jean Parrish, 'Racan's *Artenice*', *Harvard Library Bulletin* 14 (1960), 183–90 (*Artenice* having been the first play presented at Court at the Queen's instigation). Her championship of Platonic Love in plays is discussed by Kathleen Lynch in *The Social Mode of Restoration Comedy* (New York and London, 1926), 43–6. For 'Queen Henrietta Maria's Men' and a schedule of professional court performances, see G. E. Bentley, *The Jacobean and Caroline Stage*, 7 vols. (Oxford, 1941), i. 97–100, 218–59.

[85] Orgel and Strong, i. 49–75, stress the conservatism of the Queen's masques in showing the unity of Charles and his wife; Walter Montague's *The Shepherd's Paradise* (London, 1633) they describe as 'the direct expression of the Queen's will'; its purpose was

of the Restoration Queens was able (or, it seems, willing) to exert such authority. Thomas Killigrew, chatting to Pepys about the rebuilt Theatre Royal and its advantages over previous public theatres, implied that play-going in the 1660s was very much the King's business, which it had certainly not been thirty years before:

Then, the Queen seldom and the King never would come; now, not the King only for State, but all civil people do think they may come as well as any.[86]

In fact, Charles II's Catherine had made her first visit to the theatre only two months before, at the reopening of the Theatre Royal, and it was to be thirteen years before she went with anything resembling regularity. Marriage to a man who saw over four hundred professional performances of plays during a reign of twenty-five years must have provided every opportunity for involvement in the interests of the stage; none was accepted but the occasional enjoyment of a variety of plays at the theatre. Comfort may have been foremost in her mind; perhaps it is no accident that she did not attend the theatre until the Theatre Royal had been rebuilt, and that she saw no Duke's Company performances until their move from the ill-appointed Lincoln's-Inn-Fields House to the splen-dours of Dorset Garden.[87]

Her successor, Mary of Modena, overcame an unfortunate early experience of the public stage to become, with her husband, a regular if somewhat aloof spectator. The United Company presented, for her

'the education of the courtly audience in the royal virtues' (p. 63). Martin Butler, however, in *Theatre and Crisis, 1625-1642* (Cambridge, 1984), 25-34, points to the Queen's background of political dissent, and argues that the Platonic adulation which she was accorded in her masques, and particularly in *The Shepherd's Paradise*, was subversive, since it depicted her as having a power over men which she did not owe to her husband.

[86] Pepys, *Diary*, 12 Feb. 1667. Bentley, iv. 35, shows that Henrietta Maria went to the public theatre four times, and her husband not at all.

[87] Catherine's first play, on 20 Dec. 1666, was Fletcher's *The Humourous Lieutenant*; PRO, L.C.5/139, p. 129. The visit seems to have been made as a gesture of approval for the re-opening of the theatre after the Great Fire. For doubts about its propriety, see Pepys, *Diary*, 15 Oct. 1666; and CSPD Charles II: 1666, 136. From April 1680 until her husband's death, Catherine went to the theatre fourteen times, matching the number of visits made from 1666 to 1679. See PRO, L.C./139, 141, 142, 145. She was by no means averse to the racier comedies; she saw *The Souldier's Fortune* and *The Amorous Widow* twice each, and *The London Cuckolds* and *An Evening's Love* once, as well as performances of *Othello*, *Hamlet*, and a handful of plays by Fletcher. Dorset Garden Theatre opened on 9 November 1671. Discussion of its facilities (and those of the new Theatre Royal) may be found in Hotson, pp. 229-39.

birthday in August 1682, John Bankes's most recent success, *Vertue Betray'd*, or *Anna Bullen*; it was found, however, that the play, not quite the model 'ladies' play' which usually graced such occasions, forced the Duchess to keep to her bed after seeing it performed.[88] Once enthroned, Mary became an enthusiastic but passive patron. Visits to the playhouses tended to be formal in character, with the King and the Maids of Honour present on the majority of outings; towards the end of James's short reign the couple retreated for all but four productions to the theatre at Whitehall.[89] They did not, it seems, consider it in their interest to promote new plays; out of the thirty-seven plays given at Whitehall during James's reign, only one—Crowne's *Sir Courtly Nice*—was less than three years old. Conservatism and formality went before novelty and adventure.

Mary's stepdaughter and namesake, William's wife, presents an altogether more interesting case. It is well known that William himself had no time for the theatre;[90] what is less clear is the depth of uncertainty in Mary's attitude towards it. Her upbringing at the Court of Charles II involved her in showy amateur dramatics, but such things were hardly to be considered when she came to the throne. In fact, the conflict of her interests in this area defines her precisely as a patron of the late 1680s and 1690s; if the royal mistresses of the Carolean Age had been free to dabble in the theatre as their public or private interests demanded, Mary's attitudes and power were complicated by a wider range of ethical and political considerations. Like her stepmother, she suffered an early embarrassment at the theatre; this time the event appears to have a claim to historical significance which belies its actual insignificance. On 28 May 1689, her first outing to the theatre since her enthronement, she discovered what it was like to be one of 'the ladies': watching Dryden's *The Spanish Fryar*, she 'furnished the Town with discourse for a Month' by succumbing to 'some unhappy Expressions', which

put her in some disorder, and forc'd her to hold up her fan, and often look behind her and call for her palatine and hood, and anything she could next think of,

---

[88] Newdigate Newsletter of 5 Aug 1682 and letter from Juliana Brabazon to the Countess of Rutland, dated August 1682, quoted in *The London Stage*, I. 311.

[89] PRO, L.C. 5/147, pp. 68, 260, 361; 5/16, p. 124; 5/148, p. 145.

[90] *The Diary of Edward Lake*, ed. George Elliot, *Camden Miscellany I*, Camden Society, 39 (Westminster, 1847), 9. Mary made twelve visits to the public theatre as monarch, and on none of them was she accompanied by her husband. William saw one play after her death: Peter Motteux's *Europe's Revels for the Peace* (London, 1697), which was given for his birthday. See Boswell, p. 105.

while those who were in the pit before her laughed whenever their fancy led them to make any application of what was said.[91]

Neither masked nor sufficiently composed to outface the insinuations of the pit, she was embarrassed by a play which, by recent standards, was not particularly offensive. It may have been the occasional political allusion which embarrassed her; the same account reports that *The Spanish Fryar* was the only play whose performance was forbidden by her father, James II, and the only play which she was to prohibit was Dryden's *Cleomenes*, for its reflections on the government. Even so, the incident might, in 1689, have encouraged Mary to examine scrupulously the conduct of the stage and her relations with it: it embodied all that modest women traditionally suffered in the playhouse, and it took place in the year recognized now as marking 'the change in comedy'; the year when, according to J. H. Smith, the ladies pressurized the stage into regulating its comedies within truly polite limits.[92] Whether or not her anxieties were predominately political, the incident does not seem to have changed her attitude towards the stage, however; and that it did not may be attributed to a complexity rather than a want of interest.

One thing we can be sure of is that reformers of the stage considered Mary an appropriate patron of their own endeavours. After her death one newspaper, *The Observator*, enlisted her on the side of the righteous by recording that she had been 'branded for a Presbyterain . . . for no other reason than that she was not a common frequenter of play-houses'.[93] A regular play-goer she may not have been, but that did not necessarily make her of the reformers' party. The view of *The Observator* is, however, seconded by Gilbert Burnet's celebration of Mary, every sentence of which bespeaks her strong aversion to the theatre; in a number of instances, indeed, a direct sympathy with the opinions of Jeremy Collier.[94] 'The reforming the Manners of her People was one of her chief Cares,' wrote Burnet, adding that she was particularly concerned with 'raising the Reputation and Authority of the Clergy', so often, according to Collier, abused on the stage.[95] As if to suggest a dislike of what Goldsmith was later

---

[91] Sir John Dalrymple, *Memoirs of Great Britain* (London, 1771–88), quoted in *The London Stage*, i. 371. PRO, LC. 5/149, p. 154 states (somewhat surprisingly) that Elizabeth Barry was paid £25 by the Queen for her part in the performance.

[92] J. H. Smith, 'Shadwell, the Ladies, and the Change in Comedy', *Modern Philology*, 46 (1948), 31.   [93] John Tutchin, *The Observator*, 6 Mar. 1703.

[94] Gilbert Burnet, *An Essay on the Memory of the Late Queen* (London, 1695).

[95] Burnet, pp. 103, 115. For Collier on the stage's abuse of the clergy, see *A Short View*, pp. 35–41.

to call 'laughing comedy' (as opposed to 'sentimental comedy'), he records that Mary 'thought it a cruel and barbarous thing, to be merry on other People's cost; or, to make the Misfortunes or Follies of others, their Diversion'.[96] Still more significant is Mary's interest in the reforming societies, after which she inquired 'often and much'.[97] Most revealing of all, however, if perhaps not in the way it was intended, is Burnet's account of her reading habits. Predictably enough, scripture was her favourite subject for study, along with recent history and the Catholic controversy. She still found a great deal of time, however, for 'Lively Books, where Wit and Reason gave the Mind a true Entertainment', and Burnet found her to be 'a Good Judge as well as a great Lover of Poetry', a distinction which he was at pains to explain further:

she loved it best when it dwelt on the best Subjects. So tender was she of Poetry, tho' much more of Vertue, that she had a particular concern in the Defilement, or rather the Prostitution of the Muses among us.[98]

This ranks her with Collier and the editor of *The Observator* as an opponent of the stage; less partial evidence, however, shows not only that she was not that, but that she admired plays which the reformers singled out as being especially improper.

The Treasury Warrants show that three days after her dreadful excursion to *The Spanish Fryar*, Crowne's *Sir Courtly Nice*, admittedly a good-humoured play of intrigue free from obvious danger, was acted 'by the Queenes Command', and repeated at Whitehall the following year.[99] More remarkably, she took in two performances of Dryden's *Amphitryon*, which Collier found 'too much out of order to appear' in his catalogue of offensive passages and expressions;[100] and ordered a command performance (made notable for giving Cibber his first real opportunity as an actor) of Congreve's *The Double Dealer*, which had already aroused

[96] Burnet, p. 86. Oliver Goldsmith, 'An Essay on the Theatre; or, a Comparison between Laughing and Sentimental Comedy', *The Collected Works of Oliver Goldsmith*, ed. Arthur Friedman, 5 vols. (Oxford, 1966), iii. 209–13.

[97] Burnet, p. 118. For comments on the work of reforming societies, see Josiah Woodward, *An Account of the Rise and Progress of the Religious Societies* (London, 1701); and Joseph Wood Krutch, *Comedy and Conscience after the Restoration* (New York, 1924). These organizations, open only to men, were allowed to flourish in the reign of William and Mary, having been suppressed in that of James; their activity in the theatres consisted of reporting instances of blasphemy to magistrates.

[98] Burnet, pp. 78–9.

[99] L.C. 5/149, p. 368.

[100] Collier, p. 179.

opposition among the ladies and was to provoke Collier and a Middlesex
magistrate to flights of indignation.[101] The quality of Congreve's play lies
in the unusual purity of its construction, having in its design that
symmetry and beauty to appreciate which was, according to Dennis and
the central canon of the age's criticism, to identify oneself as a spectator of
true discernment.[102] It seems perfectly proper to deduce that Mary was
capable of distinguishing the play's alleged offensiveness as true satire, and
that she gave it her support on the grounds of its artistry, so little
recognised by the majority of the audience, who thought 'anything dull
and heavy which does not border upon farce'.[103]

Less controversially, Mary was also a regular admirer of the semi-
operas of Purcell; she may have been one of those who admired the
'Pastoral Dialogue' of *Amphitryon*, and she certainly saw, with her Maids of
Honour, one performance each of *The Prophetess*, *King Arthur*, and *The
Fairy Queen*. The text of *King Arthur* was recommended to her by the
Duchess of Monmouth, whose liking for that 'Fairy kind of writing',
which 'depends only on the force of imagination', led her to present the
piece for royal perusal; it was not, however, that quality which, according
to the author, appealed to the Queen, but the patriotic subject.[104]

There are further indications that Mary found more in the theatre than
literary or political satisfaction. When Aphra Behn's *The Rover* was
performed at Whitehall in November 1690, William Mountfort,
renowned for his suave, gentlemanly style of acting, played the part of
Willmore; Mary, it is said, was 'pleased to make in favour of Mountfort,
notwithstanding her Disapprobation of the Play'. The same account says
that Mountfort, 'even in that dissolute character of the Rover . . . seem'd to

---

[101] The command performance took place on 13 Jan. 1694, three months after the
opening; *The London Stage*, i. 431. For Cibber replacing Kynaston as Lord Touchwood,
Apology, p. 104. For the opposition of the ladies, Congreve, 'To the Right Honourable
Charles Mountague', *The Double Dealer*; he says that 'some of the Ladies' were concerned
that he had 'represented some Women Vicious and Affected', and replies that they should
no more expect to be complimented in a comedy 'than to be Tickled by a Surgeon when
he's letting 'em Blood'. Collier, p. 12, complains that of the four major female characters in
the play, three are 'whores': 'A Great Compliment to Quality to tell them there is not above
a quarter of them Honest!' Luttrell, *A Brief Relation*, iv. 379, records that a writ was issued
on 12 May 1698 against Congreve for writing the play and Tonson for printing it.
[102] John Dennis, *The Critical Works*, ii. 277: 'the Men of Business come to unbend, and
are incapable of appreciating the just and harmonious symmetry of a beautiful design.'
[103] Congreve, 'To the Right Honourable Charles Mountague'.
[104] Dryden, 'To the Right Honourable Marquise of Halifax', *King Arthur* (1690).
Dryden's facility in this 'Fairy kind of writing' is discussed by David Hopkins in *John Dryden*
(Cambridge, 1986), 53-5.

wash off the Guilt from Vice, and [give] it Charms and Merit'.[105] Charles
Dibdin wrote later that Mary had found it 'dangerous to see [Mountfort]
act, he made vice so alluring', a feeling which she seems to have shared
with many other women.[106] This kind of pleasure was the fruit of the
court theatricals of her late uncle's day, when instruction was given in the
art of acting, and its liveliness and dignity appreciated as a moral end in
itself.

However, notwithstanding her admiration of Mountfort, the acting
profession did not seem to be unduly upset when she died in December
1694. There was some cause for alarm among the needy, for the Lord
Chamberlain suspended all performances at the theatre from 22 December, the start of her last illness, until the following Easter; to the
disenchanted members of the United Company, Betterton at their head,
the long sojourn gave time for forces to be grouped and decisions to be
taken. By 1 April 1695, when acting was again permitted, Betterton's new
company had possession of a theatre, funds to renovate it, and the nominal
support of the King. To put it a little crudely, Mary's death offered respite
in which the rebels from the United Company could advance business
and self-esteem. Those who stayed had their salaries doubled, and in a
community ready to indulge in the most outrageous panegyric whenever
its patrons offered the slightest occasion for it, no one seems to have
suffered much grief at Mary's death.[107] The poetical tributes to her tend to
stress her dislike of 'Vulgar Sport', and the sorrow of the community of
ladies which she had gathered about her, who, their visits to the theatre
with Mary as Maids of Honour apart, appear to have had little more to do
with actively promoting the stage than their mistress.[108] Eventually,

<hr/>

[105] Cibber, *Apology*, p. 75.

[106] Highfill *et al.*, *A Biographical Dictionary*, x; Mountfort, PRO, L.C. 5/150, p. 170
records a payment to Mountfort of £10 from the Queen for his part in Bancroft's *Edward
III* (1691). For the ladies' grief at Mountfort's murder in 1691, see 'Elegy on Mountfort',
Poems on Affairs of State, ed. Cameron, v. 366. The story of his death is told in *The Player's
Tragedy* (London, 1693) and analysed in A. S. Borgman, *The Life and Death of William
Mountfort* (Cambridge, Mass., 1935), 123–7.

[107] See Cibber, *Apology*, p. 108; *A Comparison Between the Two Stages*, p. 9 (on the
'importuning and dunning' of noblemen to raise funds for the new company) and p. 10 (on
the big turn-out at the first production, *Love for Love*). Details of the legal transactions are in
the 'Petition of the Players' the 'The Reply of the Patentees' in PRO, L.C. 7/3 and PRO C.10
297/57; in *The London Stage1*, i. 433–4; and in Hotson, pp 284–95.

[108] See *A Funeral Elegy upon the Death of the Queen, Address to the Marquess of Normandy*
(London, 1695), on the 'Lovely Melancholly Train' of Mary's 'Ladies, now divested of their
pride'; and Robert Gould, *A Poem most humbly offered to the Memory of her late Sacred Majesty*
(London, 1695). Burnet, p. 84, records that Mary set an example of working vigorously,

whatever the complexity of the different moral and political considerations which bore on Mary's appreciation of the theatre, she was to take her place with her predecessors as one who could at best claim only to be an enthusiastic admirer. What Jane Hyde was to Dryden, 'a Charming Patroness' in the fullest sense, she could not be, even if she was scarcely alone in not deserving the accolade.

The relations between women at Court and the stage having been considered, it will no doubt appear that the title of the present chapter promised what could not be delivered; of patronage in the direct sense there was little. Mere enthusiasm, manipulation, and indifference took its place. Occasionally, influential bodies might form to affect the course of a particular production—the Maids of Honour in the case of *The Country Wife*, the Hyde family in that of *Cleomenes*—but there would appear to have been no regular cultivation of the interests of the stage or of the Court in relation to it. Moreover, these groups, small in number and probably short-lived, found little succour from those empowered to offer real assistance; it is no accident that the only unequivocal recorded use of the word 'Patroness' by a Restoration dramatist occurs when a woman, Jane Hyde, is praised for rescuing a play from the uncomprehending displeasure of the Queen. Such deficiencies are themselves, however, an important part of the subject in so far as it meets the question of 'the ladies' as considered by other scholars. The Court, for all the benefits of company and education it conferred on its ladies, provided them with no immediate tradition of sustained or organized influence over the stage. It will be as well to consider that, together with the variety of drama which the Court ladies (Mary included) appear to have enjoyed, as we move on to examine the question of the change in comedy and the part of 'the ladies' in it.

whether reading or stitching, 'which wrought on, not only those that belonged to her, but the whole Town to follow her'. The Maids of Honour, however, accompanied Mary on all of her visits to the public theatre: See PRO, L.C. 5/151, p. 369.

5

THE LADIES AND THE
CHANGE IN COMEDY

I

THE title of this chapter derives from that of the article which introduced
the subject of the ladies to modern students of Restoration Drama; it
therefore both acknowledges a debt and promises a reassessment. The
argument of that article—that the ladies played a significant part in
bringing about or supporting the new mode in comedy—now enjoys
universal currency, and it is not my intention to refute it. However, to
accept an argument is not, in the present instance, to forgo the right to
make a fundamental challenge to it. The paradox is allowed by Smith's
most patient critic, Robert Hume, when he refers to 'the moral element in
the audience (the ladies, as they are usually called)'.[1] This is to admit a
possible distinction between the people who went about trying to change
comedy and those in whose interest it was that comedy be changed. Actual
ladies, in other words, may have had no more to do with the changing of
comedy than with the spoiling of the reputation of The Luckey Chance; the
idea of 'the ladies', with its connotations of propriety and modesty, may
simply have lent its name to the changes which took place. If there is no
reason to doubt that comedy changed its style to suit the modesty of the
ladies, there is every reason to be sceptical about the ladies' part in
bringing the change about. Smith, it should be said, is guarded in his
claims for their involvement. He goes no further than to say that the ladies
had more to do with the shaping of comedy than had hitherto been
supposed, so it is perhaps those who have followed him too enthusiasti-
cally who need correction;[2] yet his assumptions about who the ladies were

---

[1] Robert D. Hume and Arthur H. Scouten, '"Restoration Comedy" and its Audiences,
1660–1776'; ch. 2 of Hume, The Rakish Stage (Carbondale and Edwardsville, 1983), 61. See
also Hume, The Development of English Drama in the Late Seventeenth Century (Oxford, 1976),
380–494; and his 'The Change in Comedy: Cynical versus Exemplary Comedy on the
London Stage, 1678–1693', Essays in Theatre, i (1983), 101–18.

[2] J. H. Smith, 'Shadwell, the Ladies and the Change in Comedy', p. 27. Peter Holland,
The Ornament of Action (Cambridge, 1980), 15–16, Botica, pp. 106–8 and 186, and John
Harley, Music in Purcell's London (London, 1968), 120–1, all refer to a powerful force or cabal
of ladies; this Smith is careful to avoid.

and how they exercised their alleged influence are sketchily set out (and adhered to by all his published readers except, parenthetically, Hume) and so demand the close critical attention hitherto denied them. One's debt to Smith for introducing the subject of the ladies and attempting to draw limits to it goes, therefore, with a misgiving that he may have introduced only an elaborate substitute for it.

Little that has been said so far has suggested that it is at all likely that 'the ladies' could have been directly responsible for the change in comedy in the way that Smith suggests. Factions of ladies were organized on a very occasional basis, and had different aims according to the production on offer; large numbers of ladies and gentlewomen had no objection to bawdy plays cried down in their name; and to no woman was a play dedicated during the years of change save Princess Anne, who clearly did not go to the theatre often, and the Duchess of Ormond, who sponsored Durfey for one play, *Don Quixote*, not of the new type. It would be irresponsible, however, so to dispose of the matter. So far our discussion of the ladies has not embraced the possibility of a change in their position as theatre-goers during the period in question; they have all been, in their variety and individuality, Restoration spectators. In order fairly to discuss Smith's case regarding the ladies we must first examine, therefore, the events leading up to 1688-9, the date he cites as marking the change in comedy, and their particular bearing upon the female audience. On the intellectual and social origins of the new mode in comedy there is already much good work;[3] what needs to be done here is to consider the ways in which the position of the ladies of the 1680s might have changed in such a way as to promote the kind of activity envisaged by Smith.

Among the changes which took place in those years the most significant has already been touched upon in the previous chapter: the progressive decline in the patronage of the great and its replacement by the patronage not only of booksellers and military men, but of groups of people. There are some indications of this process in the handful of plays (all unsuccessful ones) dedicated to groups rather than individuals;[4] it is more reliably witnessed in the growing number of references to factional

---

[3] See Joseph Wood Krutch, *Comedy and Conscience after the Restoration* (New York, 1924); John Loftis, *Comedy and Society from Congreve to Fielding* (Stanford, 1959); Maureen Sullivan, Introduction to *Cibber: Three Sentimental Comedies*, ed. Sullivan (Yale, 1973).

[4] James Carlisle dedicated *The Fortune Hunters* (1689) to the patentees of the United Company; George Powell *Bonduca* (1695) to the patentees and shareholders of Rich's Company; John Smyth gave *Cytherea* (1677) to the Northern Gentry; and Thomas Jevon *The Devil of a Wife* (1686) to his friends at Locket's eating house.

support in the playhouses, which appear to have replaced the authoritative judgement exercised in earlier years by men such as Rochester, Buckingham, Sedley and others.[5] Such support could not only decide the fate of a play in the theatre; it might affect the character of its performance there.[6] It may be that that the growing tendency of groups rather than individuals to create successes allowed more women to have a say in the auditorium, since the exercise of their critical prerogative had always been a matter of collective responsibility, but there is also the possibility (surely more likely) that as talk of factions and cabals became more widespread, it would have been fashionable to refer to any casual grouping of spectators in those terms. To claim that 'the ladies' took advantage of the rise in collective patronage to make their voices heard may only be to make oneself party to the loose talk of the times.

The fashionableness of faction is evident in the history of the stage during the earlier years of the 1680s, when the Popish Plot Crisis was raging. 'All run now into Politicks,' complained Shadwell, 'and you must needs, if you touch upon any humour of this time, offend one of the Parties'.[7] The conditions which produced factious behaviour in the playhouse at the beginning of the 1680s were not the same as those which produced it at the end; nevertheless, the Plot Years set some interesting precedents for behaviour among the theatre audience, and offer clues for its development in later years. The controversy surrounding Shadwell's *The Lancashire Witches* is a case in point. Catholic opponents determined to see the play banned succeeded only in having it doctored by the Master of the Revels;[8] when it came to the stage they came 'to hiss it, and many that call'd themselves Protestants, joyn'd with them', by which Shadwell meant that a number of bystanders joined in for the fun of declaring themselves and entering the faction, even if they did not quite understand

---

[5] Stacy, *The Country Gentleman's Vade Mecum*, p. 48; *The Beau's Catechism*, p. 5; Dennis, Preface, *Iphigenia* (1700); *Animadversions on Mr. Congreve's Late Answer to Mr. Collier* (London, 1699) pp. 34–6; Gildon, 'A Letter to Mr D'Urfey' in Durfey, *The Marriage-Hater Match'd* (1692); Shadwell, 'To the Reader', *The Lancashire Witches*; John Harold Wilson, 'Theatre Notes from the Newdigate Newsletters', *Theatre Notebook*, 15 (1961), 79–84; *A Comparison between the Two Stages*, p. 32; Cibber, *Apology*, p. 129.

[6] *The Post Boy* offers an amusing (if trivial) example: some sailors requested 'additional entertainments' at the day's performance of *The Tempest*; these took the form of some seafaring dances—no strong argument for the significance of such interventions.

[7] Shadwell, 'To the Reader'.

[8] Shadwell, 'To the Reader'. The changes made to the play were not significant. Expunged passages are printed in italics in the first edition, and consist of three scenes (including the first, which contains reflections on the keeping of priests in families) and a number of incidental anti-Catholic jokes.

what it was all about. It seems that the point of protests such as this was, indeed, to draw in the ordinarily silent majority. Evident public dissatisfaction with the play was what the opposition sought; a hissing faction might be countered by a clapping one, but a generally disapproving audience meant that the play would not last. In the case of Shadwell's play, vocal support eventually won the day; the author's friends went to the play for the first three days and 'quash'd all the vain attempts' of his enemies to cry it down. The opposition was hindered by a failure of common sense obvious to the rest of the audience. 'Mercenary fellows' were employed, 'who were such fools they did not know when to hiss and this was evident to all the audience'. The majority remained free from the polarities of opinion which the play's enemies sought to exploit, and it was the collective nature of the exercise which was most in evidence; the corrective derision came not from pit, box, or gallery, but from all. Allowing for the exaggeration of the triumphant playwright, it is not unreasonable to see signs here of the way the pressure of the times enforced more rigorous critical faculties upon the audience as a whole, and certainly a more concentrated kind of attention upon the spectator who demanded some expression of the playwright's political alignment. 'All run now into Politicks,' said Shadwell; while 'Humble Hodge', in a printed dialogue of 1680, boasted that 'since this damnable Popish Plot has been discovered, there have come out so many notable good and bad books on all sides that I vow to thee I am become sublime like a philosopher, and can hold out *pro* and *con* with the best of them'.[9] If the times made every dramatist a polemicist, they made many a spectator a political analyst. They urged every interested member of the audience to examine the effects of each work upon his own conscience, while the disinterested or merely indifferent were engaged at least as witnesses to a vigorous renewal of enthusiasm for drama not as a pastime but as a necessary extension to public life.[10] With the trend towards faction went an increased pressure to declare one's sympathies; even if only by reaction away from the declarations of others.

A more tangible legacy of the Plot Years was the folding of the King's Company in 1682.[11] This was, of course, occasioned by a decline in the

---

[9] *Humble Hodge his Discourse* (London, 1680).

[10] There were still occasions, of course, when indifference (or, perhaps, an affably English sense of fair play) won the day; Dryden and Lee, Preface, *The Duke of Guise*.

[11] The part played in its decline by disturbances arising from the Plot is discussed by George W. Whiting, 'Political Satire in London Stage Plays, 1680–83', *Modern Philology*, 28 (1930). Financial details may be found in Hotson, pp. 249–61.

total audience, but it appears to have had its own effects on the temper and even the size of the play-going public.[12] One newspaper complained, in the middle of the United Company's monopoly, that 'when the Two Houses were up, 'twas observable the Town had better Plays, and the Players better Audiences';[13] while Sir Charles Sedley saw the effects in terms not only of the quality of plays, but also of playhouse economics and the attitude of the audience:

> When our Two Houses did divide the Town,
> Each Faction zealously maintain'd their own,
> We liv'd on those that came to cry us down.
> Our emulation did improve your Sport:
> Now you come hither but to make your Court.[14]

Sedley believed that active interest in the theatre was aroused chiefly by the competition of two flourishing playhouses, and he reminds us how regularly the idea of the competing theatres arises in the documentation of the Restoration Stage.[15] One important instance of the kind of benefits he had in mind has already been quoted in the previous chapter, and demands further consideration here; in leading the Court away from Settle's controversial success, *The Female Prelate*, and going to see *Macbeth* at the Duke's Theatre instead, the Duchess of Portsmouth clearly did not harm the poet as she had thought, but merely added to the controversy and, inevitably, to his reputation.[16] It must partly have been because of her factious support for the other house that the play succeeded as it did;[17] had

---

[12] For the decline in the audience after 1678, Botica, pp. 133–4; Edward A. Langhans, 'New Restoration Theatre Accounts', *Theatre Notebook*, 17 (1963), 134; Hotson, p. 288.

[13] *The Lacedemonian Mercury*, 7 Mar. 1691/2.

[14] Sedley, Prologue, *Bellamira* (1687).

[15] It is not for nothing that the first history of the Restoration Stage was called *A Comparison Between the Two Stages*; the idea of having more than two patent companies was rejected at an early stage (see William Cavendish, Duke of Newcastle, Bodleian Library Clarendon MS 109 f.74) and the repertoire and personnel of the King's and Duke's Companies established by statute (see PROL, C. 5/139 and 5.12, and John Freehafer, 'The Formation of the London Patent Companies in 1660', *Theatre Notebook*, 20 (1965) 6–30). Shipman, Prologue, *Henry the Third of France* (1678), acclaims the arrangement as a celebration of the audience's love of 'the brisk delightfulness of *change* ': one house was as tiresome as one spouse.

[16] Theophilus Cibber, *Lives*, iii. 72, writing about the years of the Plot, records, 'However contemptible Settle was as a Poet, yet such was the prevalence of parties at that time, that, for some years, he was Dryden's rival on the stage.'

[17] There are only three recorded performances of *The Female Prelate*, although the prologue to Otway's *The Souldier's Fortune*, first given over two weeks after the last recorded performance of Settle's play, speaks of Settle's success in drawing the crowds away from the Duke's House. See *The London Stage*, i. 286–7.

it not been given the Duchess's chances of success might have been greater. 'We liv'd on those that came to cry us down,' said Sedley; crying down could clearly be just as profitable if it took the indirect form of a conspicuous snub. This may have important implications for the events of the late 1680s which this chapter is devoted to considering. It suggests, as Sedley claimed, that the dual patent was more likely to produce factious (but profitable) behaviour; but it also argues that such instances of factious behaviour as did take place were likely to have a more immediate effect on the practice of the theatre generally. When the two stages were concentrated into one, everyone needed to be more concerned about members of the audience who disliked particular kinds of plays; in the days of the dual patent, there was always the other house for such people to content themselves with, an arrangement which might benefit both companies, whereas during the Union they might stop coming altogether. Something of the difficulty may be recognized in the attempts of dramatists to make fun of diversions which drew people away from the theatre.[18] If the two stages provided a stimulus to argument, an awakening of critical interest, they also provided an easy means for both theatre and public to shirk active critical responsibility. This, and not simply the fact that the audience had already shrunk since the 1660s and 1670s, may explain why, in 1676, Wycherley was able to produce in *The Plain Dealer* a play just as offensive to those whom its predecessor, *The Country Wife*, had offended, while in 1683 Ravenscroft was constrained to offer, in *Dame Dobson*, an apology for its predecessor, *The London Cuckolds*, which had 'pleas'd the Town, and divert the Court', but which had also aroused the fury of certain women who 'made Visits with Design to cry it down'. Now that there was only one stage no one could afford to be cavalier about upsetting any substantial group of spectators, whatever the sport of others, especially since the audience in general was held by some dramatists to have become more chary of the satirist's lash.[19]

The early years of the 1680s provide two important indications, then, of how the disposition of the audience may have changed in such a way as to make possible the trends of later years identified by Smith; in both

[18] Aphra Behn was the first to complain, in her prologue to *Abdelazer* (1677), of the attractions of the card-table; Durfey, in the dedication of *The Fool's Preferment* (1688), found similar cause for complaint, while Southerne, 'To the Right Honourable Thomas Wharton', *The Wives Excuse* (1691), records the disapproval which greeted his satire of music-meetings.

[19] See Durfey, Prologue, *The Fool's Preferment*; Shadwell, Epilogue, *The Lancashire Witches*; Shadwell, Prologue, *The Squire of Alsatia* (1688); Durfey, Prologue and Epilogue, *Bussy d'Ambois* (1691).

instances the changes are ones which might strongly have influenced the power and temper of 'the ladies'. One more such indication introduces us to the real difficulty of the subject, that of determining who the powerful ladies of 1688–9 were; or at least, whom they represented. J. H. Smith offers as a definition of 'the ladies' of 1688–9 'the respectable female patrons of the theatre'. This is rather broad even by the standards of the prologues which were his chief evidence, and his main concern was to dissociate the change in comedy from those women who romped about in masks. Nevertheless, it may serve as a social as well as a moral distinction. It has long been a commonplace that reform of the stage at this time was very much a middle-class occupation, and the distinctive anxieties of 'the men of business' about 'the men of wit' are well established.[20] Chief among them were two concerns which were shared by 'the ladies': the morality of wit and the misrepresentation of women on the stage. Those issues were inseparable in the minds of the leading reforming critics, just as they were in the experience of ladies in the playhouse, where the bawdy jest correctly understood was a satirical blow in itself. Blackmore complained that the stage's picture of feminine accomplishment involved merely 'confident discourses, immodest repartees, and prophane raillery'; there the ideal woman despised her parents, scoffed at the prudence of 'the best of her sex', and was 'thoroughly instructed in intrigues and assignations'. He further complained that city-wives were always made to despise their husbands.[21] Steele put such misrepresentation down to the tendency of 'the charming force of wit' to travesty its subject, so that 'things in their own nature of a dark and horrid aspect can be cast in so bright a disguise, that they have half persuaded us that a whore may still be a beauty, and an adultress no villain'.[22] It is not surprising that in earlier years the interest of the ladies should have been thought to coincide with that of the 'citizens';[23] or that Otway, in his prologue to *The Orphan* (1680), should have been able to detect something like a faction of women critical

[20] See Richard Steele, Preface, *The Christian Hero: An Argument* (London, 1701); John Loftis, *Comedy and Society from Congreve to Fielding* (Stanford, 1959), 20–42; Sir Richard Blackmore, Preface to *Prince Arthur*, in J. E. Spingarn, ed., *Critical Essays of the Seventeenth Century*, 3 vols. (Oxford, 1909) iii. 227–41; Blackmore, *A Satyr Against Wit*, in Spingarn, iii. 325–33; Behn, Prologue, *The False Count*; Sullivan, xxxiv–xxxv.

[21] Blackmore, Preface, *Prince Arthur*, pp. 230–1.

[22] Steele, Preface, *The Christian Hero*. It was not the prerogative of the reformers to argue such a case; similar thoughts are to be found, ironically, in Engine's soliloquy in III. i. of *The London Cuckolds*.

[23] Durfey, Prologue, *The Virtuous Wife* (1680): 'My part [that of the virtuous wife] can take with none / But Women, or some Citt, that pays half a Crown.'

of the stage within the ranks of the stolidly bourgeois. In this latter
instance, however, it is suggested that there may have been differences
between the city's case regarding its women and that of the ladies:

> He ne're with Libel treated yet the Town,
> The names of honest Men bedaub'd and shown,
> Nay, never once lampoon'd the harmless Life
> Of suburb Virgin, or of City-Wife.

Here, fifteen years before Blackmore's realization of bourgeois discontent
with the stage's representation of the city-wife, is some indication that
dramatists were already aware of the problem and the pressure to do
something about it.[24] There are, naturally, obscurities in the terms of social
description: 'Town' and 'City' converge to confuse traditional allegiances;
'City-Wife' conforms to one half of her conventional image, while
'suburb Virgin' is a wholly new type, allied both with the city-wives and
'honest Men', the latter being not of the city but of the 'Town'. Nevertheless, there are potentially useful distinctions to be made. The women
mentioned by Otway clearly do not belong to the group usually identified
as 'the ladies', nor are their chief concerns the same. Two years before *The
Orphan*, in the prologue to *Friendship in Fashion*, Otway had shown his
understanding of what the ladies were worried about most: the issue of
bawdy humour.[25] It was very probably only the few most conspicuous
spectators who needed to worry about that; for the others, who could
expect to go to the theatre without suffering the scrutiny of men prying
for signs of experience, what was important was (according to Otway and
Blackmore) that the stage should offer the just and respectable an accurate
image of themselves. Bawdy humour might be distasteful, but it was not a
risk. This contrasts interestingly with the view of the ladies offered by
Robert Hume on the basis of close analysis of the comedies which they
admired and the ones they did not. Hume accounts for the success of two
plays among the ladies, *Friendship in Fashion* and Shadwell's *The Squire of
Alsatia*, on the grounds that they incorporated all the risks, seductions, and
intrigues of the 'Wycherlean' plot while eschewing the hated *double
entendre*;[26] a somewhat different account from the one given by J. H.

[24] See also Behn, Prologue, *The False Count*, for the anxiety of 'the Reverend
Bruminghams o'th'City' about 'smutty Scenes' and 'Love that so debauches all [their]
Daughters'.

[25] Otway protests that he 'took such care to work it chaste and fine, / He disciplined
himself at every line;' an elegant turn of phrase which offers its own *double entendre*, and in
doing so affirms the currency of the concern.

[26] Hume and Scouten, '"Restoration Comedy" and its Audiences', pp. 62–4; Hume, *The
Development of English Drama*, pp. 353–4, 367–79.

Smith, who claims that 'the ladies had for long been anxious to see *risqué* wit, facetious lovemaking, and perhaps even coquetry replaced on the stage by decency, sincerity, and honest love'.[27] These would have been the anxieties of Otway's suburb virgins and city-wives. There is further evidence to support this intimation of a division between 'factions' of female taste according to class. At the same time as Otway and Aphra Behn were acknowledging the concern of the city for the drama's treatment of women, Sir George Raynsford offered a view of the ladies' chief interests which, for all its bullying raillery, does not differ in essence from the scrupulously researched conclusions of Hume:

> But now I spy Tyrannick Judges here;
> What Pity 'tis so Fair, and so Severe!
> Fine Lady Criticks—on whose fragrant Breath
> Depends the Play's long Life, or sudden Death.
> From them the Poet must receive his Doom,
> Just as affairs succeed with them at Home;
> We hope the Paraquit and Squirrel's well,
> Else we are dammn'd to th'very pit of hell.
> Sir John is kind, and nothing goes amiss,
> Else we shall have a scurvy night of this!
> If we should here present a husband cross,
> And the revenge neglected by his spouse,
> 'Twere death in us—nay some of 'em would rage,
> Because he's not made cuckold on the stage.[28]

Again there are problems of social description; if these are ladies they are not the same kind of ladies as the 'bright stars' of other prologues, not only in temperament but in social background. It is established that the Court, a brief flurry of activity from 1684 to 1685 apart, was rapidly losing interest in the public stage; it preferred to select its own favourites from the repertoire and have them performed at Whitehall. In consequence there was not the substantial turn-out of, for example, the Maids of Honour who in previous years had been significant opponents of at least one bawdy play;[29] so it seems perfectly likely that the 'ladies' of the prologues and epilogues of the 1680s were closer than before in their social

[27] J. H. Smith, 'Shadwell, the Ladies, and the Change in Comedy', p. 31.

[28] Raynsford, Prologue to Nahum Tate, *The Ingratitude of a Commonwealth* (1681). The ladies are not the only faction referred to here.

[29] The Maids of Honour attended the public theatre in an official capacity only twice between Oct. 1686 and May 1689, compared, for instance, with seven visits between Apr. 1681 and Dec. 1682 (PRO, L.C. 5/145, p. 120; 5/147, pp. 68, 260; 5/148, p. 145; 5/149, p. 368.

constituency to those women referred to as city-wives or suburb virgins. It is certainly the case, at least, that the number of references in prologues and epilogues to married women increases during the late 1680s and 1690s; to that extent there is a greater emphasis on the reality of the bourgeois domestic establishment.[30] This is precisely what emerges in Raynsford's assault on the 'Fine Lady Criticks', who, with their titled husbands and fashionable toys, need represent no one more exalted than, say, the wife of Pepys's colleague, Sir William Batten; or, her husband apart, Margery Pinchwife. The difficulty of making a social distinction here must encourage caution in assigning different aims to different social groups, but we can at least be sure that in so far as women were able to apply to the stage for changes in the style of comedy, they were unlikely all to want the same kind of changes; and Hume's analysis of comedies admired by women shows above all how many different kinds of plots and heroines were permissible.[31]

Such analysis, by showing the variety of preferences declared by the female audience during the years of the change in comedy, does not argue strongly for the 'ladies' faction' of 'respectable female patrons' which Smith proposed; if anything, it suggests that there were almost as many factions as there were new plays, and—possibly—that the intentions of such factions varied with their social origin. It is true that those developments in the 1680s which we have looked at—the growth of collective patronage, the increase in factious behaviour, the theatre monopoly— suggest that the later years of the decade should have provided ample opportunities for the kind of pressure envisaged by Smith, but there is a great deal of evidence to show that such opportunities, if they were felt, were scarcely acted upon in the way he claims. We may best begin to examine the evidence by heading for the centre-piece of Smith's argument, the allegedly seminal success of Shadwell's *The Squire of Alsatia*. The departures in that play from dramatic convention are unquestionable; what must be scrutinized is Smith's sense of Shadwell's attitude towards his audience, and the precise circumstances of the play's success.

[30] A. H. Scouten, 'Notes Towards A History of Restoration Comedy', *Philological Quarterly*, 45 (1966), 62–70, notices this, and keys it to the shift in comic plots charted by J. H. Smith, *The Gay Couple in Restoration Comedy* (Cambridge, Mass., 1948), from the depiction of unmarried 'gay couples' in consideration of the problems of marriage.

[31] And, indeed, how plays could succeed by mixing different comic modes, thereby satisfying the variety of opinion among the audience. The outstanding example of deliberate mixing, Cibber's *Love's Last Shift* (1696), is discussed by Hume, *The Development of English Drama*, pp. 411–12, and (at greater length) by Paul E. Parnell, 'Equivocation in Cibber's *Love's Last Shift*', *Studies in Philology*, 57 (1960), 519–34.

The tone of satirical raillery set by the prologue is, even by the usual standards of the form, abrupt. It strongly resembles that of Sir George Raynsford in his prologue to *The Ingratitude of a Commonwealth*; it is bullying in manner, and charged with suspicion about the trappings of the female world:

> Our Poet begs you who adorn this Sphere,
> This shining Circle, will not be severe;
> Here no *Chit-Chat*, here no *Tea Tables* are.

That is the language of the suspicious Mirabell who requires his future wife to restrict herself to 'genuine and authorised tea-table talk, such as mending of fashions, spoiling reputations, railing at absent friends, and so forth'.[32] It may be raillery, but it shows little desire seriously to engage 'the ladies' as moral arbiters of a new style of comedy. If it be objected that no prologue, of its nature, could do that, we must point to what indicates more directly a satirical intention, those lines which look forward to the play's use of the latest fashionable talk about town:

> The *cant* be hopes will not be long unknown.
> 'Tis almost grown the language of the Town.

Surprisingly enough, it was this very feature which made the play so popular—a fact apparently unknown both to Smith and to Hume, who attribute the play's success to the rethinking of the relationship between hero and heroine so that rakishness would eventually be subdued by beauty and virtue. That that pattern was to become as familiar as it did in the subsequent twenty years is no doubt a reliable indication of its popularity; but such patterns may often be initiated through coincidental alliance with other, more immediate factors.[33] Such was the case with *The Squire of Alsatia*. A letter describing its success (evidence more reliable than the prologue so liberally used by Smith) shows how:

there is nothing in [*The Squire of Alsatia*] extraordinary—except it is a Latin song—but the thin reason why it takes soe well is, because it brings severall of the cant words uppon the stage which some in towns have invented, and turns them into ridicule.[34]

If that was so, the play's success owed less to its answering to the severe demands of the ladies than to the ladies happily failing to appreciate what

---

[32] *The Way of the World*, iv. i. 235-7.
[33] For its development, see Smith, *The Gay Couple in Restoration Comedy*, ch. 5.
[34] HMC Rutland, ii. 119.

it was they wanted when it was offered them. The epilogue to the play, furthermore, speaks not of the fulfilment of long-frustrated ambitions for the stage, but of a challenge to existing standards of taste. 'No Princess frowns,' warns Shadwell, 'no Hero rants and whines'; such extravagances should, he urges, be the diversion of chambermaids, so that ladies might forgo 'the silly Authors of Romances' and be 'reconcil'd to Comedy'. There are other indications that Shadwell was most certainly not, as both Smith and Robert Hume have claimed, aware of addressing a new kind of audience.[35] The author trots out familiar warnings and provisos with as much sense of novelty as a teacher facing the start of yet another term's work, and the compliments to the ladies are appropriately stale.[36]

The point is this. It is likely that there was what Hume and Scouten call 'a changing climate of opinion' in the theatre of the late 1680s; all our evidence that it issued from a faction of ladies comes, however, from a number of prologues and epilogues which merely mumble through the longest-established clichés about the female audience. Peter Holland, thinking to correct Smith's historical sense of the ladies and their critical principles, objects that 'the ladies [had] had no compunction about attacking bawdiness from the beginning', and quotes one instance of women throwing fruit at the actors for performing the 'damn'd bawdy' play, *The Custom of the Country*, in 1667.[37] The trouble with this argument is not only that Smith actually does state that the problem was a long-standing one;[38] it is that it fails to recognize that the problem was so long

---

[35] Smith, 'Shadwell, the Ladies, and the Change in Comedy', p. 32; Hume, *The Development of English Drama*, p. 378; Hume and Scouten, 'Restoration Comedy and its Audiences', pp. 63–4. One reason for this claim is the opening of Shadwell's prologue, 'Our Poet found your gentle Fathers kind'; a rallying nod at the author's seven-year absence from the stage since the trouble over *The Lancashire Witches* which is not accompanied by any sense that the 'new' audience would behave differently.

[36] For example, 'For when we make you merry you must own / You are much prettier when you frown. / With charming smiles you use to conquer still, / The melancholy look's not apt to kill.' Even the lines quoted by Hume, *The Development of English Drama*, p. 378, as evidence of 'speedy re-assurance', toy with the attitudes of the conventional gallant: 'Baudy the nicest ladies need not fear, / The quickest fancy shall extract none here: / We will not make 'em blush, by which is shown / How much their bought Red differs from their own.'

[37] Holland, *The Ornament of Action*, pp. 15–16. The throwing of 'peares and fruites' at Fletcher and Massinger's *The Custom of the Country* is reported in Evelyn Legh, Lady Newton, *The House of Lyme* (London, 1917), 240. It may have been unusual for 'stock' or 'old' plays to prompt such reactions; Aphra Behn, in her preface to *The Luckey Chance*, wonders why her play should have been criticized for indecency when *The London Cuckolds* and *The Man of Mode*, still being played, were not.

[38] See Smith, 'Shadwell, the Ladies, and the Change in Comedy', p. 27.

standing that it had ceased to be, at least in the documentary evidence of it, merely a problem. Dramatists had been exercising their ingenuity in the rhyming couplets of prologues and epilogues for over thirty years before Sir Robert Howard complained, in his prologue to *The Vestal Virgin* of 1664, that there was nothing left to write about.[39] It is no surprise, therefore, that there is little distinction to be made between the 'ladies' evoked by the prologues of Brome, Shirley, and Massinger, and those whom Shadwell is supposed to have been writing about in the prologue to *The Squire of Alsatia*.[40] There is talk of 'soft influences', and of the ravages of bawdy on the 'smooth Alabaster of the brow';[41] authors disown bawdy for the ladies' sake, appeal to 'kinder Stars', yet scorn the 'Lady Criticks'.[42] Divisions between the ladies and the young men in the theatre are also emphasized, yet talk of this is adduced by Smith as conclusive proof of movements to reform comedy in the late 1680s.[43] Everything, in short, that Shadwell is said to have found by way of uniform critical opinion among the ladies inhered in the forms he used to describe them. This is not to deny that some women remained concerned about the matters consistently raised there;[44] it is to show that any idea of a 'ladies' faction' depends entirely on a literal reading of worn-out evidence. If the terms used to describe the middle classes of London were obsolete, incapable of dealing with people like the Pepyses, so were those used to represent the ladies; all they could do was to trudge over well-trodden ground, colliding occasionally, like the 'citizen' of the prologues and epilogues, with the

[39] 'Would you would tell him which of all the ways / You like in Prologues, us'd to help out Plays.' He proceeds to give an inventory of conventional topics. See also his prologue to *The Surprisall* (1662): 'this excise on wit, / Though undiscern'd, consumes the Stock so fast, / That no new Fancy will be left at last.

[40] Occasionally, as in Fletcher's prologue to *The Coronation* (1635), there are appeals to the Platonic sensibility which are more precise in their terms than anything found after 1660.

[41] Fletcher, Epilogue, *The Coronation*; Shirley, Prologue, *The Imposture* (1640).

[42] William Habington, 'Prologue at the Fryers', *The Queene of Arragon* (1640); Davenant, Prologue, *The Witts* (1636); Glapthorne, Prologue, *The Ladies Priviledge* (1637).

[43] Davenant, Epilogue, *The Platonick Lovers* (1634), and Epilogue, *The Unfortunate Lovers* (1643); Fletcher, 2nd Epilogue (1625), *Wit at Several Weapons* (1609); Brome, Epilogue, *The Court Beggar* (1632). See also Brome, Prologue, *The Weeding of the Covent-Garden* (1632); Massinger, Prologue, *The Emperor of the East* (1631); and Davenant, Prologue, *The Fair Favourite* (1638). Glapthorne, 'Prologue to a Reviv'd Vacation Play', in *The Poems of Mr. Henry Glapthorne* (London, 1639), 21, notes the Caroline citizens taking their 'Wives and Daughters to a Play', as does Aston Cockain, Prologue, *The Obstinate Lady* (1639).

[44] The outcry over Durfey's *Don Quixote, Part III* in 1695 shows that real protests might yet be made.

interests of the genuine article. Hume's words, 'the moral element in the audience (the ladies, as they are usually called)' seem peculiarly apt. Quite how apt they are may be confirmed by consideration of the efforts made on behalf of the ladies by other reformers of the stage; this will demonstrate more precisely the inadequacies of the traditional ways of talking about female spectators, and it will begin to show how those interested in reform tried to address themselves to the problems faced by 'the ladies' in general, without reference to any faction or cabal.

We shall begin with the most significant case, Jeremy Collier. *A Short View* has attracted more attention for the legal wrangling, caution, and suspicion it provoked than for any of its intrinsic merits; even those who have praised Collier have done so not because of the quality of the work itself, but because of its author's courage and tenacity.[45] *A Short View* is, however, a valuable and sometimes acute book; it is also a manifesto for reform according to the time-honoured wishes of 'the ladies', whose part Collier takes with as complete a command of the established issues and terms as any playwright, and with the air of a courtly sentimentalist—more a Davenant than a Prynne.[46]

What concerned Collier was that the theatre was an affront to all people of all breeding. If they were to enjoy it, they would have to leave their better qualities at home, for people of breeding, he insists, have the same expectations of behaviour and conversation at the theatre as they do at home or anywhere else; and just as it is especially rude, as all the courtesy books point out, to use obscene words when talking to ladies, so it is especially offensive of the stage to put on indecent plays when it is known that ladies are in the audience. This equation leads readily to the pervasive notion that a woman reveals her experience of the world through her taste in plays, and Collier reveals some bafflement with it:

Whence comes it to pass that those Liberties which disoblige so much in Conversation, should entertain upon the Stage? Do the Women leave all the

---

[45] The most substantial work on the subject offers the least interesting account of it: Sister Rose Anthony, *The Jeremy Collier Stage Controversy, 1698–1726* (New York, 1937). Repercussions of the controversy are alluded to in Susannah Centlivre, Preface, *The Perjur'd Husband* (1700), and Thomas Brown, *Letters from the Dead to the Living* (London, 1704), 62, and discussed in *A Comparison Between the Two Stages*, p. 95, Krutch, pp. 72–81, and Loftis, *Comedy and Society*, pp. 45–59.

[46] Other reformers also defended the traditional rights of 'the ladies': see Josiah Woodward, *Some Thoughts Concerning the Stage in a Letter to a Lady* (London, 1704); Tutchin, *The Observator*, 13–17 Mar. 1703. Collier was not, unlike Prynne, a royal-hater; for his allegiance to James II rather than to William and Mary, see Thomas Durfey, Preface, *The Campaigners* (1698).

Regards to Decency and Conscience behind them when they come to the Playhouse? Or does the Place transform their Inclinations, and turn their former Aversions into Pleasure? Or were their Pretences to Sobriety elsewhere nothing but Hypocrisy and Grimace?[47]

The questions are ostensibly empty ones, raised only for what Collier reckons to be their absurdity, yet they are largely real ones which, on the whole, demand affirmative answers. It would not be pretentious, indeed, to suggest that what Collier is struggling with here is the idea of leisure. We have seen how the courtesy literature is a little shy of admitting the value of diversion as opposed to instruction in visits to the theatre, as reckoning reluctantly with the current habits of London life; and it has long been acknowledged that the Restoration period saw an acceleration in the significance of that part of London known as 'the Town', which was defined not so much by geographical location or by the nature of its business but by the opportunities it offered for leisure, or 'conspicuous consumption'.[48] It is precisely this phenomenon which causes Collier difficulty. 'Instruction' is unlikely to be the aim of people who go to the theatre to satisfy their craving for conspicuous leisure; what they seek is 'diversion', entertainment which takes them beyond the concerns of their daily lives. In such cases, Collier's 'former Aversions' might very well be turned into 'Pleasure' without exposing daily sobriety as 'nothing but Hypocrisy and Grimace'. This (to us) startlingly obvious conclusion evaded Collier as well as all those dramatists who contributed to the long-running debate about the place of bawdy humour in comedy; in that respect the regular equation of a woman's experience of drama and her moral status is a relic of outdated economic assumptions.

Among Collier's opponents only one dramatist grasped fully the degree to which *A Short View* misunderstood the female patrons of the stage. Charles Gildon's eminently sensible reply to Collier points out simply that plays to which he took exception were encouraged by unexceptionable women:

---

[47] *A Short View*, p. 7.
[48] See E. A. Wrigley, 'A Simple Model of London's Importance in Changing English Society and Economy, 1650-1750', *Past and Present*, 37 (1967), pp. 44-70; F. J. Fisher, 'The Development of London as a Centre of Conspicuous Consumption in the Sixteenth and Seventeenth Centuries', *Transactions of the Royal Historical Society*, 4th Series (1948), 37-50; Emrys Jones, 'The First West End Comedy', *Proceedings of the British Academy*, 68 (1982), 215-58; Lawrence Stone, 'The Residential Development of the West End of London in the Seventeenth Century', *After the Reformation*, ed. Barbara C. Malament (Manchester, 1980), 167-212.

with all the persons of the highest Quality, Virtue, and Learning of the other Sex, he has fix'd an Infamy ... on all Ladies of Honour, Piety, and Sense who remarkably encourag'd those very Plays he would render so monstrous. He must argue them guilty of want of *Honesty* or *Understanding* ...[49]

Precisely so. Were the honesty and understanding of Queen Mary in doubt because she twice saw *Amphitryon* and commanded a performance of *The Double Dealer*? Collier's political sympathies might have led him to conclude that they were, but then his own honesty and understanding would have been in doubt. The effect of Gildon's simple observation is to lend those outraged rhetorical questions of Collier's a tone of misogyny far stronger than anything in Wycherley. Any woman who enjoyed a play on Collier's extensive blacklist must, by his definition, have been of doubtful virtue; where Wycherley believed some theatre-going women to be hypocrites, Collier believed that a virtuous woman was a hypocrite the moment she entered a theatre, and in his inadvertent vilification of such women he slips easily into the characteristic Wycherlean vocabulary: 'hypocrisy', 'grimace', and 'aversion'. He had indeed, in Gildon's words, adopted 'a very awkward method' to 'insinuate himself with the ladies'.

In his sense of who 'the ladies' were, and what they expected of the theatre, this most important reformer was clearly wide of the mark; as wide, indeed, and for the same reasons, as J. H. Smith was in suggesting that their preference was for 'decency, sincerity, and honest love', rather than the more liberal diet described by Robert Hume. In his understanding of the problems faced by those women who conformed to his notional type of the lady, however, he was acute. Of the conspiring offence given by lewd dialogue, he writes,

They can't discover their Disgust without Disadvantage, nor Blush without Disservice to their Modesty. To appear with any Skill in such Cant, looks as if they had fallen upon ill conversation; or managed their Curiosity amiss.[50]

Of course, the conspiracy was sustained by Collier's own belief that theatre-going reflected private morality, but he was right to contend that a man who scrutinized the face of a conspicuous woman during a bawdy scene was bound, if he felt so inclined, to find something to her disadvantage. He was right, too, to contend that dramatists could themselves so conspire by offering *double entendres* which really permitted

---

[49] Charles Gildon, Preface, *Phaeton* (1698).
[50] *A Short View*, p. 8.

no ambiguity at all;[51] and he presents an account of the moral bias of certain comedies which anticipates precisely those changes chronicled by Smith and Hume. Collier was sufficiently acute as a critic to see that there was something wrong with comedy which could not be checked by the mere pruning of profanities which his *Short View* provoked; further, that what was a wrong was a rooted enmity to the interests of women.[52] Over this matter he agreed substantially with George Farquhar, the author of what is usually taken to be the first fully-fledged 'sentimental comedy'.[53] In his epilogue to that play, *The Constant Couple* (1699), Farquhar witnesses the obsolescence of the usual address of dramatist to ladies, and claims to have taken into account the women in the audience far more completely than any of his predecessors; although it is interesting to see how tenaciously he clings to old-style compliments:

> The Ladies Censure I'd almost forgot,
> Then for a Line or two t'engage their Vote:
> But that way's old, and below our Author's Aim,
> No less than his whole Play is Compliment to them.
> For their sakes then the Play can't miss succeeding,
> The Criticks may want Wit, they have good Breeding.
> They won't, I'm sure, forfeit the Ladies Graces,
> By showing their ill Nature to their Faces.

Farquhar's insistence on 'good breeding' and 'Graces' does something to diminish the force of the old equation, 'be civil to a lady and she will be civil to you', but the invitation to sexual commerce remains intact; even though he is plainly no less insistent that more should be done, beyond the usual bland assurances of the prologue, to cater for the interest of women. It is the whole play which must answer to their needs and forestall their censure. The notion of the faction persists with the language of compliment which betrays allegiance to the courtly outrage of Collier.

Agreement over the extent of what was needed to allow comedy to

---

[51] *A Short View*, p. 12: 'when the sentence has two Handles, the worst is generally turn'd to the Audience. The matter is so contriv'd that the Smut and Scum of the Thought rises uppermost.'

[52] For Collier 'On the Courtship of the Stage', *A Short View*, pp. 170-2. On 4 June 1697 and 18 Feb. 1698, the Lord Chamberlain ordered that all scurrilous and profane expressions be excluded from performances and printed texts (L.C. 5/152, p. 19). For the effects of Congreve's submission to the ruling, see Holland, pp. 125-37.

[53] For the significance of *The Constant Couple* and its success, see Hume, *The Development of English Drama*, p. 446; and Shirley Strum Kenny, 'Theatrical Warfare, 1695-1710', *Theatre Notebook*, 27 (1973), 130-45.

meet the wishes of the ladies was reached early on between the reformers of the stage and the stage's own reformers; argument over the nature of what was achieved has been diverse and largely informative. Particularly valuable have been J. H. Smith's extensive commentary on the reassigning of supremacy in the game of stage courtship and David S. Berkeley's ingenious tracing in the new comedy of themes and figures expressing female power from heroic tragedy.[54] Still, however, some crucial questions have been ignored. Why, for instance, was there this sudden concern with the interests of women? The idea of a powerful 'ladies' faction' is, we have seen, extremely dubious, so we must investigate other sources of pressure in order to make full sense of the new style in comedy. It should also be asked whether there was nothing more to the new comedy's representation of women than a reassigning of supremacy in the game of courtship: did this go with a genuine rethinking of values, or was it merely 'sentimental' in the sense of promoting an unreal vision of harmony between the sexes?

The answer to these questions lies initially in one feature of the intellectual environment of the late eighties and nineties which none of the existing accounts of the new comedy mentions, but which has long attracted the attention of historians of English women: the sudden arousal of interest in the position of woman in society. This is represented for us by a body of writing in books, newspapers, and magazines which reveals a range of cogent consideration of the problems faced by women, and it will be my contention that some of that cogency was imparted to the leaders in the field of so-called sentimental comedy. I do not pretend that 'women's writing' was the only effective influence upon the new form; nor do I seek to analyse others which have already been properly explained. I do intend to show, however, that such writing informed the stock scenes of popular comedy in the 1690s, finding understanding and consent among the audience, and giving the plays a strength and seriousness which other critics have refrained from allowing them. It is a strength which comes of a real attempt to create a comic style for 'the ladies', not through pressure from any cabal or faction, but through the responsiveness to new thinking which was being digested by a far wider public.

---

[54] David S. Berkeley, 'The Penitent Rake in Restoration Comedy', *Modern Philology*, 49 (1953), 223–31.

II

One rather dismaying fact about the 'women's writing' of the 1680s and 1690s had better be stated at once: little of its analysis of the position of women in society so much as alludes to their role as patrons of the theatre. One anonymous publication devotes a chapter to 'Diversions'—actual and recommended—among married couples, and going to the theatre does not appear in either category; the more conservative contributors to the published debate simply recommend that it should be avoided.[55] It was not generally the case, we know, that theatre-going was thought sufficiently wicked to be proscribed by the courtesy literature; what is implied by its absence from the new writing is that the playhouse was not regarded as a battleground where rights and privileges had to be fought for, but at most as an implicit adjunct to issues being pondered seriously elsewhere. Whatever Collier might say about the dire offence caused to women at the theatre, it seems that those who wrote about women's rights, many women among them, did not see the playhouse as something which seriously compromised the sex. That is one reason, too, why success or failure in the playhouse continued to depend on matters remote indeed from matters of political concern. Durfey found that his play, *The Richmond Heiress*, which shows a virtuous heiress triumphantly dismissing all pressure from basely-inclined relatives and suitors, failed less because of its content than for its undue length; if moral earnestness and approval were responsible for any of the 'general Applause' which parts of the play gained, they were severely taxed by little more than three hours' exercise.[56] Let that be a warning to anyone out to define too straightforwardly the interest of women in sentimental drama.

[55] *The Womens Advocate: or Fifteen Real Comforts of Matrimony, written by a Person of Quality of the Female Sex* (London, 1683), ch. 8. This is a complementary reply to *The XV Comforts of Rash and Inconsiderate Marriage, Done out of French* (London, 1683), which criticizes young couples for 'fancying nothing but Musick, Dancing, Balls and Plays, where the Variety of Female Objects fire the young Sparks'.

[56] Durfey, Preface, *The Richmond Heiress* (1693). The play was, he says, lengthened 'a little beyond the common Time of Action' by the insertion of a number of songs and dances, one of which, the 'Mad Song', Dryden found 'wonderfully diverting'; the rest, however, was 'woefull stuff, & concluded with Catcalls' (Dryden, *Letters*, pp. 52-3). The song he admired may be heard on Henry Purcell, *Theatre Music—Vol. V*. With Judith Nelson, Emma Kirkby, Martyn Hill, and David Thomas. Directed by Christopher Hogwood. The Academy of Ancient Music (London: DSLO 561, 1981). Hume and Scouten, '"Restoration Comedy" and its Audiences', p. 61, shows unique good sense in suggesting that 'the ladies' may not have considered the play sufficiently diverting or good to merit their lasting support.

However, the fact that the new writing did not take much account of the theatre naturally does not mean that the theatre did not take much account of the new writing and the issues which prompted it. As we have remarked, comedies of the 1690s dealt increasingly with the problems of the married rather than the 'gay' couple,[57] and this reflects a growing interest in the poverty of the institution among the books and journals which carried the debate over women's rights to the public. The poor reputation of marriage in the late seventeenth century has received some attention already; the debate of the late 1680s and 1690s involved a marked diversification of approaches to it, from the religious and ethical to the legal and political.[58] The somewhat desperate intensity of argument is reflected in the prophetic tone of some of the contributors. Mary Manley claimed that consummation was often achieved only because it was legally required, and that future generations would suffer as a result, the offspring of such unions being 'void of generous Fire, of that Sparkling Genius, the product of free-born Love' (an old idea pressed into service in difficult times);[59] and one anonymous projector, similarly dismayed, argued that all men should be legally bound to marry at twenty-one, when they were most fit for the production of vigorous children. Such an arrangement, the author protests, would strengthen the arts and industry, and promote godliness and sobriety.[60]

The intensity and variety of the debate were not only the effects of long sufferance. In one respect they were the fruit of the major constitutional measure of the later years of the century, the passing of the Bill of Rights in 1689, which set out for the first time the basic rights of the subject and his elected representatives in relation to the monarch.[61] As we have seen, the ideas embodied in the Bill had great significance for observers of the theatre from the 1680s onwards; they defined the audience's rights of approval or disapproval, and in doing so cast 'the ladies' in the role of benign outsiders to the critical democracy of the playhouse. If such ideas

---

[57] Scouten, 'Notes Towards a History of Restoration Comedy'; Smith, *The Gay Couple*; and Gellert Spencer Alleman, *Matrimonial Law and the Materials of Restoration Comedy* (Wallingford, Philadelphia, 1942).

[58] See e.g. *The Case of Clandestine Marriages* (London, 1691); *A Representation of the Prejudices that may arise in Time from an Intended Act, concerning Matrimony* (London, 1692); Mary Astell, *Some Reflections upon Marriage* (London, 1696).

[59] Mary Manley, *The New Atlantis* (London, 1704), 27.

[60] *Marriage Promoted in a Discourse* (London, 1693), 30. A similar analysis may be found in *Female Grievances Debated* (London, 1707).

[61] An account of its terms may be found in David Ogg, *England in the Reigns of James II and William III*, 3rd edn. (Oxford and New York, 1984), 241-5.

were to have their impact on the women who attended the theatre, they were certainly to charge the indignation of many others who probably did not. 'If mere Power gives a Right to Rule,' wrote Mary Astell, 'there can be no such thing as Usurpation ... Again, if Absolute Sovereignty be not necessary in a State, how comes it to be so in a family?'[62] Not only did the terms of the Bill give a charge to indignation; they lent the indignant the vocabulary with which to argue. It is interesting to see this constitutional terminology being used in what otherwise was a fairly casual publication, *The Gentleman's Journal*, a paper for the salon and the coffee-house. The autumn editions of 1693 carry a series of versified correspondence on the subject of marriage from people calling themselves Orithya, Placidia, and Urania; the editor hands them to his readers with a complete assurance of their being grasped and pondered without prejudicial comment from him, and what follows is an often strongly reasoned discussion (perhaps from the editor's own pen) of personal experience and general principle. Constitutional vocabulary is adopted from the first. Orithya begins by lamenting the futility of marriage for women:

> Nature to us strong charms and freedom gave;
> What free-born woman then would be a slave?
> Yet we, fond fools, give our birth-rights away,
> Stoop to the yoke, and a blind homage pay.[63]

Placidia counters by arguing, more tamely but in accordance with legal precedent, that 'Women are Subjects born', that they must surrender all rights first to their parents and then to their husbands; the only freedom should be in choosing their man, and here Placidia adopts the language of heroic tragedy:

> What greater Glory can a Virgin have,
> Than to make him a King, who was her Slave?[64]

The felicity of having such a choice was, Orithya replies, peculiar to only a few women such as Placidia; in general, she continues, if parents choose 'a Fool, or Sot' for the sake of 'Int'rest', 'We must submit, nor must the Yoke refuse',[65] (even Hannah Woolley, who was in some respects a liberal defender of women, believed that a girl had no right to disobey her parents

---

[62] Astell, *Some Reflections upon Marriage*, p. 31. The popularity of the book is witnessed by the appearance of a third edn. in 1706, ten years after the first.

[63] *The Gentleman's Journal*, Oct. 1693, p. 343. There was a recent precedent for this kind of debate, called *The Triumphs of Female Wit in Some Pindarick Odes* (London, 1683).

[64] *The Gentleman's Journal*, Nov. 1693, pp. 368–9.

[65] *The Gentleman's Journal*, Dec. 1693, p. 405.

in any matter, least of all that of marriage[66]). The third correspondent, Urania, now enters the field in support of Orithya, declaring that man's ignorance of woman's rights within marriage was so widespread that many women would sooner remain single than 'herd among the servile Drove' who married for the sake of obedience or economic security.[67]

It is easy to laugh at the Platonic affectations of this correspondence, but it does at least indicate that concern about the effects of marriage on the liberty of women extended far beyond the works of radical thinkers such as Mary Astell. The matter crops up again in *The Gentleman's Journal*, in the form of articles about the equality of the sexes and the tyranny of social custom in enforcing male supremacy and preventing men and women from understanding the real iniquity of their relative positions in society and marriage;[68] it figures in works sponsored by the journalist and publisher, John Dunton;[69] as well as in a number of occasional poems, books, and pamphlets.[70] The subject of women's rights was becoming a popular, perhaps a fashionable one, and through the variety of approaches it attracted and the range of vocabulary it adopted and developed, it was fast becoming a science.

The theatre was well placed to take advantage of its currency. Political terminology already figured significantly in the way poets described and entertained the female audience in prologues and epilogues, while current anxieties about the schooling and general upbringing of girls inform the

[66] Woolley, *The Gentlewoman's Companion*, p. 24.

[67] *The Gentleman's Journal*, Dec. 1693, p. 406. H. J. Habakkuk, 'Marriage Settlements in the Eighteenth Century', in *Transactions of the Royal Historical Society*, 4th Series, 32 (1950), 15–30, notes in the last two decades of the seventeenth century 'an increasing subordination of marriage to the increase of landed wealth, at the expense of other motives for marriage' (p. 17).

[68] *The Gentleman's Journal*, Oct. 1693, pp. 340–3. The same edition carries a poem on female constancy, an article on modesty, and one entitled, 'That Women may apply themselves to Liberal Arts and Sciences'. Motteux's article, 'On the Equality of the Sexes' (p. 341) owes much to A. L., *The Woman as Good as the Man, or the Equality of Both Sexes* (London, 1677), from Poulain de la Barre, *De L'Égalite des Deux Sexes* (Paris, 1673). The debate continued into some edns. of 1694.

[69] *The Athenian Mercury*, 4 Nov. 1693. John Dunton's *The Ladies Dictionary* (London, 1694), like the *Mercury*, provides some radical moral counselling as well as 'Love Secrets' and 'Characters' of women and their admirers. The intimacy of the newspaper in these matters led to its suppression in 1692: see John Dunton, *The Life and Errors of John Dunton* (London, 1705), 258.

[70] See Lady Chudleigh, *The Ladies Defence* (London, 1699); *The Fair Counsellor, or The Young Lady's Guide after Marriage* (London, 1699); *An Essay in Defence of the Female Sex* (London, 1696); Daniel Defoe, *An Essay on Projects* (London, 1697); William Walsh, *A Dialogue Concerning Women, Being a Defence of the Sex* (London, 1691).

stock scenes of fathers discussing their daughters' education. The extracts from *The Gentleman's Journal* shown above indicate some allegiance between the terms of the new debate and those of heroic tragedy. The work of J. H. Smith shows conclusively, moreover, that the evolution of the 'gay couple' in comedy supplied the theatre audience with a highly individual and extensive notation for discussing the relationship between the sexes.[71] The materials were there, in short, to be extended and deepened by the recent acceleration of thought about the position of women in marriage and society; there for the audience to focus its understanding of the issues involved, and to cultivate a critical vocabulary commensurate with contemporary thinking.

How dramatists of the 1690s took account of this thinking, and with what success, we must now consider. Some terms of reference should be established first. No purpose would be served by attempting to 'key' plays and scenes to particular aspects of the wider public debate about women as it appeared in print; as the previous paragraph has indicated, the theatre made its own contribution to understanding by adapting its special traditions to new currents of thought. It is, in any case, in the nature of any such controversy that the printed texts form only a fraction of public debate, and that similar arguments and phrases are repeated endlessly; in such circumstances, the topicality of a lively nod towards the subject of debate is not necessarily diminished by a failure to discover its precise direction. Nor is it necessary to offer a broad survey of 'types' after the fashion, for example, of Robert Hume; it will be more productive to examine in detail three individual plays, two of which did well at the box-office and one which did not. Consideration of the ways in which these plays addressed themselves to the audience and its different expectations will gauge the importance of women and their interests among the theatre-goers of the nineties. It may then be clear what, precisely, their authors had in mind when they claimed to be speaking for and to 'the ladies'.

We shall start with the popular failure, Thomas Southerne's *The Wives Excuse* of 1691. Since its rescue from critical neglect by J. H. Smith, the

---

[71] For the fine discrimination of tragedy and romance, Paul Salzman, *English Prose Fiction, 1558-1700* (Oxford, 1985), 171-95; for those made in response by one reader, Dorothy Osborne, *Letters of Lady Dorothy Osborne to Sir William Temple*, ed. Herbert Parry (London, 1888), 39. Heroic tragedy could offer its own *éducation sentimentale*: Kathleen M. Lynch, 'Conventions of Platonic Drama in the Heroic Plays of Orrery and Dryden', *PMLA* 44 (1929), 456-71; Scott C. Osborn, 'Heroical Love in Dryden's Heroic Drama', *PMLA* 73 (1958), 480-90; and Jean Gagen, 'Love and Honour in Dryden's Heroic Plays', *PMLA* 77 (1962), 208-20.

play has come to be recognized by most specialists in Restoration Comedy as one of the major achievements of the form.[72] We do not know how long its first (and very probably its only) production lasted, but we do know that it was an immediate failure. There is substantial documentary evidence of the reasons why. First witness is Dryden, who was sufficiently impressed by the play to write a poem in praise of it.[73] He found it worthy of comparison, for complexity of plotting and purity of diction, with the comedies of Terence; praised Southerne's moral understanding of lewdness, and consoled him for the play's failure with the public by declaring that it would win fame among readers rather than 'Hearers', who, he said, had felt the lack of a good comic role for an actor such as James Nokes. Dryden, weary of the stage, was no doubt eager to give high status to any play more suited to the salon than the theatre;[74] but Southerne clearly had no such honour in mind when he offered the play to the United Company. His previous comedy, *Sir Anthony Love*, had been a great success, and all the prominent actors had substantial roles in the new play, including Betterton, Barry, Bracegirdle, and Mountfort; as Peter Holland has shown, the distribution of parts cunningly exploited the actors' conventional 'lines' no less than their popular reputations.[75] The Company wanted—or believed it had got—a play in which its different talents could be shown in an unusually favourable light. Moreover, the piece reveals a mastery of dialogue for which Southerne was famous in his own day; as one commentator put it, 'there's a Spirit of Conversation in everything he writes'.[76]

---

[72] Smith, *The Gay Couple*, pp. 144–8, ranks it among the five best comedies of the age. His enthusiasm is shared by Hume, *The Development of English Drama*, pp. 364–5; Scouten, 'Notes Towards a History'; Holland, *The Ornament of Action*, p. 187; and James Sutherland, *English Literature of the Late Seventeenth Century* (Oxford, 1969), 145. There is also a sympathetic article by Anthony Kaufman, '"This Hard Condition of A Woman's Fate": Southerne's *The Wives Excuse*', in *Modern Language Quarterly*, 34 (1973), 36–47. Earlier commentators are dismissive: 'not a very good play', says Nicoll, p. 228; 'a drearier round of cuckolding and wenching would be hard to find', says John Wendell Dodds in his *Thomas Southerne, Dramatist* (New Haven, 1933) 104.

[73] Dryden, 'To Mr. Southern; on his Comedy, called the *Wives Excuse*', in *Poems and Fables*, p. 464.

[74] His Preface to *Don Sebastian* (1690) complains that the 'Humours of Comedy are spent', and that he is 'still condemn'd to dig in those exhausted Mines'.

[75] Holland, *The Ornament of Action*, pp. 187–90.

[76] *A Comparison Between the Two Stages*, p. 19. Kaufman comments further. It soon became a cliché of Southerne criticism: see *The Gentleman's Journal*, Jan. 1693, p. 28 on Southerne's next play, *The Maid's Last Prayer*, and Thomas Evans, 'An Account of his Life and Writings', in *The Plays of Thomas Southerne*, ed. Evans, 2 vols. (London, 1774), i. 9–10.

It does not seem enough to cite the play's alleged untheatricality as a reason for its failure. Modern critics have opted instead for the view that its satire was too keen for a sensitive audience;[77] the author himself observed that the music-meeting shown in the first act, introduced, Southerne says, 'as a fashionable scene of bringing good company together', was thought merely to abuse 'what everybody likes'.[78] A reading of the scene today suggests that the audience was right to find it unpleasant;[79] and it seems to have been part of Southerne's plan from the first to please 'the more reasonable part of mankind' by showing up the unreasonable. The reasonable ones were 'the ladies'. Wellvile, Southerne's representative in the play, explains:

I have a Design upon a Play ... I am scandaliz'd extremely to see the Women upon the Stage make Cuckolds at that insatiable Rate they do in our modern Comedies; without any other Reason from the Poets, but, because a Man is married he must be a Cuckold: now, Sir, I think the Women are most unconscionably injur'd by this general Scandal upon their Sex; therefore to do 'em what Service I can in their Vindication I design to write a Play, and call it ... *The Wives Excuse: or, Cuckolds make themselves*.[80]

His companions, Friendall and Wilding, remark that such a play was likely to be 'popular among the women' and 'true among the men'; vindication of the one party was to be achieved by pointed satire against the other. Such forthright intentions lend an air of seriousness to the raillery of the prologue: the 'gallants' are urged to make up for the stage's likely want of wit with their 'she-neighbours in the pit,' for, after all, jokes Southerne,

> On the Stage whate'er we do, or say,
> The Vizard-Masks can find you better Play.

[77] Hume, *The Development of English Drama*, p. 387, describes it as an 'angry, ugly, and effective' satire. The author of *A Comparison* noted that Southerne's 'acquaintance with the best Company entered him into the secrets of their Intrigues, and no Man knew better the Way and Disposition of Mankind' (p. 19).

[78] Southerne, 'To the Right Honourable Thomas Wharton', *The Wives Excuse*.

[79] *The Wives Excuse*, I. ii. I quote from the first edn of 1692; the play is now available in *The Works of Thomas Southerne*, ed. Robert Jordan and Harold Love, 2 vols. (Oxford, 1987). The scene is an extremely skilful representation of a large party of fashionable people disguising lewd intentions with polite conversation; in its management of 'cross-talk' and movement around the stage it has no peer in Restoration Drama. Southerne can hardly have been ingenuous in claiming to have been hurt by criticism of the scene; he shared his opinion of the music-meeting with the bluff Mrs Teazall in the fifth act of the play: 'Your Musick-Meetings ... are all but pretences to bring you together: And when you meet, we know what you meet for well enough.'   [80] *The Wives Excuse*, III. ii.

This complacency was no good-humoured invention of the poet's; it was a force to be reckoned with and, in this case, flattered. The title of the new play was *The Wives Excuse: or, Cuckolds make themselves*; it sported a prologue with exhortations to sexual commerce; and that prologue was spoken by an actor famous for his portrayals of libido untrammelled, Thomas Betterton.[81] The play can have promised little to the less reasonable part of mankind but two hours' traffic of complete sexual licence; and it appears to have been part of Southerne's intention not to disappoint them, while showing at the same time to 'the ladies' that their interest had been accounted for too. Referring in the dedication to the treacherous Mrs Witwoud and the virtuous Mrs Friendall (the wife of the title of the play), he laments that the former 'was no more understood to the advantage of the man, than the Wife was receiv'd in favour of the women'.

The element of satire in the play which was to be directed against the so-called gallants' party was to be apparent to the ladies, for it was to vindicate them, and be invisible (or unimportant) to the men; it was hoped that they might be bought off with characters who flattered them sufficiently to divert attention from the vindication of female virtue which lies at the centre of the play. In that respect *The Wives Excuse*, like *Love's Last Shift*, was designed as a 'mixed' play, not because it had both a comic and a 'serious' plot, but because it opportunistically attempted to satisfy the wishes of opposing interests in the audience. Paul E. Parnell has shown how, in Cibber's play, 'both Restoration trickery and virtuous sentiment prevail', representing a victory for both sides, and he celebrates Cibber as 'the most suave and devious of literary entrepreneurs'.[82] *The Wives Excuse* certainly makes an attempt upon devious impartiality, but its very failure at the box-office may be enough to indicate that its author fell short of Cibber in achieving it; and if we examine the events which produce the climax of the play it should be clear how far Southerne's conviction that 'the ladies' should be vindicated exceeded his business sense.

The plot, as Wellvile has partly informed us, concerns a fine young woman who has for three months been married to a cowardly, good-for-nothing coxcomb. It has taken no longer for the husband, Friendall, to announce to half the young men in town that he is bored with marriage

---

[81] For Betterton's line in comic roles, from the 'rake hero' in plays such as *The Man of Mode* and *Epsom Wells* to 'darker roles' such as Don John, Maskwell, and Fainall, see Holland, pp. 80–1.

[82] Parnell, 'Equivocation in Cibber's *Love's Last Shift*', pp. 522 and 530.

and might not care particularly if his wife received attentions from them. Lovemore takes up the offer, and he preys upon Mrs Friendall's knowledge of her husband's weakness, plotting to expose it fully to her and to the town. She, however, remains sufficiently composed to rescue her husband from the insults duly practised upon him, and she continues to the last to resist Lovemore's advances and her own ill opinion of her husband. Eventually Friendall is revealed, by a parting of the scenes at the evening masquerade in the fifth act, *in flagrante delicto* with a woman he has mistaken for someone else. The central question of the play is thereby raised with renewed clarity: what chance has Lovemore now with the comprehensively disabused Mrs Friendall? She can, it seems, no longer pretend; more a victim than anyone of her husband's exposure, how can she continue to resist her suitor? Husband and wife agree to part but remain married in name, and they pursue a grim and casual parody of the familiar proviso scene (here the provisos are laid down for their separation) before Mrs Friendall concludes, 'I must be still your Wife, and still Unhappy'; the only option open to her by law.[83] It appears that no one can claim victory.

None the less, we are left with Lovemore, conscious of the uncertainty of his position, but flattering himself that he has at least improved it. It is to him that we turn, moreover, for the last lines of the play, and what appears to be the moral of the piece:

> This must you all expect, who marry Fools;
> Unless you form 'em early in your Schools,
> And make 'em, what they were design'd for, Tools.[84]

The effect is disconcerting if we come to these lines, as Southerne undoubtedly did, in the knowledge of Molière's *L'École des maris*, whose last couplet runs as follows:

> Vous, si vous connaissez des maris loup-garous,
> Envoyez-les au moins a l'école chez nous.[85]

Molière assigned his lines to the sensible and disinterested maid, Lisette, while Southerne's go to a man who is very obviously neither of those things; Lovemore has far too much at stake to offer a useful reflection on

---

[83] Alleman, *Matrimonial Law and the Materials of Restoration Comedy*, pp. 17-35, has shown how many comedies of the period engineer happy endings by legal agreements which would have been impossible in real life: *The Virtuoso*, *Sir Courtly Nice*, *The Beaux Strategem* and Southerne's own *Sir Anthony Love* among them.

[84] *The Wives Excuse*, v. v.

[85] *L'École des maris*, III. ix. 1113-14, Œuvres Completes, i. 399.

the subject of the play. He is there to claim victory, to persuade those who might be expected to identify with him that it is they who have been vindicated, and not the wife and her party. The appeal to the baser instincts is scarcely veiled; within Lovemore's proposal that husbands should be used as 'tools', as a means of procuring lovers, lies the kind of *double entendre* favoured by a more celebrated literary wife, of Bath, who needed no excuses. Such is the immediate appeal of bawdy that it scarcely matters that the joke is gained from a suggestion which is contrary to Lovemore's interest. The device was employed with a full consciousness of its likely effect; it is, to make use of a famous analogy, the bit of meat thrown to the dog to keep it quiet. Only in that respect was it what John Wendell Dodds called it: a feeble crack to save a dying evening.[86]

There is, however, an inadvertent accuracy in Lovemore's summary of the action, one which shows both that Southerne was interested in achieving more than the entrepreneurial impartiality of *Love's Last Shift*, and that he was really capable of the psychological depth for which James Sutherland has praised him.[87] Lovemore's words do offer an acute comment on Mrs Friendall's behaviour, the import of which has certainly not eluded him in the course of the play, but which he now can scarcely begin to appreciate: the wife has all along been using her husband as a tool, not to procure herself lovers, but to defend herself from them. She cares no more for him in the latter capacity than she would in the former. It is not only submission to law which makes her say, after the final exposure of her husband, 'I must be still your Wife, and still Unhappy'; it is her victory after the fashion of the virtuous wife, a familiar figure in the first attempts at 'sentimental comedy'.[88] There should be confusion here only if we have attended to the action as Lovemore and his supposed party have attended to it. They assume that the final unmasking of Friendall must invalidate all his wife's resistance to her suitor; what it really does is to vindicate it. Lovemore has the last word only in the literal sense. What we might expect of Mrs Friendall at this moment is a sudden invasion of insecurity; what we get is the moment of greatest security. Separated from her husband at the end of the play, she loses her defence against lovers, but she also forfeits any excuse she might have for countenancing them. This

---

[86] Dodds, *Thomas Southerne, Dramatist*, p. 106.

[87] Sutherland, p. 145.

[88] For a discussion of the virtuous wife in comedy, see Kathleen M. Lynch, 'Thomas D'Urfey's Contribution to Sentimental Comedy', in *Philological Quarterly*, 9 (1930) 249–59; and DeWitt C. Croissant, 'Early Sentimental Comedy', in *The Parrott Presentation Volume* (Princeton, NJ, 1935), 47–71.

is the most that Mrs Friendall can achieve in a world where marriage and adultery are equally unsatisfactory; a state of half-marriage in which she can be true to herself and her husband without having to put up with his company. The inconclusiveness of this frustrated, half-achieved state is implicit in the half-fulfilled promise of the title of the play: the wife excuses herself, the cuckold makes himself, but the one needs excusing no more than the other is actually made a cuckold. Mrs Friendall's victory is a bitterly equivocal one.

If we examine her case in terms of what the female audience was generally held to admire in stage women, it is clear that she must have presented great problems to those people whom Southerne intended to please most. The epilogue of the play is particularly useful in revealing the different ways in which Mrs Friendall was thought likely to be regarded by her first audience. It was Elizabeth Barry, in the title role, who spoke it:

> Our Author has his Ends, if he can show,
> The Women ne'er want Cause for what they do:
> For, Ladies, all his Aim is pleasing you.
> Some mettled Sparks, whom nothing can withstand,
> Your Velvet-Fortune-Hunters, may demand,
> Why, when the means were in the Lady's Hand,
> The Husband civil, and the Lover near,
> No more was made of the Wife's Character?
> Damn men, cries one, had I been Betterton,
> And struts, and cocks, I know what I had done;
> She should not ha'got clear of me so soon.
> You only fear such Plays may spoil your Game.

Character and actor step forward in justification of the play, which is to say the central part;[89] it is plain from the reference to 'Betterton' rather than his role that the actor was identified with the role and the two together with the aspirations (and, no doubt, fantasies) of certain members of the audience.[90] The 'Velvet-Fortune-Hunters' could not support failure in a Lovemore, but felt themselves scorned, their virile attractions slighted as his had been. Their conception of 'character', in so far as it dealt with Mrs Friendall, seems to have depended on the amount of sexual energy

[89] In the prologue to *Love's Last Shift*, Cibber urges the ladies to be kind to the play 'for *Amanda's* sake'; as so often, women were expected to applaud qualities in a stage character which they would expect to own (or be thought to own) themselves.

[90] S. C., *The Art of Complaisance*, pp. 64-5, writes of young men going to the theatre, intoxicated by its representation of 'compleat gentlemen', and wanting to follow the example set by rake-heroes who whored and drank.

expended rather than on any criteria of consistency or variety: she might have been an interesting character, more might have been made of her, had she gone to bed with Lovemore. As it is, her example is to be feared in so far as it might be followed. Already it is clear that the 'exemplary' qualities of the play are designed to be more than placid reflections of the virtues of self-adoring fine ladies in the audience. They are to enlighten and equip.

If fullness of character meant sexual energy to the young male audience, Southern wanted it to mean something more inward and rational to the female. 'No more' was made of the wife's character because he wanted to please by explanation and justification rather than by action; to show the causes of action rather than the thing itself. The range of Mrs Friendall's active power within the play, her power over her own fate, is, we have seen, as depressingly limited as that of most of her intended supporters. She stands in marked contrast to the heroines of two plays by Southerne which received loud applause from women, *Sir Anthony Love* and *Oroonoko*.[91] Both of these plays, significantly, are set abroad, *Sir Anthony Love* in France and *Oroonoko* in Surinam; removed from the claustrophobic meetings and visits of London, Lucia (*Sir Anthony*) and the Welldons are free to pursue their fortunes and their men as energetically as they please. In *The Wives Excuse* the appeal to 'the ladies' was decidedly unconventional; there is little of exaltation, and much of earnest assistance. They become objects of compassionate consideration, not simply the bright originals of Southerne's study. The moral interests of the virtuous heroine and her female advocates had always been assumed to be identical; in this play Southerne insists on close circumstantial identification as well, in order that the experience of the virtuous wife might provide her hoped-for supporters not only with a renewed sense of moral dignity but also with the means of rationalizing their actions independently of the insinuations of men.

Nowhere is this more clear than in the encounter of Mrs Friendall and her admirer in the third act of the play.[92] A long and central confrontation of female virtue with rakish insouciance, the scene takes its place in the tradition of transformation scenes identified by David S. Berkeley, but as a wry criticism of it.[93] Here there is plainly no possibility of a transformation

---

[91] *A Comparison Between the Two Stages*, p. 19, describes *Oroonoko* as 'the Favourite of the Ladies'; *The Gentleman's Journal*, Jan. 1691/2, pp. 51–2, says that *Sir Anthony Love* was 'lik'd so well' by the Town and the Ladies.

[92] *The Wives Excuse*, III. iii.

[93] Berkeley, 'The Penitent Rake'.

in the hero; Lovemore emerges as a stupid braggart, incapable of dealing
with Mrs Friendall's contempt except by muttering the banalities of his
profession. Asked what encouragement he has received from her that he
treats her thus, he can only reply, 'A Lover makes his Hopes'—a fine
miniature of his drab rakish outlook. The wife answers her own question
more effectively by drawing attention to the dangerous conventionality of
her suitor's behaviour; here the intimate psychological struggle which
commentators have admired in the play is turned outwards in a rhetorical
contribution to current matters of debate:

Perhaps 'tis from the general encouragement of being a marry'd woman,
supported on your side by that honourable opinion of our sex, that because some
women abuse their husbands, every woman may. I grant you indeed, the custom
of England has been very prevailing in that point.

This is not the struggle of the heroine of Lee's *The Princesse of Cleve* (a play
whose grim inconclusiveness, however, closely resembles that of *The
Wives Excuse*[94]), torn between duty and desire; here the attractions of the
suitor are dismissed a little too easily.[95] Mrs Friendall's difficulty is to
credit her own integrity in a world mindlessly enslaved to doubting it. As
she puts it, 'how have I behav'd myself? What have I done to deserve this?'
The honesty of Southerne's registration of the problem keeps Lovemore
from understanding what the fuss is about; he remains convinced to the
last of his entitlement to his prize.[96] Relentless in its exposure of the
idiocies of certain men, the failings of marriage, and the want of any
commendable solution to women's experience of them, the play must
have been both galling to gallants and depressing for women. At the end of
the play both wife and suitor have some claim to be vindicated, so
anticipating what Parnell has called the businesslike equivocation of *Love's
Last Shift*, but it is clear that the claims of the one are as brash as the victory
of the other is without reward. Neither party could have been satisfied.

---

[94] Discussion of the 'darker elements' of the two plays may be found in Hume, 'Nat.
Lee's *The Princess of Cleve* ', in *The Rakish Stage*, pp. 82–106; Holland, *The Ornament of Action*,
p. 144, discusses the pairing of Betterton and Barry as the conflicting lover and wife in both
plays.

[95] Mrs Friendall exclaims ironically in III. iii, 'Who would not stay to see her
Worshipper upon his knees, thus prais'd, and thus ador'd? . . . Mr Lovemore, you might
have known me better, than to imagine your Flattery could softly sing me into a Consent to
Anything my Virtue had abhorr'd.' This kind of rhetoric belongs to the tradition of the
sentimental virtuous heroine; what elevates the play above that tradition is its analysis of
the involuntary assumptions which underlie flattery and praise.

[96] *The Wives Excuse*, v, v.: 'What Alteration this may make in my Fortune with her, I
don't know, but I'm glad I've parted them.'

It would be tempting to argue that *The Wives Excuse* was ahead of its time. It should have appealed, as Dryden remarked, to the female audience—its language was clean, its recognition of licence profoundly moral, and its heroine nobly resistant—yet little of it seems to have been even understood by those whom it was designed to please. Mrs Friendall was not, as her creator said, received in favour of the women. Even so, Southerne's concern to show how women could be compromised by a more than merely personal disrespect was continuous with the interests of some of his contemporaries in the status of women in society;[97] so it may be that it was simply his fate to find a medium for it which was guaranteed to produce the maximum of inconclusiveness. With this in mind, it is possible to find in the frustrated captivity of the central character the playwright's own frustrations with the dramatic form to which he had committed himself. The disastrous misjudgement of the play by Dodds has an inadvertent accuracy which says a little more about the real distinctiveness of *The Wives Excuse* than James Sutherland's enthusiastic praise. Sutherland describes the play as putting 'the whole business of cuckolding on a psychological basis', which suggests that Southerne felt at home with the medium of the cuckolding plot and wanted to delve beneath its usually boisterous surface (the title of the play implied no less); whereas Dodds, in lamenting the 'dreary round of cuckolding and wenching', gives us something of Southerne's unease with his material.[98] The resolution of *The Wives Excuse* is dreary and inconclusive by the standards of the conventional structure which Southerne adopted, but it is precisely the discrepancy between the medium and the way the dramatist wished to fashion it that makes the play so interesting and, in its distinctive way, so intense. Here, in a comedy about the wrongs done to women, author and protagonist share the frustration of received forms and ideas to produce a dead-end of conflict which we may now pronounce, with a confidence which its first audience could not summon, to be the point of the play. In no other Restoration play, with the possible exception of Wycherley's *The Plain Dealer*, is such power generated by the very risk of artistic failure.

The Wives Excuse shows a playwright consciously addressing himself to 'the ladies' through a larger consideration of their position in society,

---

[97] Even Tate, in his Preface to *A Present for the Ladies*, has two pages on the 'hard Fortune of Ladies' who 'create Enemies by their Repulses' having already been insulted by unlooked-for advances. For similar thoughts more comprehensively explored, see Astell, *A Serious Proposal*, pp. 81–4.

[98] Sutherland, p. 145; Dodds, p. 98.

confident of being understood and supported, and failing because he chose a medium which proved unsympathetic to his thinking. The two plays I shall examine next, Cibber's *Love's Last Shift* and Farquhar's *The Constant Couple*, were considerable successes to which modern critics have not on the whole been kind, and I intend to show that their success had much to do with the way they both solve the problem which had defeated Southerne: that of finding the right medium in which to convey the new concern about women's status which confronted the literate Londoner in books, journals, and newspapers.

We have as much documentation of the success of *Love's Last Shift* as we have of the failure of *The Wives Excuse*, and it is now generally agreed that its popularity was the result less of the rapture caused by the transformation of Loveless in the fifth act than of Cibber's shrewd business sense: 'Cibber was trying to provide something for everybody in this potpourri,' as Robert Hume has put it.[99] That being agreed, it is perhaps not surprising that no one who has sought to explain Cibber's triumph with this, his first play, has attempted (or dared) to suggest that it reflects with much credit on the intelligence of its supporters. Nicoll charged the play and its famous conversion scene with superficiality and even hypocrisy, and no one has really challenged him.[100] Inflation and mediocrity of expression, and thinness of characterization there may be, but the play as a whole and the conversion scene in particular ponder matters quite as serious as those explored in *The Wives Excuse*; it is clear that *Love's Last Shift* was designed to engage the minds and not just the sensibilities of its female audience.

Crucial differences between it and Southerne's play immediately

[99] Hume, *The Development of English Drama*, p. 412, taking up the detailed account given by Paul E. Parnell; Sullivan, too, follows Parnell's lead, xvii–xix. Earlier criticism is heavily indebted to Thomas Davies's description of the effect of the conversion scene upon its first audience, in *Dramatic Miscellanies*, 3 vols. (London, 1759) III. 504: 'The joy of unexpected reconcilement, from Loveless's remorse and penitence, spread such an uncommon rapture of pleasure in the audience, that never were spectators more happy in easing their minds by uncommon and repeated plaudits.' For accounts of the play influenced by this, treating it as the first sentimental comedy, see Ernest Bernbaum, *The Drama of Sensibility* (Cambridge, Mass., 1915); DeWitt C. Croissant, 'Studies in the Work of Colley Cibber', *Bulletin of the University of Kansas Humanistic Studies*, I (1912) 1–69; J. W. Krutch, *Comedy and Conscience*, pp. 202–4; and Richard Hindry Barker, *Mr Cibber of Drury Lane* (New York, 1939), 20–9. Lynch, 'Thomas D'Urfey's Contribution to Sentimental Comedy', challenges the view that Cibber's play was the first sentimental comedy; Arthur Sherbo, *English Sentimental Drama* (New Haven, 1957), pp. 99–102, argues that it is not 'sentimental' at all.

[100] Nicoll, p. 266. Sherbo, p. 100, thinks the conversion scene a parody of the excesses of heroic tragedy; this takes Davies too lightly.

become apparent if we accept Cibber's invitation, in his prologue, to be kind to him 'for Amanda's sake'. Amanda is a virtuous wife who has been abandoned somewhat more comprehensively than Mrs Friendall; her husband, Loveless, left her ten years before the first events of the play for the pleasures of the single life, and she has remained faithful to his memory, believing him dead. Upon hearing of his return to London, however, she plans to make love to him *incognito*, and eventually inspires him with her beauty, virtue, and money to reform his ways. It is clear that the hardship she suffers at the beginning of the play is, compared with that of Mrs Friendall, one which her audience could contemplate with a certain emotional luxuriance, in spite of its tragic pretensions. She is definitely not someone with whom the female audience could have been expected to identify in the full circumstantial sense demanded by Southerne in offering them Mrs Friendall. She belongs in fashionable London, but her social and economic circumstances give her more power and self-determination than any of her supporters could have wished for: her husband having been absent for so long, he is presumed dead, and she has a settlement of two thousand pounds placed with her by a recently deceased uncle.[101] She is as well-placed as any woman could be in a comedy about life in the world inhabited by her audience. The dialogue at once labours the point and seeks to diminish its significance to an admirable woman like Amanda. 'Methinks the Death of a Rich Old Uncle shou'd be a Cordial to your Spirits,' announces her companion, Hillaria; 'That adds to 'em,' returns Amanda, 'for he was the only Relation I had left, and was as tender of me, as the nearest!' Hillaria will have none of it: 'He was better than some Fathers to you; for he dyed, just when you had occasion for his Estate.' This is dramatic manipulation after the fashion of a modern soap-opera; the women in the audience must simply have been coerced into admiring Amanda because her economic advantages were so conspicuously enviable, yet so openly disdained. Other things are more important to Cibber's heroine: 'All the Comfort of my Life is, that I can tell my Conscience, I have been true to Virtue.'[102]

Nevertheless (and this may be a further symptom of Cibber's entre-preneurial sense), the high-spirited Hillaria gains partial consent through laughter, and allows room at this stage for attitudes which would be unseemly in Amanda herself; the end of the play, as we shall see, shows the heroine attaching greater value to her independence than this first scene

---

[101] See Antonia Fraser, *The Weaker Vessel: Women's Lot in Seventeenth-Century England* (London, 1984), 81–99, on the benefits of widowhood at this time.

[102] *Love's Last Shift*, II, i.

suggests, so Hillaria's case is by no means dismissed. Cibber would not have been the cunning business man we now know, moreover, if he had not seen the possibility of working in a line or two to engage the vote of anyone, like Hillaria, angered by Amanda's disregard for her envied independence; when Amanda asks Young Worthy why he told the errant Loveless that she was dead, he replies, 'Because I wou'd not see him rob your House', thereby raising laughter to mock the law's unfair provision for the irresponsible husband.[103] Amanda's virtuous disdain for her economic advantages did not, therefore, mean that they could not be valued by her admirers.

The result is that the scene in which she hands over her two thousand pounds to her returned husband could be made much more serious than her behaviour in the first scene might promise; a real issue is manufactured as she pronounces with confidence that her late uncle left her 'in the possession of two thousand pounds a year, which I now cannot offer as a gift, because my duty, and your lawfull right, makes you the undisputed master of it'.[104] If her sober humility prompts derision now, it may be rash to assume that it would have been instantly palatable to all in 1696. It appears in what is a familiar scene of a down-at-heel gallant getting his reward in beauty and money-bags, but that is kept in the background of the important action, which depicts a conscious surrendering of rights and independence, however the sobriety of that action may have been engineered at the cost of dramatic consistency. The scene appears designed to occasion not a collapse into sentimental approval, but a sudden and perhaps even shocking challenge to the true importance of the only kind of independence its female audience could realistically imagine; it is precisely Cibber's laborious insistence on the economic facts of the relationship which has generated such an effect. This is not to say that the play sheds the emotional luxuriance which characterizes the presentation of Amanda at her first appearance. Moral sympathy and approval continue to be enlisted without effort as we are given unimpeded access to Amanda's consciousness in a series of pointedly public speeches: 'Can I justify, think you, my intended Design upon my Husband?' she asks Hillaria and, implicitly, the entire audience;[105] naturally there is no doubt

---

[103] *Love's Last Shift*, II. i.

[104] *Love's Last Shift*, v, i.

[105] *Love's Last Shift*, III, i. It is typical of Cibber's business tact that it should not be Amanda who forms the plan to win back her husband, but Young Worthy (in II. i.); she is therefore spared the imputation of too much subtle ingenuity, just as she is only allowed to value her fortune when it does her most credit.

that she can. Her dilemma is not complicated; it involves little more than a variety of re-statements of her original moral position, and it is not hard to approve where there is for the most part so little of the bracing challenge of circumstances which we find in *The Wives Excuse*. Nevertheless, the working out of her dilemma does examine carefully and soberly questions which the earlier play had explored, and shows the reformation of Loveless not to be an implausible or hypocritical volte-face, but a popularly rendered answer to a problem which had concerned women throughout the age. We cannot read the crucial scene carefully and doubt it.

The scene begins with Amanda's appearance after her night of passion with Loveless. 'Thus far,' she reports, with customary distance from the fact, 'my Hopes have all been answered, and my Disguise of vicious Love has charm'd him ev'n to a Madness of Impure Desire: But now I tremble to pull off the Mask, lest bare-faced Virtue shou'd fright him from my Arms for ever,'[106] The metaphor of the mask is not accidental. How is Amanda to continue to interest a man who sees that she no longer carries the badge of what he takes to be her profession? What will he think of her when she shows herself to be more than merely the most refined prostitute he has encountered? Scant hope is offered by his replies to her questions about his wife: he says that she was virtuous because he was never jealous of her, and that he was fond of her because she was only his third conquest. His thuggishness is as apparent as Lovemore's and it required no further comment from Cibber. Amanda then questions him on the subject of virtue, having offered him first a riddle the solving of which will reveal her identity: she is, in spite of appearance, a virtuous wife who was never false to her husband. He fails to understand, but proceeds to offer an account of women and virtue in general. This is the essential first step in his reformation. Most women, he contends, 'confound the very name of Virtue, for they wou'd live without Desires', which is not, he argues, real virtue, but 'the Defect of unperforming nature'. Virtue is alone in that woman 'whose Conscience and whose Force of Reason can curb her warm Desires', and he admits the possibility that such a one may exist. It is this admission that signals hope for Amanda, who, taking him up, puts to him in the abstract the case of a woman abandoned by her husband for ten years, yet faithful to him—is such a woman not truly virtuous? Guilt asserts itself and he stands 'in a fixed posture'. Once he has been subdued, she can solve the riddle of her identity by declaring herself his wife. Of

[106] *Love's Last Shift*, v, i.

course, 'identity' in this play is very much a matter of moral stereotyping—Amanda's monologues, we have seen, simply reiterate her moral status in the action—so that what she reveals is not only that she is Loveless's wife but that she is, after all, a virtuous woman. The real riddle for Loveless is to think of her, a woman, as something more than the recipient of his sexual attentions, and once he begins to think himself out of that customary equation by admitting that there may be such a thing as a woman capable of complete restraint he shows himself worthy of the assistance which Amanda duly offers. Her stated riddle, that she is a virtuous wife never false to her husband, is a metaphor for the larger riddle which forms the subject of *The Wives Excuse*: how can a woman, being a woman, remain above the insulting suspicions of men? The difference between Southerne's play and Cibber's is that the former, more pessimistic, does not portray a man who can solve it. 'What have I done to deserve this? What encouragement have I given you?' pleads Mrs Friendall. 'A lover makes his hopes,' replies the impenetrably assertive Lovemore. Thus, in the conclusion to *Love's Last Shift*, however deviously engineered, lies a real challenge to the female audience's understanding of what, for Amanda, constitutes the real freedom: economic independence, or the self-respect born of knowing that she represents more than an object of desire to every gallant. Her sacrificing her fortune to her husband at the end of the play is therefore more than 'sentimental'; it is the result of a choice whose importance the thinness of her characterization does not diminish. The similarities between *Love's Last Shift* and *The Constant Couple* have long been apparent; as yet no one has considered the precise implications of Farquhar's borrowing of the conversion scene from Cibber's play.[107] 'Borrowing' will not quite do to describe Farquhar's use

---

[107] Bonamy Dobree, *English Literature in the Early Eighteenth Century* (Oxford, 1959), 233, considers Farquhar's play a 'dreary re-hash' of Cibber's; Virgil Hutton, *The Aesthetic Development of George Farquhar in his Early Plays* (High Wycombe, 1966), 50–73, takes him to task for the verdict, and points to the greater precision and complexity of Farquhar's dialogue. Many critics mention Farquhar's debt to Cibber without considering the conversion scene which is central to both plays: Willard Connely, *Young George Farquhar* (London, 1949), pp. 67–8; Ronald Berman, 'The Comedy of Reason', *Texas Studies in Literature and Language*, 7 (1965), p. 161; A. J. Farmer, *Farquhar* (London, 1966), 19–20; Eric Rothstein, *George Farquhar* (New York, 1967), 44–5; Eugene Nelson James, *The Development of George Farquhar as a Comic Dramatist* (The Hague and Paris, 1972), 60–2, 126–7. *The Constant Couple* is now seen as the first complete 'sentimental comedy'; it eschewed the opportunistic mixing of styles pursued by Cibber, while managing to be popular with everyone. *A Comparison Between the Two Stages*, p. 32, records the pleasure of the footmen as well as those who sat in 'Pit, Box and Stage'; Farquhar's preface says that the ladies were 'pleased' and 'diverted'.

of the scene, however; he quotes it, signals its imminence to the audience in a way which confirms both Thomas Davies's indication of the fame which the original obtained, and my own account of its true significance.

The Constant Couple deals with the return from the Continent of the brave but rakish Sir Harry Wildair and his wooing of the virtuous Angelica, whom he presumes, owing to a trick played upon both by his rival, Vizard, to be a prostitute. Angelica, happy in the ardour of her suitor but nervous of the impurity of his advances, owes something to Cibber's Amanda in the midst of her plot to recover Loveless. She is also an outspoken critic of the impositions which life and the theatre put upon women, and she surprises Wildair at one point by suggesting that his protestations smack more of gallantry than of love, a distinction which he does not grasp.[108] In their final confrontation, which results in the reformation of Sir Harry, the pattern of behaviour is almost identical to that set down by Cibber. Angelica feels sure that there is 'something generous' in Wildair's soul; Wildair confesses that her words 'turn the wild current of [his] blood, and thrill through all [his] veins', and upon Angelica's seeking some assurance of the purity of his 'flame' he affirms that her conduct has 'quench'd the gross material flame, but rais'd a subtil piercing fire' which disdains 'common fuel' and instead gains nourishment from 'the nobler part, the Soul'.[109] Platonic terminology apart, that is just the stage which Loveless reaches when he declares a belief in the possibility of a truly virtuous woman: in this case Wildair has to admit that he is inspired by something more than lust. Accepting the signal, Angelica, hoping his words are true, can put to him the central question of their relationship so far: what motives caused him 'thus to affront [her] virtue' by behaving as if she was a prostitute? His reply refers us beyond the immediate machinations of their intrigue, towards the larger issue: 'Your question, madam, is a riddle, and cannot be resolved.' How can she be anything more than an object of desire, being a woman? So Farquhar incorporates the riddle which Cibber had made the crux of the scene of Loveless's transformation in *Love's Last Shift*, and once again it is the fulcral point upon which the plot turns; a narrative device which, if it is to work, must serve a purpose beyond mere narration: that of representing a

---

[108] *The Constant Couple*, III. i. The scene also contains Angelica's reflections on the female prerogative of modesty: 'our much boasted modesty is but a slavish restraint. The strict confinement on our words makes our thoughts ramble the more; and what preserves our outward fame, destroys our inward quiet'. Cp. Olivia in Mary Manley's *The Lost Lover*, IV. i.

[109] *The Constant Couple*, V, i.

new set of attitudes about relations between the sexes. Vizard's plot, revealed at the end of the play, seems a perfect imitation of the wider conspiracy which the riddle scene, and the published debate about women's rights which helped to make it fashionable and comprehensible, attempted to correct. As Angelica exclaims, 'What have I suffer'd? to be made a prostitute for sale!—'Tis an unequall'd curse upon our sex, that women's virtue shou'd so much depend on lying fame, and scandalous tongues of men.'

In so far as they were conceived for 'the ladies', the plays examined here—usually described as 'sentimental'—clearly sought not to satisfy the demands of a faction but to respond to concerns which were alive among the population at large. As such, they did not necessarily predict a collapse into sentimental approval; to the extent that they expected full sympathetic involvement, they also demanded a measure of patient consideration of new ideas. The fact that Cibber and Farquhar sustained a note of optimism in their plays which seems, by contrast with Southerne's acerbity, merely mechanical, should not blind us to the contiguous fact that they also examined perils and insults more damaging than the word 'sentimental' promises. Their having done so, and in a manner crucial to the basic unfolding of the plot, indicates a female audience united less by faction than by a developing awareness of its insecurity in the modern world.

Bibliography

PRIMARY SOURCES

Manuscripts

BL Add. MS 36916.

Bodleian Library Ballard MS 33.

Bodleian Library MSS North, C. 10.

BRUNET, FRANÇOIS, 'Voyage d'Angleterre', BL Add. MS 35177.

CAVENDISH, WILLIAM, Duke of Newcastle. Bodleian Library Clarendon MS 109.

DERING, Sir EDWARD, 'Notebook', BL Add. MS 33892.

PRO, C. 10 297/57.

PRO, L.C. 5/12.

PRO, L.C. 5/16.

PRO, L.C. 5/139-45.

PRO, L.C. 5/147-52.

PRO, L.C. 7/1.

PRO, L.C. 7/3.

Newspapers

DUNTON, JOHN, *The Athenian Mercury* (London, 1691-6).

The Daily Courant (London, 1702-4).

Domestic Intelligence (London, 1679-80).

MOTTEUX, PETER, *The Gentleman's Journal* (London, 1691-5).

The Lacedemonian Mercury (London, 1683-94).

WARD, EDWARD, *The London Spy* (London, 1698-1700).

TUTCHIN, JOHN, *The Observator* (London, 1699-1703).

The Post Boy (London, 1685-1703).

The Post-Boy Robb'd of his Mail (London, 1692).

The True News; or Mercurius Anglicanus (London, 1680).

Printed Books

ADDISON, JOSEPH, *The Spectator, 61 & 62, Selections from* The Tatler *and* The Spectator, ed. Angus Ross (Harmondsworth, 1982), 341-9.

ALLESTREE, RICHARD, *The Ladies Calling* (Oxford, 1673).

Animadversions on Mr Congreve's Late Answer to Mr Collier (London, 1699).

ASTELL, MARY, *A Serious Proposal to the Ladies* (London, 1694).

—— *Some Reflections upon Marriage* (London, 1696).

ASTON, ANTHONY, *A Brief Supplement to the Life of Mr Colley Cibber: An Apology for the Life of Mr Colley Cibber*, ed. R. W. Lowe, 2 vols. (London, 1889), ii, 297-318.

BANCROFT, JOHN, *The Tragedy of Sertorius* (London, 1679).

—— *King Edward the Third* (London, 1691).

BANKES, JOHN, *The Rival Kings* (London, 1677).
— *The Unhappy Favourite* (London, 1681).
BARKSDALE, CLEMENT, *A Letter Touching a College of Maids or a Virgin Society* (London, 1675).
BATCHILER, JOHN, *The Virgin's Pattern* (London, 1661).
The Beau's Catechism (London, 1703).
BEHN, APHRA, *The Forc'd Marriage* (London, 1670).
— *The Dutch Lover* (London, 1673).
— *The Debauchee* (London, 1677).
— *Abdelazer* (London, 1677).
— *Sir Patient Fancy* (London, 1678).
— *The Feign'd Curtezans* (London, 1679).
— *The Second Part of the Rover* (London, 1680).
— *The False Count* (London, 1682).
— *The City-Heiress* (London, 1683).
— *The Luckey Chance* (London, 1686).
— *Oroonoko* (London, 1688).
— *The Widow Ranter* (London, 1689).
— 'The Court of the King of Bantam', *The Works of Aphra Behn* ed. Montague Summers, 6 vols. (London and Stratford, 1915), v. 13-34.
BETTERTON, THOMAS, *The Amorous Widow* (London, 1670).
— *The Prophetess* (London, 1690).
BOYER, ABEL, *Achilles* (London, 1700).
BOYLE, ROGER, Earl of Orrery. *Parthenissa that Most Fam'd Romance*, 6 vols. (London, 1654-69).
— *Altemira* (London, 1664).
— *Mr Anthony* (London, 1694).
BRATHWAITE, RICHARD, *The English Gentlewoman* (London, 1631).
— *Time's Treasury* (London, 1641).
BROME, RICHARD, *The Court Beggar* (London, 1632).
— *The Weeding of the Covent-Garden* (London, 1632).
BROWN, THOMAS, *Amusements Serious and Comical* (London, 1700).
— *Letters from the Dead to the Living* (London, 1704).
BURNET, GILBERT, *An Essay on the Memory of the Late Queen* (London, 1695).
C., S., *The Art of Complaisance* (London, 1673).
The Calendar of State Papers (Domestic): Charles I.
The Calendar of State Papers (Domestic): Charles II.
The Calendar of Treasury Books, iv (1672-5).
CARLISLE, JAMES, *The Fortune Hunters* (London, 1689).
The Case of Clandestine Marriages (London, 1691).
CAVELLI, La Marquise CAMPANA DI, *Les Derniers Stuarts*. 2 vols. (Paris and London, 1871), i.
CAVENDISH, MARGARET, Duchess of Newcastle, *Plays written by the Thrice Noble,*

Illustrious and Excellent Princess, The Lady Marchioness of Newcastle (London, 1662).

CENTLIVRE, SUSANNAH, *The Perjur'd Husband* (London, 1700).

CHAMBERLAYNE, EDWARD, *Angliae Notitia* , 9 vols. (London, 1669–77).

The Character of a Coffee-house (London, 1665).

The Character of a Town-Gallant (London, 1675).

CHARLETON, WALTER, *The Ephesian Matron* (London, 1659).

CHILD, JOSIAH, *Brief Observations Concerning Trade and the Interest of Money* (London, 1665).

—— *A New Discourse of Trade* (London, 1694).

CHUDLEIGH, Lady, *The Ladies Defence* (London, 1699).

CIBBER, COLLEY, *An Apology for the Life of Mr Colley Cibber, Comedian* , ed. B. S. Fone (Ann Arbor, 1968).

—— *Love's Last Shift* (London, 1696).

CIBBER, THEOPHILUS, *The Lives of the English Poets* , 3 vols. (London, 1773).

COCKAIN, ASTON, *The Obstinate Lady* (London, 1639).

COLLIER, JEREMY, *A Short View of the Immorality and Prophaneness of the English Stage* , 3rd edn. (London, 1698).

A Comparison Between the Two Stages (London, 1702).

A Congratulatory Folio presented to Her Grace the Duchess of Newcastle (London, 1671).

CONGREVE, WILLIAM, *The Double Dealer* (London, 1693).

—— Prologue, *A Very Good Wife*, by George Powell (London, 1693).

—— *The Mourning Bride, Poems and Miscellanies*, ed. Bonamy Dobree (Oxford, 1928).

—— *The Way of the World* , ed. Brian Gibbons (London, 1971).

CORDEMOY, L. G. DE, *A Philosophical Discourse Concerning Speech, Conformable to the Cartesian Principles: Englished out of French* (London, 1668).

CORYE, JOHN, *The Generous Enemies* (London, 1672).

CROWNE, JOHN, *Juliana* (London, 1671).

—— *The History of Charles the Eighth of France* (London, 1671).

—— *Calisto* (London, 1674).

—— *The Destruction of Jerusalem, Part II* (London, 1677).

—— *The Ambitious Statesman* (London, 1679).

—— *Henry VI* (London, 1681).

—— *Sir Courtly Nice* (London, 1685).

—— *Darius King of Persia* (London, 1688).

—— *The English Friar* (London, 1690).

—— *The Married Beau* (London, 1694).

CURLL, EDMUND, *A History of the English Stage* (London, 1741).

DALRYMPLE, Sir JOHN, *Memoirs of Great Britain* (London, 1771).

DAUNCEY, JOHN, *The History of the Thrice Illustrious Princess Henrietta Maria de Bourbon, Queen of England* (London, 1660).

DAVENANT, Sir WILLIAM, *The First Dayes Entertainment at Rutland House by*

Declamations and Musick: after the Manner of the Ancients. The Dramatic Works of Sir William Davenant, ed. James Maidment and W. D. Logan, 5 vols. (Edinburgh, 1874), iii. 196–247.

— *The Platonick Lovers* 2nd edn. (London, 1634).

— *The Witts* (London, 1636).

— *The Fair Favourite* (London, 1638).

— *The Unfortunate Lovers* (London, 1643).

— *The Siege of Rhodes*, 3rd edn. (London, 1661).

— *The Rivals* (London, 1664).

— *The Man's the Master* (London, 1668).

DAVIES, THOMAS, *Dramatic Miscellanies*, 3 vols. (London, 1759).

DEFOE, DANIEL, *An Essay on Projects* (London, 1697).

DENNIS, JOHN, *The Critical Works of John Dennis*, ed. Giles N. Hooker, 2 vols. (Baltimore, 1939).

— *A Plot and No PLot* (London, 1697).

— *Iphigenia* (London, 1700).

A Dialogue between the D[uchess] of C[leveland] and the D[uchess] of P[ortsmouth] at their Meeting in Paris with the Ghost of Jane Shore (London, 1682).

The Dictionary of National Biography.

DILKE, THOMAS, *The Lover's Luck* (London, 1696).

— *The City Lady* (London, 1697).

DOVER, JOHN, *The Mall* (London, 1674).

DOWNES, JOHN, *Roscius Anglicanus* (London, 1708).

DRYDEN, JOHN, *The Poems and Fables of John Dryden*, ed. James Kinsley (Oxford, 1970).

— *Of Dramatick Poesy and Other Essays*, ed. George Watson, 2 vols. (London, 1962).

— *The Letters of John Dryden*, ed. Charles E. Ward (Durham, NC, 1942).

— *Secret Love* (London, 1667).

— *Sir Martin Mar-All* (London, 1667).

— *An Evening's Love* (London, 1668).

— *The Conquest of Granada, Part I* (London, 1670).

— *Marriage à-la-Mode* (London, 1672).

— *All for Love* (London, 1677).

— *The Kind Keeper* (London, 1678).

— *The Vindication of the Duke of Guise* (London, 1683).

— *Don Sebastian* (London, 1690).

— *Amphitryon* (London, 1690).

— *King Arthur* (London, 1691).

— *Cleomenes* (London, 1692).

DRYDEN, JOHN, and NATHANIEL LEE, *Oedipus* (London, 1678).

— *The Duke of Guise* (London, 1683).

DU BARTAS, GUILLAUME, *La Semaine* (Paris, 1578).

The Duchess of C[leveland]'s Memorial (London, 1708).
DUFFETT, THOMAS, *The Spanish Rogue* (London, 1673).
—— *New Poems, Songs, Prologues and Epilogues* (London, 1676).
DUNTON, JOHN, *The Ladies Dictionary* (London, 1694).
—— *The Life and Errors of John Dunton* (London, 1705).
DURFEY, THOMAS, *The Siege of Memphis* (London, 1676).
—— *Madam Fickle* (London, 1676).
—— *A Fond Husband* (London, 1677).
—— *The Fool Turn'd Critick* (London, 1678).
—— *Trick for Trick* (London, 1678).
—— *The Virtuous Wife* (London, 1679).
—— *The Commonwealth of Women* (London, 1685).
—— *The Banditti* (London, 1686).
—— *The Fool's Preferment* (London, 1688).
—— *Love for Money* (London, 1690).
—— *Collin's Walk Through London and Westminster* (London, 1690).
—— *Bussy d'Ambois* (London, 1691).
The Marriage-Hater Match'd (London, 1692).
—— *The Richmond Heiress* (London, 1693).
—— *The Comical History of Don Quixote* (London, 1694).
—— *The Comical History of Don Quixote: The Third Part* (London, 1695).
—— *Cinthia and Endimion* (London, 1696).
—— *The Campaigners* (London, 1698).
ELSTOB, ELIZABETH, *An English-Saxon Homily on the Birthday of St. Gregory* (London, 1709).
English Army Lists and Commission Registers: 1660-1714, ed. Charles Dalton, 6 vols. (London, 1892-4).
An Essay in Defence of the Female Sex (London, 1696).
ETHEREGE, Sir GEORGE, *She Would if She Could* (London, 1668).
—— *The Man of Mode* (London, 1676).
EVANS, THOMAS, 'An Account of his Life and Writings', *The Plays of Thomas Southerne*, 2 vols. (London, 1774), i, 1-29.
EVELYN, JOHN, *The Diary of John Evelyn*, ed. Esmond S. de Beer. 6 vols. (Oxford, 1955).
—— *The Life of Mrs Godolphin*, ed. Samuel, Lord Bishop of Oxford (London, 1847).
The Fair Counsellor, or the Young Lady's Guide after Marriage (London, 1699).
FANE, SIR FRANCIS, *Love in the Dark* (London, 1675).
FARQUHAR, GEORGE, *Love and a Bottle* (London, 1699).
—— *The Constant Couple* (London, 1699).
Female Grievances Debated (London, 1707).
The XV Comforts of Rash and Inconsiderate Marriage, Done out of French (London, 1683).
FLECKNOE, RICHARD, *Damoiselles à-la-Mode* (London, 1667).
—— *Euterpe Reviv'd* (London, 1675).

FLETCHER, JOHN, *Wit at Several Weapons* (London, 1609).

—— *The Coronation* (London, 1635).

FOUNTAINHALL, Lord, *Historical Observes of Memorable Occurents* (Edinburgh, 1840).

FULLER, THOMAS, *A History of the Worthies of England* (London, 1662).

A Funeral Elegy upon the Death of the Queen, Addrest to the Marquess of Normandy (London, 1695).

GILDON, CHARLES, *Phaeton* (London, 1698).

—— *The Life of Mr. Thomas Betterton* (London, 1710).

GLANVILL, JOSEPH, *Palpable Evidence of Spirits and Witchcraft* (London, 1668).

GLAPTHORNE, HENRY, *The Ladies Priviledge* (London, 1637).

—— *The Poems of Mr. Henry Glapthorne* (London, 1639).

—— *Wit in a Constable* (London, 1641).

GOLDSMITH, OLIVER, *She Stoops to Conquer* (London, 1773).

—— 'An Essay on the Theatre: or, a Comparison between Laughing and Sentimental Comedy'. *The Collected Works of Oliver Goldsmith*, ed. Arthur Friedman, 5 vols. (Oxford, 1966), iii, 209-13.

GOULD, ROBERT, *Poems* (London, 1689).

—— *A Poem most humbly offered to the Memory of Her Late Sacred Majesty* (London, 1695).

The Gracious Answer of the most Illustrious Lady of Pleasure the Countess of Castlemaine to the Poor-Whores Petition (London, 1668).

GRANVILLE, GEORGE, *The She-Gallants* (London, 1695).

GUILLIM, JOHN, *A Display of Heraldry*, 5th edn. (London, 1664).

HABINGTON, WILLIAM, *The Queene of Arragon* (London, 1640).

HALIFAX, GEORGE SAVILE, Marquis of, *Complete Works*, ed. J. P. Kenyon (Harmondsworth, 1969).

HAMILTON, ANTHONY, *Memoirs of the Life of the Count de Grammont* trans. Abel Boyer (London, 1714).

HARRIS, JOSEPH, *The City Bride* (London, 1690).

The Hatton Correspondence, ed. Edward Maunde Thompson, Camden Society, NS 23, 2 vols. (Westminster, 1878).

HAWKESWORTH, JOHN, *Oroonoko* (London, 1759).

HMC 8th Report, Appendix, Pt I, Sec. 2.

HMC 12th Report, Appendix V, Rutland MSS, II.

HMC 12th Report, Appendix VII, Fleming MSS.

HOPKINS, CHARLES, *Boadicea* (London, 1697).

HORTON, GEORGE, *Now or Never: Or a New Parliament of Women* (London, 1656).

HOUGHTON, JOHN, *A Collection for the Improvement of Husbandry* (London, 1683).

HOWARD, SIR ROBERT, *The Surprizall* (London, 1662).

—— *The Vestal Virgin* (London, 1664).

Humble Hodge his Discourse (London, 1680).

HUTCHINSON, LUCY, *Memoirs of Colonel Hutchinson*, 3rd edn. 2 vols. (London, 1810).

JANEWAY, JAMES, *Invisibles, Realities, demonstrated* (London, 1673).

JEVON, THOMAS, *The Devil of a Wife* (London, 1686).

JONSON, BEN, *Collected Works of Ben Jonson*, ed. C. H. Herford and Percy and Evelyn Simpson, 11 vols. (Oxford 1925-52), v. 435-549.

JOSCELINE, MRS ELIZABETH, *The Mother's Legacie to her Unborne Child* (London, 1622).

KILLIGREW, ANNE, *Poems by Mrs Anne Killigrew* (London, 1686).

KING, GREGORY, *Natural and Political Observations*, in George Chalmers, *An Estimate of the Comparative Strength of Great Britain* (London, 1804), 38-49.

L., A., *The Woman as Good as the Man, or the Equality of Both Sexes* (London, 1677).

L., T., Letter, *The Theatrical and Monthly Inquisitor and Monthly Mirror* (London, July 1816), 25-6.

LA CALPRANEDE, GAUTHIER DE COSTES DE, *Cassandra*, trans. Sir Charles Cotterell, 10 vols. (London, 1652).

—— *Cleopatra*, trans. Richard Loveday, 12 vols. (London, 1652-5).

LACY, JOHN, *Sawney the Scot* (London, 1667).

—— *The Old Troop* (London, 1672).

The Ladies Catechism (London, 1703).

LAKE, EDWARD, *The Diary of Edward Lake*, ed. George Elliot, in *Camden Miscellany I* (Westminster, 1847).

LANGBAINE, GERARD, *An Account of the English Dramatick Poets* (London, 1691).

LEANERD, JOHN, *The Counterfeits* (London, 1679).

LEE, NATHANIEL, *Sophonisba* (London, 1675).

—— *Gloriana* (London, 1676).

—— *Mithridates* (London, 1678).

—— *Theodosius* (London, 1680).

—— *Lucius Junius Brutus* (London, 1680).

—— *The Massacre at Paris* (London, 1689).

LEGH, EVELYN, Lady NEWTON, *The House of Lyme* (London, 1917).

LEIGH, MRS DOROTHY, *The Mother's Blessing* (London, 1630).

A Letter to A. H. Esq.: Concerning the Stage (London, 1698).

Letters of Love and Gallantry (London, 1693).

LUTTRELL, NARCISSUS, *A Brief Historical Relation of State Affairs*, 6 vols. (Oxford, 1857).

M., W., *The Female Wits* (London, 1697).

MACKY, JOHN, *A Journey Through England in Familiar Letters*, 2 vols. (London, 1714).

MAGALOTTI, Count LORENZO, *The Travels of Cosmo the Third Grand Duke of Tuscany, Through England* (London, 1821).

MAKIN, BATHSUA, *An Essay to Revive the Antient Education of Gentlewomen* (London, 1673).

MANLEY, MARY DELARIVIÈRE, *The Lost Lover* (London, 1696).

—— *The New Atlantis* (London, 1704).

—— *The Adventures of Rivella* (London, 1714).

MANNING, FRANCIS, *The Generous Choice* (London, 1700).

Marriage Promoted in a Discourse (London, 1693).

MARVELL, ANDREW, *Complete Poems*, ed. Elizabeth Story Donno (Harmondsworth, 1972).

MASSINGER, PHILLIP, *The Emperor of the East* (London, 1631).

MISSON, HENRI, M. *Misson's Memoirs and Observations*, trans. John Ozell (London, 1719).

The Modern World Disrob'd (London, 1708).

MOLIÈRE (JEAN-BAPTISTE POQUELIN), *Œuvres Complètes*, ed. Georges Mongredien, 4 vols. (Paris, 1965).

MONCONYS, BALTHASAR DE, *Journal des voyages de Monsieur de Monconys*, 2nd edn. (Lyons, 1666).

MONTAGUE, WALTER, *The Shepherd's Paradise* (London, 1633).

MOTTEUX, PETER, *Love's a Jest* (London, 1696).

—— *Europe's Revels for the Peace* (London, 1697).

—— *The Island Princess* (London, 1698).

—— *Beauty in Distress* (London, 1698).

MOUNTFORT, WILLIAM, *Greenwich Park* (London, 1691).

NEVILLE, HENRY, *Newes from the New Exchange, or the Commonwealth of Ladies* (London, 1650).

OLDMIXON, JOHN, *A History of England During the Reign of the Royal House of Stuart*, 3 vols. (London, 1709).

OSBORNE, DOROTHY, *Letters of Lady Dorothy Osborne to Sir William Temple*, ed. Herbert Parry (London, 1888).

OTWAY, THOMAS, *Don Carlos* (London, 1676).

—— *Friendship in Fashion* (London, 1678).

—— *The Orphan* (London, 1680).

—— *The Souldier's Fortune* (London, 1681).

—— *Venice Preserv'd* (London, 1682).

Ovid's Metamorphoses, trans. George Sandys (London, 1640).

The Parliament of Women (London, 1640).

PAYNE, HENRY NEVIL, *The Fatal Jealousie* (London, 1672).

—— *The Rambling Justice* (London, 1678).

PEPYS, SAMUEL, *The Diary of Samuel Pepys*, ed. Robert Latham and William Matthews, 11 vols. (London, 1970–83).

—— *Shorthand Letters of Samuel Pepys*, transcribed and ed. by Edwin Chappell (Cambridge, 1933).

PHILLIPS, KATHERINE, *Pompey* (Dublin, 1663).

—— *Letters from Orinda to Poliarchus* (London, 1705).

PHILLIPS, WILLIAM, *The Revengeful Queen* (London, 1698).

PIX, MARY, *Ibrahim the Thirteenth Emperour of the Turks* (London, 1696).

—— *The Spanish Wives* (London, 1696).

—— *The Innocent Mistress* (London, 1697).

The Player's Tragedy (London, 1693).

PLAYFORD, JOHN, *Musick's Delight on the Cithern* (London, 1666).

Poems on Affairs of State, 7 vols. (London, 1703).

The Poor Whores Petition to the most splendid, illustrious, serene, and eminent lady of pleasure, the Countess of Castlemayne (London, 1668).

PORDAGE, SAMUEL, *The Siege of Babylon* (London, 1677).

PORTER, THOMAS, *The French Conjurer* (London, 1677).

POWELL, GEORGE, *Alphonso, King of Naples* (London, 1691).

—— *Bonduca* (London, 1695).

—— *Brutus of Alba* (London, 1696).

The Rambling Rakes (London, 1679).

RAVENSCROFT, EDWARD, *The Citizen Turn'd Gentleman* (London, 1671).

—— *The London Cuckolds* (London, 1681).

—— *Dame Dobson* (London, 1683).

RAWLINS, ?, *Tom Essence* (1677).

The Reasons of Mr. Joseph Hains Conversion (London, 1690).

Remarques on the Humours and Conversations of the Gallants of the Town (London, 1673).

A Representation of the Prejudices that may arise in Time from an Intended Act, concerning Matrimony (London, 1692).

RICCOBONI, LUIGI, *An Historical and Critical Account of the Theatres of Europe* (London, 1741).

The Rules of Civility, or Certain Ways of Deportment observed in France amongst all Persons of Quality. Translated out of French (London, 1673).

ST. SERFE, THOMAS, *Tarugo's Wiles* (London, 1667).

SAUNDERS, CHARLES, *Tamerlane the Great* (London, 1681).

SCUDERY, MADELEINE DE, *Artamenes, or Grand Cyrus*, trans. F. G., 5 vols. (London, 1653–5).

—— *Clelia*, trans. John Davies and George Havers, 5 vols. (London, 1656–61).

SEDLEY, Sir CHARLES, *Bellamira* (London, 1687).

Select Papers chiefly relating to English Antiquities: Published from the Originals, in the Possession of John Ives (London, 1773).

SETTLE, ELKANAH, *The Empress of Morocco* (London, 1673).

—— *Love and Revenge* (London, 1674).

—— *Pastor Fido* (London, 1674).

—— *The Female Prelate* (London, 1679).

—— *Distress'd Innocence* (London, 1690).

SHADWELL, THOMAS, *The Sullen Lovers* (London, 1668).

—— *The Royal Shepherdess* (London, 1669).

—— *Epsom Wells* (London, 1672).

—— *Psyche* (London, 1675).

—— *The Virtuoso* (London, 1676).

—— *A True Widow* (London, 1678).

—— *The Woman Captain* (London, 1679).

—— *The Lancashire Witches* (London, 1681).

—— *The Squire of Alsatia* (London, 1688).

—— *Bury Fair* (London, 1689).

SHAKESPEARE, WILLIAM, *The First Folio of Shakespeare: The Norton Facsimile*, ed. Charlton Hinman (London and New York, 1968).

—— *Macbeth*, altered by Sir William Davenant (London, 1673).

SHIPMAN, THOMAS, *Henry the Third of France* (London, 1678).

SHIRLEY, JAMES, *The Imposture* (London, 1640).

SHIRLEY, JOHN, *The Illustrious History of Women* (London, 1686).

SIDNEY, HENRY, *Diary of the Life and Times of Charles the Second by the Honourable Henry Sidney*, ed. R. W. Blencowe, 2 vols. (London, 1843).

SMITH, HENRY, *The Princess of Parma* (London, 1699).

SMYTH, JOHN, *Cytherea* (London, 1677).

SORBIÈRE, SAMUEL DE, *Relation d'un Voyage en Angleterre* (Paris, 1664).

SOUTHERNE, THOMAS, *The Works of Thomas Southerne*, ed. Robert Jordan and Harold Love (Oxford, 1987).

—— *The Disappointment* (London, 1682).

—— *Sir Anthony Love* (London, 1690).

—— *The Wives Excuse* (London, 1691).

—— *The Fatal Marriage* (London, 1694).

—— *Oroonoko* (London, 1695).

SOUTHLAND, THOMAS, *Love à-la-mode* (London, 1663).

STACY, *The Country Gentleman's Vade Mecum* (London, 1699).

STEELE, Sir RICHARD, *The Christian Hero: An Argument* (London, 1701).

—— *The Funeral* (London, 1701).

SWIFT, JONATHAN, 'Hints Towards an Essay on Conversation'. In *The Prose Works of Jonathan Swift*, ed. Herbert Davis, 14 vols. (Oxford, 1957–68), iv. 91–6.

SWINNOCK, GEORGE, *The Christian Man's Calling* (London, 1662).

SYLVESTER, JOSEPH, *Divine Weeks and Workes* (London, 1641).

TATE, NAHUM, *The History of King Richard the Second* (London, 1681).

—— *The History of King Lear* (London, 1681).

—— *A Present to the Ladies* (London, 1694).

TILLIÈRES, LE COMTE DE, *Mémoires*, ed. M. C. Hippeau (Paris, 1863).

TORRIANO, GIOVANNI, *Mescolanze dolce di varie historiette* (London, 1673).

The Town-Misses Catechism (London, 1703).

The Town-Misses Declaration and Apology (London, 1675).

The Triumphs of Female Wit in Some Pindarick Odes (London, 1683).

TROTTER, CATHERINE, *Fatal Friendship* (London, 1698).

—— *The Revolution in Sweden* (London, 1706).

TUKE, Sir SAMUEL, *The Adventures of Five Hours* (London, 1663).

USHER, JAMES, *A Body of Divinity* (London, 1645).

VANBRUGH, Sir JOHN, *The Relapse* (London, 1696).

—— *Aesop Part II* (London, 1697).

VERNEY, FRANCES PARTHENOPE (ed.), *Memoirs of the Verney Family during the Seventeenth Century*. 4 vols. (London, 1892).

VILLIERS, GEORGE, Duke of Buckingham, *The Rehearsal*, in *Burlesque Plays of the Eighteenth Century*, ed. Simon Trussler (Oxford, 1969), 3–54.

WALLER, WILLIAM, *Pompey the Great* (London, 1664).

WALSH, WILLIAM, *A Dialogue Concerning Women, Being a Defence of the Sex* (London, 1691).

The Wand'ring Whore (London, 1661).

WILD, ROBERT, *Iter Boreale* (London, 1660).

WILKES, THOMAS, *A General View of the Stage* (Dublin, 1759).

WILMOT, JOHN, Earl of Rochester, *Valentinian* (London, 1684).

Wits Led by the Nose (London, 1681).

The Womens Advocate: or Fifteen Real Comforts of Matrimony, written by a Person of Quality of the Female Sex (London, 1683).

WOOD, ANTHONY, *Athenae Oxoniensis*, ed. H. Bliss. 4 vols. (Oxford, 1813).

—— *The Life and Times of Anthony Wood*, ed. A. Clark, 5 vols. (Oxford, 1891–1900).

WOODWARD, JOSIAH, *An Account of the Rise and Progress of the Religious Societies* (London, 1701).

—— *Some Thoughts Concerning the Stage in a Letter to a Lady* (London, 1704).

WOOLLEY, HANNAH, *The Gentlewoman's Companion* (London, 1675).

—— *The Queen-like Closet* (London, 1684).

WRIGHT, JAMES, *Historia Histrionica* (London, 1699).

WRIGHT, THOMAS, *The Female Vertuosoes* (London, 1693).

WYCHERLEY, WILLIAM, *The Plays of William Wycherley*, ed. Peter Holland (Cambridge, 1981).

Recordings

PURCELL, HENRY, *Theatre Music—Volume IV*, with Judith Nelson, Martyn Hill, and Christopher Keyte, directed by Christopher Hogwood, The Academy of Ancient Music, London DSLO 550, 1978.

—— *Theatre Music—Volume V*, with Judith Nelson, Emma Kirkby, Martyn Hill, and David Thomas, directed by Christopher Hogwood, The Academy of Ancient Music, London DSLO 561, 1981.

SECONDARY SOURCES

ALLEMAN, GELLERT SPENCER, *Matrimonial Law and the Materials of Restoration Comedy* (Philadelphia, 1942).

ASHTON, JAMES, *A History of English Lotteries* (London, 1893).

ATKINS, J. W. H., *English Literary Criticism: 17th and 18th Centuries* (London, 1951).

AVERY, EMMET L.; 'The Restoration Audience', *Philological Quarterly*, 45 (1966), 54–61.

BARKER, RICHARD HINDRY, *Mr Cibber of Drury Lane* (New York, 1939).

BEAR, ANDREW S., 'Criticism and Social Change: The Case of Restoration Drama', *Komos*, 2 (1969), 23–31.

BENICHOU, PAUL, *Morales du Grand Siècle* (Paris, 1948).

BENTLEY, G. E., *The Jacobean and Caroline Stage*, 7 vols. (Oxford, 1941).

BERKELEY, DAVID S., 'The Penitent Rank in Restoration Comedy', *Modern Philology*, 49 (1953), 223–31.

BERMAN, RONALD, 'The Comedy of Reason', *Texas Studies in Literature and Language*, 7 (1965), 158–180.

BERNBAUM, ERNEST, *The Drama of Sensibility* (Cambridge, Mass., 1915).

BONE, QUENTIN, *Henrietta Maria, Queen of the Cavaliers* (London, 1973).

BORGMAN, A. S., *The Life and Death of William Mountfort* (Cambridge, Mass., 1935).

BOSWELL, ELEANOR, *The Restoration Court Stage* (Cambridge, Mass., 1932).

BOTICA, ALLAN RICHARD, 'Audience, Playhouse and Play in Restoration theatre, 1660–1710', D.Phil. thesis (Oxford, 1985).

BUTLER, MARTIN, *Theatre and Crisis, 1625-1642* (Cambridge, 1985).

CAMERON, WILLIAM J. (ed.) *Poems on Affairs of State*, 7 vols. (New Haven and London, 1971).

CARTWRIGHT, JULIA, *Madame: A Life of Henrietta, daughter of Charles I and Duchess of Orleans* (London, 1891).

CHAPMAN, A. BEATRICE WALLIS and CHAPMAN, MARY WALLIS, *The Status of Women under the English Law* (London, 1909).

CLARK, ALICE, *The Working Life of Women in the Seventeenth Century* (London, 1919).

CONNELY, WILLARD, *Brawny Wycherley* (New York, 1930).

—— *Young George Farquhar: The Restoration Drama at Twilight* (London, 1949).

CROISSANT, DEWITT C., 'Studies in the Work of Colley Cibber', *Bulletin of the University of Kansas Humanistic Studies* I (1912) 1–69.

—— 'Early Sentimental Comedy', *The Parrott Presentation Volume* (Princeton, NJ, 1935), 47–71.

DANCHIN, PIERRE, 'Le Public des théâtres londoniens à l'époque de la Restauration d'après les prologues et les épilogues', *Dramaturgie et Société: XVIᵉ et XVIIᵉ siècles*, ed. Jean Jacquot (Paris, 1968), 847–88.

DOBREE, BONAMY, *English Literature in the Early Eighteenth Century*, Oxford History of English Literature, vii (Oxford, 1959).

DODDS, JOHN WENDELL, *Thomas Southerne, Dramatist* (New Haven, 1933).

EDE, MARY, *Arts and Society in England under William and Mary* (London, 1979).

FARMER, A. J., FARQUHAR. Writers and their Work, 193 (London, 1966).

FISHER, F. J., 'The Development of London as a Centre of Conspicuous Consumption in the Sixteenth and Seventeenth Centuries', *Transactions of the Royal Historical Society*, 4th Series (1948) 37–50.

FLETCHER, I. K., 'ITALIAN COMEDIANS IN ENGLAND IN THE SEVENTEENTH CENTURY', *Theatre Notebook*, 8 (1954).

FORNERON, HENRI, *Louise de Keroualle, Duchess of Portsmouth* (London, 1887).

FRASER, ANTONIA, *The Weaker Vessel: Woman's Lot in Seventeenth Century England* (London, 1984).

FREEHAFER, JOHN, 'The Formation of the London Patent Companies in 1660', *Theatre Notebook* 20 (1965), 6–30.

GAGEN, JEAN, 'Love and Honour in Dryden's Heroic Plays', *Publications of the Modern Language Association of America*, 77 (1962), 208–20.

GILLET, J. E., *Molière en Angleterre* (Brussels, 1913).

GOREAU, ANGELINE, *Reconstructing Aphra: A Social Biography of Aphra Behn* (Oxford, 1980).

GOULDING, RICHARD W., *Margaret Lucas, Duchess of Newcastle* (Lincoln, 1925).

GRANT, DOUGLAS, *Margaret the First* (London, 1957).

HABAKKUK, H. J., 'Marriage Settlements in the Eighteenth Century', *Transactions of the Royal Historical Society*, 4th Series, 32 (1950).

HALLBAUER, OTTO, *The Life and Works of George Farquhar* (Holzminden, 1880).

HAMILTON, ELIZABETH, *Henrietta Maria* (London, 1976).

—— *The Illustrious Lady* (London, 1980).

HARLEY, JOHN, *Music in Purcell's London* (London, 1968).

HIGHFILL, PHILIP H., BURNIM, KALMIN A., and LANGHANS, EDWARD A., *A Biographical Dictionary of Actors, Actresses, Musicians, Dancers, Managers and Other Stage Personnel in London, 1660–1800*, 10 vols. (Carbondale, Ill., 1973–   ).

HILL, CHRISTOPHER, *The World Turned Upside Down* (Harmondsworth, 1975).

HILL, HERBERT WYNFORD, *La Calpranede's Romances and the Restoration Drama*, 3 vols. (Nevada, 1910–11).

HISCOCK, W. G., *John Evelyn and Mrs Godolphin* (London, 1951).

HOLLAND, PETER, *The Ornament of Action* (Cambridge, 1979).

HOLLINGSWORTH, T. H., 'A Demographic Study of the British Ducal Families', *Population in History*, ed. D. V. Glass and D. E. C. Eversley (Chicago, 1965), 1–18.

HOPKINS, DAVID, *John Dryden* (Cambridge, 1986).

HORN-MONVAL, M., 'French Troupes in England during the Restoration', *Theatre Notebook*, 7 (1953).

HOTSON, LESLIE, *The Commonwealth and Restoration Stage* (Cambridge, Mass., 1928).

HUGHES, DEREK, *Dryden's Heroic Plays* (London and Basingstoke, 1981).

HUGHES, LEO, *The Drama's Patrons: A Study of the Eighteenth Century Audience* (Austin and London, 1971).

HUME, ROBERT D., *The Development of English Drama in the Late Seventeenth Century* (Oxford, 1976).

—— '"The Change in Comedy": Cynical versus Exemplary Comedy on the London Stage, 1678–1693', *Essays in Theatre*, i. (1983), 101–18.

—— and SCOUTEN, A. H., '"Restoration Comedy" and its Audiences, 1660–1776', in Robert D. Hume (ed.), *The Rakish Stage, Studies in English Drama 1660–1800* (Carbondale and Edwardsville, 1983), 46–81.

Hutton, Virgil, *The Aesthetic Development of George Farquhar in his Early Plays* (High Wycombe, 1966).

Jackson, W. A., and Parrish, Jean, 'Racan's *Artenice*', *Harvard Library Bulletin*, 14 (1960), 183–90.

James, Eugene Nelson, *The Development of George Farquhar as a Comic Dramatist* (The Hague and Paris, 1972).

Jones, Emrys, 'The First West End Comedy', *Proceedings of the British Academy*, 68 (1982), 215–58.

Jordan, R., 'Some Restoration Playgoers', *Theatre Notebook*, 35 (1981), 51–7.

Kaufman, Anthony, '"This Hard Condition of a Woman's Fate": Southerne's *The Wives Excuse*', *Modern Language Quarterly*, 34 (1973), 36–47.

Kenny, Shirley Strum, 'Theatrical Warfare, 1695–1710', *Theatre Notebook*, 27 (1973), 130–45.

Kenyon, J. P., *The Popish Plot*, 2nd edn. (Harmondsworth, 1974).

Kirsch, Arthur C., *Dryden's Heroic Drama* (Princeton, 1965).

Knights, L. C., 'Restoration Comedy: the Reality and the Myth', *Scrutiny* 6 (1937), 131–48.

Krutch, Joseph Wood, *Comedy and Conscience after the Restoration* (New York, 1924).

Langhans, Edward A., 'New Restoration Theatre Accounts', *Theatre Notebook*, 17 (1963), 118–34.

Loftis, John, *Comedy and Society from Congreve to Fielding* (Stanford, 1959).

—— *The Politics of Drama in Augustan England* (Oxford, 1963).

Lough, John, *Paris Theatre Audiences in the Seventeenth and Eighteenth Centuries* (London, 1957).

Love, Harold, 'The Myth of the Restoration Audience', *Komos*, 1 (1968), 49–56.

—— 'Bear's Case Laid Open: Or, A Timely Warning to Literary Sociologists', *Komos*, 2 (1969), 72–80.

—— 'Who were the Restoration Audience?' *The Yearbook of English Studies*, 10 (1980), 21–44.

Luckett, Richard, Sleeve notes, *Dido and Aeneas*, by Henry Purcell, with Emma Kirkby, Judith Nelson and David Thomas, conducted by Andrew Parrott, The Taverner Choir and Taverner Players (London, ABRD 1034, 1981).

Lynch, Kathleen M., *The Social Mode of Restoration Comedy* (New York and London, 1926).

—— 'Conventions of Platonic Drama in the Heroic Plays of Orrery and Dryden', *Publications of the Modern Language Association of America*, 44 (1929), 456–71.

—— 'Thomas D'Urfey's Contribution to Sentimental Comedy', *Philological Quarterly* 9 (1930), 249–59.

McArthur, Ellen, 'Women Petitioners and the Long Parliament', *English Historical Review*, 24 (1909), 698–709.

Milhous, Judith, 'The Duke's Company's Profits, 1674–1677', *Theatre Notebook*, 32 (1978), 76–87.

MORGAN, FIDELIS (ed.), *The Female Wits: Women Playwrights on the London Stage, 1660–1720* (London, 1981).

NICOLL, ALLARDYCE, *A History of Restoration Drama*. 3rd edn. (Cambridge, 1940).

OGG, DAVID, *England in the Reign of Charles II*, 2nd edn. (Oxford, 1984).

—— *England in the Reigns of James II and Willilam III*, 3rd edn. (Oxford and New York, 1984).

OLLARD, RICHARD, *Pepys: A Biography*, 2nd edn. (Oxford, 1984).

ORGEL, STEPHEN, and STRONG, ROY, *Inigo Jones: The Theatre of the Stuart Court*, 2 vols. (Berkeley and Los Angeles, 1973).

OSBORN, SCOTT C., 'Heroical Love in Dryden's Heroic Drama', *Publications of the Modern Language Association of America*, 73 (1958), 480–90.

PARNELL, PAUL E., 'Equivocation in Cibber's *Love's Last Shift*', *Studies in Philology*, 57 (1960), 519–34.

PINTO, V. DE SOLA, 'Rochester, Dryden, and the Duchess of Portsmouth', *The Review of English Studies*, 16 (1940), 177–8.

RAYNOR, HENRY, *Music in England* (London, 1980).

REYNOLDS, MYRA, *The Learned Lady in England, 1650–1750* (New York, 1920).

ROSE ANTHONY, Sister, *The Jeremy Collier Stage Controversy, 1698–1726* (New York, 1937).

ROSENFELD, SYBIL, *Foreign Theatrical Companies in Great Britain in the 17th and 18th Centuries*, Society for Theatre Research Pamphlet Series, No. 4 (London, 1955).

ROTHSTEIN, ERIC, *George Farquhar* (New York, 1967).

SALZMAN, PAUL, *English Prose Fiction, 1558–1700* (Oxford, 1985).

SAWYER, P., 'The Seating Capacity and Maximum Receipts of Lincoln's-Inn-Fields Theatre', *Notes and Queries*, 199 (1954), 290.

SCHWEITER, JEROME W., 'Dryden's Use of Scudery's *Almahide*', *Modern Language Notes*, 54 (1939), 190–2.

—— 'Another Note on Dryden's Use of George de Scudery's *Almahide*', *Modern Language Notes*, 62 (1947), 262–3.

SCOUTEN, A. H., 'Notes Towards a History of Restoration Comedy', *Philological Quarterly*, 45 (1966), 62–70.

SHERBO, ARTHUR, *English Sentimental Drama* (New Haven, 1957).

SMITH, JAMES L., Introduction, *The Plain Dealer* by William Wycherley (London, 1979).

SMITH, JOHN HARRINGTON, 'Shadwell, the Ladies, and the Change in Comedy', *Modern Philology*, 46 (1948), 22–33.

—— *The Gay Couple in Restoration Comedy* (Cambridge, Mass., 1948).

SOUERS, PHILIP WEBSTER, *The Matchless Orinda* (Cambridge, Mass., 1931).

SPINGARN, J. E. (ED.), *Critical Essays of the Seventeenth Century*, 3 vols. (Oxford, 1909).

STONE, LAWRENCE, 'The Residential Development of the West End of London in the Seventeenth Century', *After the Reformation*, ed. Barbara C. Malament (Manchester, 1980), 167–212.

Bibliography

—— *The Family, Sex and Marriage in England, 1500–1800*, 2nd edn. (Harmondsworth, 1983).

STYAN, J. L., *Restoration Comedy in Performance* (Cambridge, 1986).

SUCKLING, NORMAN, 'Molière and English Restoration Comedy', *Restoration Theatre*, Stratford-upon-Avon Studies, vi, ed. J. R. Brown and B. Harris (London, 1965), 93–107.

SULLIVAN, MAUREEN (ED.), *Cibber: Three Sentimental Comedies* (New Haven and London, 1973).

SUMMERS, MONTAGUE, *The Restoration Theatre* (London, 1934).

SUTHERLAND, JAMES, *English Literature of the Late Seventeenth Century*, Oxford History of English Literature, vi. (Oxford, 1969).

THOMAS, K. V., 'Women and the Civil War Sects', *Crisis in Europe, 1560–1660*, ed. T. Aston (London, 1965), 95–117.

THOMPSON, GLADYS SCOTT, *Life in a Noble Household* (London, 1937).

—— *The Russells in Bloomsbury* (London, 1940).

THOMPSON, ROGER, *Women in Stuart England and America* (London and Boston, 1974).

—— *Unfit for Modest Ears: A Study of Pornography in the Seventeenth Century* (London and Basingstoke, 1979).

VAN LENNEP, WILLIAM, 'Nell Gwyn's Playgoing at the King's Expense', *Harvard Library Bulletin*, 4 (1950), 405–8.

—— (ed.), *The London Stage, 1660–1800*; Part I: 1660–1700 (Carbondale, Ill. 1965).

VEBLEN, THORSTEIN, *The Theory of the Leisure Class* (New York, 1925).

WHITING, GEORGE W., 'The Condition of the London Theatres, 1679–83', *Modern Philology*, 25 (1927), 195–206.

—— 'Political Satire in London Stage Plays, 1680–83', *Modern Philology*, 28 (1930), 29–43.

WILCOX, JOHN, *The Relation of Molière to Restoration Comedy* (New York, 1938).

WILEY, AUTREY NELL, 'Female Prologues and Epilogues in English Plays', *Publications of the Modern Language Association of America*, 48 (1933), I. 1060–79.

—— *Rare Prologues and Epilogues* (London, 1940).

WILSON, J. HAROLD, 'Rochester, Dryden, and the Rose-Street Affair', *The Review of English Studies*, 15 (1939), 294–301.

—— *Nell Gwyn, Royal Mistress* (London, 1952).

—— 'Theatre Notes from the Newdigate Newsletters', *Theatre Notebook*, 15 (1961).

WILSON, JOHN, *Roger North on Music* (London, 1959).

WRIGLEY, E. A., 'A Simple Model of London's Importance in Changing English Society and Economy', *Past and Present*, 37 (1967).

ZIMMERMAN, FRANKLIN B., *Henry Purcell* (London and Basingstoke, 1967).

Index